PART II THE NATURE OF COMPETITIVE ADVANTAGE 77

PART III   STRATEGIES   157

Chapter 5   Building Competitive Advantage Through Functional-Level Strategy   158

Chapter 6   Business-Level Strategy   202

Chapter 7   Competitive Strategy and the Industrial Environment   233

PART TWO

The Nature of Competitive Advantage

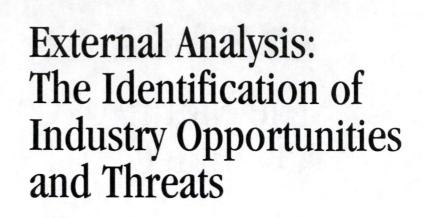

3 External Analysis: The Identification of Industry Opportunities and Threats

OPENING CASE

On-line Firms Revolutionize the Stockbrokerage Industry

FOR YEARS, although trading on the stock market has been electronic, only professional stockbrokers with expensive computer hardware could trade on-line. If an individual investor wanted to buy or sell a stock, she had to call her stockbroker and place an order. The stockbroker would charge a commission for this service. At full-service stockbrokers such as Merrill Lynch—which offered their clients detailed research reports, stock recommendations, and financial planning services—these commissions could run to 2.5 percent of the value of the order. Thus, an order worth $10,000 could generate $250 in commissions.

The situation began to change in 1994 when a small discount broker, K. Aufhauser, took advantage of new technology to become the first to offer its clients the ability to trade on-line over the Internet, effectively bypassing stockbrokers. The offering allowed Aufhauser to operate with fewer personnel. The cost saving was passed on to consumers in the form of lower commissions. Initially, on-line trading was merely a curiosity, but several things changed this. First, the Internet started to make rapid inroads into the homes of individual Americans. Second, within a short space of time, a vast amount of investment information was being offered on the Internet. Individual investors soon found that they could go to sites such as the Motley Fool at America Online or Yahoo!'s finance site and get much of the information that they needed to make informed investment decisions. No longer did they have to call their stockbrokers to ask for information. Third, a number of small companies quickly followed Aufhauser's lead and took advantage of the Internet to offer their clients on-line trading for commissions that were significantly below those offered by full-service stockbrokers in the physical world. Finally, America's long bull market attracted ever more individuals to the stock market, particularly among America's large baby-boom generation, who were drawn to investing in order to build up funds for retirement. Increasingly, these newcomers set up on-line trading accounts.

The effects of these trends were dramatic. By 1999, there were 70 firms offering on-line trading via the Internet. Many of these companies did not even exist in 1994. The arrival of the Internet had lowered barriers to entry and allowed these companies to enter the stockbrokerage industry and compete against incumbents such as Merrill Lynch. As the competition for the business of on-line investors started to heat up, commissions started to fall. By early 1999, on-line brokerages such as E*Trade were charging deep discount fees of $14.95 per market order for trades of up to 5,000 shares. Thus, while an order for 1,000 shares of a stock trading at $20 a share could cost the client of a full-service broker as much as $500 in commission, the same trade could be executed vie E*Trade for $14.95! Attracted by such low prices, from little more than a trickle in 1994, the volume of on-line trades grew to account for 30–35 percent of all stock trades by individuals as of mid 1999.

At first, full-service brokers derided on-line trading as dangerous and justified their high commissions by claiming that they offered their clients sound financial advice and proprietary research reports. However, with as many as 40 percent of all stockbrokers lacking much in the way of experience, and with the rapid increase in the amount of investment information that could be accessed on-line, such arguments sounded increasingly shrill and self-serving. By early 1999, it was becoming apparent that full-service brokers need to adapt to the new technology or risk seeing their client base evaporate. The landmark event occurred in June 1999, when Merrill Lynch, the world's largest full-service broker, bowed to the inevitable and announced that it, too, would soon offer its clients the ability to trade on-line for a fee of $29.95 for trades of up to 1,000 shares. An internal Merrill report estimated that as a result its army of 14,800 well-paid stockbrokers, who were paid chiefly in commissions, might initially see their incomes decline by 18 percent as a result of this move. Merrill knew that it faced a potential rebellion from its stockbrokers, but it also knew that it had no choice, given the forecasts suggesting that more than 50 percent of stock trades by individuals would be on-line by 2001.[1]

OVERVIEW

The Opening Case illustrates the impact that changing market conditions can have on prices and strategies in an industry. The rise of a new technology, the Internet, has lowered barriers to entry into the stockbrokerage industry, allowing upstarts like E*Trade and Ameritrade to compete head-to-head with incumbents such as Merrill Lynch for the business of individual investors. As hordes of these new enterprises entered the industry, prices (fees and commissions) plunged and demand shifted from high-priced full-service stockbrokers toward discount on-line brokers. The revolutionary nature of this process was illustrated by Merrill Lynch's decision in June 1999 to offer its clients on-line trading for a flat fee of $29.95 per trade of 1,000 shares or less. In effect, Merrill substantially reduced the price it charged individual investors and altered the way it delivered its service so that it might maintain its revenues and profits in the face of a fundamental change in the environment of the stockbrokerage industry.

Consistent with the theme introduced in the Opening Case, in this chapter we consider the influence of the industry environment in which a company competes on its performance. First, we discuss a number of models that can assist managers in analyzing the environment. The models provide a framework for identifying environmental opportunities and threats. **Opportunities** arise when a company can take advantage of conditions in its external environment to formulate and implement strategies that enable it to earn higher profits. Thus, the advent of the Internet provided an opportunity for discount stockbrokers to capture business from full-service brokers by offering services on-line. **Threats** arise when conditions in the external environmental endanger the integrity and profitability of the company's business. On-line stock trading threatened incumbent full-service stockbrokers such as Merrill Lynch. Second, we consider the competitive implications that arise when groups of companies within an industry pursue similar strategies. Third, we examine the nature of industry evolution and discuss in detail how the globalization of the world economy is affecting the competitive forces at work in an industry environment. Finally, we assess the impact of conditions within a nation on competitive advantage. By the end of the chapter, you will understand that to succeed a company must either fit its strategy to the industry environment in which it operates or be able to reshape the industry environment to its advantage through its chosen strategy.

ANALYZING INDUSTRY STRUCTURE

An **industry** can be defined as a group of companies offering products or services that are close substitutes for each other. Close substitutes are products or services that satisfy the same basic consumer needs. For example, the metal and plastic body panels used in automobile construction are close substitutes for each other. Despite different production technologies, auto supply companies manufacturing metal body panels are in the same basic industry as companies manufacturing plastic body panels. They are serving the same consumer need, the need of auto assembly companies for body panels.

The task facing managers is to analyze competitive forces in an industry environment in order to identify the opportunities and threats confronting a company. Michael E. Porter of the Harvard School of Business Administration has developed a framework that helps managers in this analysis.[2] Porter's framework, known as the **five forces model,** appears in Figure 3.1. This model focuses on five forces that shape competition within an industry: (1) the risk of new entry by potential competitors; (2) the degree of rivalry among established companies within an industry; (3) the bargaining power of buyers; (4) the bargaining power of suppliers; and (5) the threat of substitute products.

Porter argues that the stronger each of these forces, the more limited is the ability of established companies to raise prices and earn greater profits. Within Porter's framework, a strong competitive force can be regarded as a threat since it depresses profits. A weak competitive force can be viewed as an opportunity, for it allows a company to earn greater profits. The strength of the five forces may change through time as industry conditions change, as illustrated by the Opening Case. The task facing managers is to recognize how changes in the five forces give rise to new opportunities and threats, and to formulate appropriate strategic responses. In addition, it is possible for a company, *through its choice of strategy,* to alter the strength of one

FIGURE 3.1

The Five Forces Model

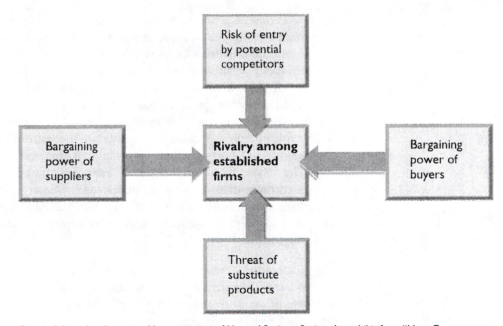

or more of the five forces to its advantage. This is discussed in the following chapters. In this section, we focus on understanding the impact that each of the five forces has on a company.

■ Potential Competitors

Companies that are not currently competing in an industry but have the capability to do so if they choose are **potential competitors**. For example, electric utilities are potential competitors to telecommunications companies in the markets for phone service and Internet access. In order to be able to deliver electricity to residential and commercial property, many electric utilities have been granted rights of way by state and local governments. They have laid electric cables down these rights of way, but there is nothing to stop them from putting in fiber-optic lines along these rights of way and offering high-bandwidth communication services to residential and commercial customers. In fact, a number of utilities have started to do this. For example, Tacoma City Light in Washington State has used its rights of way to run fiber-optic lines to several commercial buildings in the city of Tacoma and take away business from the dominant telecommunications service provider in the region, US West. Tacoma City Light is also laying coaxial cable to homes in its service region and offering a cable television service in direct competition with the local cable provider, TCI.[3]

Incumbent companies (those already operating in an industry) try to discourage potential competitors from entering the industry, since the more companies enter, the more difficult it becomes for established companies to hold their share of the market and to generate profits. For example, TCI's response to the potential entry of Tacoma City Light into the cable TV business in Tacoma was to threaten intense competition on both price and service offerings. Thus, a high risk of entry by potential competitors represents a threat to the profitability of established companies. On the other hand, if the risk of new entry is low, incumbent companies can take advantage of this opportunity to raise prices and earn greater returns.

The strength of the competitive force of potential rivals is largely a function of the height of barriers to entry. **Barriers to entry** are factors that make it costly for companies to enter an industry. The greater the costs that potential competitors must bear to enter an industry, the greater are the barriers to entry. High entry barriers keep potential competitors out of an industry even when industry returns are high. The classic work on barriers to entry was done by economist Joe Bain. He identified three main sources of barriers to new entry: brand loyalty, absolute cost advantages, and economies of scale.[4] To Bain's list we can add two more entry barriers of considerable significance in many situations: switching costs and government regulation.

Brand Loyalty   Buyers' preference for the products of incumbent companies is termed **brand loyalty**. A company can create brand loyalty through continuous advertising of brand and company names, patent protection of products, product innovation achieved through company research and development programs, an emphasis on high product quality, and good after-sales service. Significant brand loyalty makes it difficult for new entrants to take market share away from established companies. Thus, it reduces the threat of entry by potential competitors since they may see the task of breaking down well-established consumer preferences as too costly.

Absolute Cost Advantages   Sometimes incumbent companies have an absolute cost advantage relative to potential entrants. **Absolute cost advantages** seem to derive from three main sources. These are (a) superior production operations, due to past experience, patents, or secret processes; (b) control of particular inputs required for production, such as labor, materials, equipment, or management skills; and (c) access to cheaper funds because existing companies represent lower risks than companies that are not yet established. If incumbent companies have an absolute cost advantage, then the threat of entry decreases.

Economies of Scale   The cost advantages associated with large company output are known as **economies of scale**. Sources of scale economies include cost reductions gained through mass-producing a standardized output, discounts on bulk purchases of raw-material inputs and component parts, the advantages gained by spreading of fixed costs over a large production volume, and economies of scale in advertising. If these cost advantages are significant, then a new entrant faces the dilemma of either entering on a small scale and suffering a significant cost disadvantage or taking a very large risk by entering on a large scale and bearing significant capital costs. A further risk of large-scale entry is that the increased supply of products will depress prices and result in vigorous retaliation by established companies. Thus, when established companies have economies of scale, the threat of entry is reduced.

Switching Costs   When it costs a consumer to switch from the product offering of an incumbent company to the product offering of a new entrant, **switching costs** arise . When these costs are high, consumers can be **locked in** to the product offerings of incumbents, even if new entrants offer better products.[5] A familiar example of switching costs concerns the costs associated with switching from one computer operating system to another. If an individual currently uses Microsoft's Windows operating system, and has a library of related software applications (such as word-processing software, spreadsheet, games) and document files, it is expensive for that individual to switch to another computer operating system, such as the Macintosh OS produced by Apple Computer. The reason is simple; to effect the change the individual will have to buy a new set of software applications because applications written for Windows will not run on the Macintosh OS. Moreover, the individual will have to devote considerable time and effort to convert her document files so that they can be used by applications written for the Macintosh OS. Faced with such an expense of money and time, most people are unwilling to make the switch *unless* the competing operating system offers a *substantial* leap forward in performance (and arguably, the Mac OS does not). Thus, at this point one might argue that high switching costs have created barriers to entry into the market for a personal computer operating system and that competing operating systems have been locked out of the market. At the same time, it is important to understand that if a competitor offers an operating system that represents a substantial improvement over Windows, then users will switch to that operating system. In this regard, the Linux operating system, which is being sold by Red Hat Software, is viewed by some as a potential threat to Microsoft's market dominance.

Government Regulation   Historically, government regulation has constituted a major entry barrier in many industries. For example, until recently in the United States, government regulation prohibited providers of long-distance telephone service, such as AT&T, MCI, and Sprint, from competing for local telephone service with the Regional Bell Operating Companies (RBOCs) such as US West and Bell Atlantic. Moreover, the RBOCs were prohibited from entering the long-distance telephone market. Other potential providers of telephone service, including cable television service companies such as TCI Communications and Viacom (which could in theory use their cables to carry telephone traffic as well as TV signals), were prohibited from entering the market altogether. These regulatory barriers to entry significantly reduced the level of competition in both the local and long-distance telephone markets, enabling telephone companies to earn higher profits than might otherwise have been the case. All this changed in January 1996 when the U.S. government deregulated the industry, removing all barriers to entry. In the months that followed this announcement, the RBOCs, long-distance companies, and cable TV companies all announced their intention to enter each other's markets. A significant increase in competitive intensity is to be expected. A similar move toward deregulating telephone service can be seen in many other countries. The member states of the European Union, for example, deregulated their telephone markets on January 1, 1998.

Entry Barriers and Competition   If established companies have built brand loyalty for their products, have an absolute cost advantage with respect to potential competitors, have significant scale economies, are the beneficiaries of high switching costs, or enjoy regulatory protection, the risk of entry by potential competitors is greatly diminished. When this risk is low, established companies can charge higher prices and earn greater profits than would have been possible otherwise. Clearly, it is in the interest of companies to pursue strategies consistent with raising entry barriers. Indeed, empirical evidence suggests that the height of barriers to entry is one of the most important determinants of profit rates in an industry.[6] Examples of industries where entry barriers are considerable include pharmaceuticals, household detergents, and commercial jet aircraft. In the first two cases, product differentiation achieved through substantial expenditures for research and development and for advertising has built brand loyalty, making it difficult for new companies to enter these industries on a significant scale. So successful have the differentiation strategies of Procter & Gamble and Unilever been in household detergents that these two companies dominate the global industry. In the case of the commercial jet aircraft industry, the barriers to entry are primarily due to the enormous fixed costs of product development (it cost Boeing $5 billion to develop its new wide-bodied jetliner, the 777) and the scale economies enjoyed by the incumbent companies, which enable them to price below a potential entrant's costs of production and still make a significant profit. A more detailed example of entry barriers appears in Strategy in Action 3.1, which discusses the barriers to entry in the Japanese brewing industry.

■ Rivalry Among Established Companies

The second of Porter's five competitive forces is the extent of rivalry among established companies within an industry. If this rivalry is weak, companies have an opportunity to raise prices and earn greater profits. But if rivalry is strong, significant price competition, including price wars, may result. Price competition limits profitability by reducing the margins that can be earned on sales. Thus, intense rivalry among established companies constitutes a strong threat to profitability. The extent of rivalry among established companies within an industry is largely a function of three factors: (1) industry competitive structure, (2) demand conditions, and (3) the height of exit barriers in the industry.

Competitive Structure   Competitive structure refers to the number and size distribution of companies in an industry. Structures vary from **fragmented** to **consolidated** and have different implications for rivalry. A fragmented industry contains a large number of small or medium-sized companies, none of which is in a position to dominate the industry. A consolidated industry may be dominated by a small number of large companies (in which case it is referred to as an oligopoly), or in extreme cases, by just one company (a monopoly). Fragmented industries range from agriculture, video rental, and health clubs to real estate brokerage and sun tanning parlors. Consolidated industries include aerospace, automobiles, and pharmaceuticals.

Many fragmented industries are characterized by low entry barriers and commodity-type products that are hard to differentiate. The combination of these traits tends to result in boom-and-bust cycles as industry profits rise and fall. Low entry barriers imply that whenever demand is strong and profits are high there will be a flood of new entrants hoping to cash in on the boom. The explosion in the number of video stores, health clubs, and sun tanning parlors during the 1980s exemplifies this situation.

Often the flood of new entrants into a booming fragmented industry creates excess capacity. Once excess capacity develops, companies start to cut prices in order to utilize their spare capacity. The difficulty companies face when trying to differentiate their products from those of competitors can worsen this tendency. The result is a price war, which depresses industry profits, forces some companies out of business, and deters potential new entrants. For example, after a decade of expansion and booming profits, many health clubs are now finding that they have to offer large discounts in order to hold on to their membership. In general, the more com-

STRATEGY *in* ACTION

Entry Barriers in the Japanese Brewing Industry

In 1565, an English visitor to Japan noted that the Japanese "feed moderately but they drink largely." This is still the case today; the Japanese have one of the highest levels of beer consumption per capita of any country in the world. In 1998, for example, fifty liters of beer were sold for every man, woman, and child in the country, making Japan's level of beer consumption per capita similar to that of big beer-drinking nations such as Australia, Britain, and Germany.

The Japanese market is dominated by four companies: Kirin, Asahi, Sapporo, and Suntory. In 1998, these four had a combined market share of around 97 percent. Collectively, these companies enjoy one of the highest profit rates of any industry in Japan. Despite this high level of profitability, however, there has been very little entry into this industry over the last three decades. Suntory has been the only successful new entrant in the last thirty years, and its market share stands at no more than 6 percent.

Normally, a lack of new entry into a profitable industry indicates the presence of high entry barriers, and that is certainly the case here. Like large brewers all over the world, Japan's big four spend heavily on advertising and promotions. Moreover, Japan's big brewers have been aggressive in the area of product development. During the 1990s, Asahi gained significant share from its competitors by pushing its "Super Dry" beer. The resulting product differentiation and brand identification have certainly helped to limit the potential for new entry. But some argue that there is more to it than this. Japan's big brewing companies have also benefited from significant regulatory barriers to entry. Brewers in Japan must have a license from the Ministry of Finance (MOF). Prior to 1994, the MOF would not issue a license to any brewer producing less than 2 million liters annually. This restriction represented an imposing hurdle to any potential new entrant. Interestingly enough, the reason for the licensing scheme was bureaucratic convenience rather than a desire to protect brewing companies from new entry; it is easier to collect tax from 4 companies than from 400.

Another significant barrier to entry has been Japan's distribution system. In Japan, there are often close ties between distributors and manufacturers, and this is the case in the brewing industry. Roughly half the beer consumed in Japan is sold in bars and restaurants. Their owners appear to be loyal to the big brewers and reluctant to take on competing brands that might alienate their main supplier. Small liquor stores are another main distribution outlet for beer, and they, too, have traditionally maintained close ties with the big brewers and are unwilling to sell the products of new entrants for fear that their main suppliers might "punish" them by denying them access to adequate supplies.

However, it now appears that some of the barriers to entering Japan's brewing industry are being lowered. As part of an economic liberalization plan, in 1994 the MOF reduced the production threshold required to gain a license from 2 million liters to 60,000 liters. This was low enough to allow the entry of microbreweries using the same technology that is now found in many brew pubs in the United States and Britain. Moreover, regulatory changes have also permitted the establishment of large new discount stores in Japan. (Until 1994, small retailers could effectively block the establishment of a large discount store in their region by appealing to the local authorities). Unlike traditional small retailers, large discount retailers are motivated more by price and profit than by loyalties to an established supplier and seem willing to sell the beer of foreign companies and microbreweries, in addition to that of Japan's big four.

Given the decline in barriers to entry associated with regulation and distribution channels, many observers thought that Japan's big four brewers would have to face new competitors in the years after 1994. So far, however, that has not happened. Instead, Japan's big four brewers continue to dominate the domestic market—a testament perhaps to the significance of advertising, promotions, and product differentiation as barriers to entry. On the other hand, Japan's brewers are facing indirect competition from an alternative alcoholic beverage, wine, which is starting to become fashionable among younger people.[7]

modity-like an industry's product, the more vicious will be the price war. This bust part of the cycle continues until overall industry capacity is brought into line with demand (through bankruptcies), at which point prices may stabilize again.

A fragmented industry structure, then, constitutes a threat rather than an opportunity. Most booms will be relatively short-lived because of the ease of new entry and will be followed by price wars and bankruptcies. Since it is often difficult to differentiate products in these industries, the best strategy for a company to pursue may be cost minimization. This strategy allows a company to rack up high returns in a boom and survive any subsequent bust.

The nature and intensity of rivalry in consolidated industries is much more difficult to predict. Because in consolidated industries companies are *interdependent*, the competitive actions of one company directly affect the profitability of others in the industry, and the impact on the market share of its rivals forces a response from them. The consequence of such competitive interdependence can be a dangerous competitive spiral, with rival companies trying to undercut each other's prices, pushing industry profits down in the process. The fare wars that have racked the airline industry in the early 1990s provide a good example. When demand for airline travel fell during 1990 as the U.S. economy slipped into a recession, airlines started cutting prices to try to maintain their passenger loads. When one airline serving a particular route cut its prices, its competitors would soon follow. The result was a particularly severe downward price spiral. So intense did price competition become that between 1990 and 1992 the industry lost a staggering $7.1 billion, more than had been made during its previous fifty years, and some long-established carriers, such as Pan American, disappeared into bankruptcy.

Clearly, high rivalry between companies in consolidated industries and the possibility of a price war constitute a major threat. Companies sometimes seek to reduce this threat by following the price lead set by a dominant company in the industry. However, they must be careful, for explicit price-fixing agreements are illegal, although tacit agreements are not. (A tacit agreement is one arrived at without direct communication). Instead, companies watch and interpret each other's behavior. Often tacit agreements involve following the price lead set by a dominant company.[8] However, tacit price-leadership agreements often break down under adverse economic conditions, as is beginning to occur in the beer industry. For most of the 1980s, Anheuser-Busch was the acknowledged price leader in this industry. The resulting absence of price competition helped keep industry profits high. However, slow growth in beer consumption during the late 1980s and early 1990s put pressure on the earnings of all beer majors and persuaded Miller Brewing—a division of Philip Morris—and Adolph Coors to break ranks and institute a policy of deep and continuous discounting for most of their beer brands. In 1990, market leader Anheuser-Busch announced that it would start offering similar discounts in order to protect its sales volume. Thus, after the breakdown of a tacit price-leadership agreement, the beer industry seemed to be sliding toward a price war.

More generally, when price wars are a threat, companies tend to compete on nonprice factors such as advertising and promotions, brand positioning, and product quality, functionality, and design. This type of competition constitutes an attempt to differentiate the company's product from those of competitors, thereby building brand loyalty and minimizing the likelihood of a price war. The effectiveness of this strategy, however, depends on how easy it is to differentiate the industry's product. Although some products (such as cars) are relatively easy to differentiate, others (such as airline travel) are difficult. Moreover, as Strategy in

Action 3.2 demonstrates, in practice nonprice competition in consolidated industries can often be as vigorous, expensive, and damaging as price competition.

Demand Conditions An industry's demand conditions are another determinant of the intensity of rivalry among established companies. Growing demand stemming from new customers or from additional purchases by existing customers, tends to moderate competition by providing greater room for expansion. Growing demand tends to reduce rivalry because all companies can sell more without taking market share away from other companies, and high profits are often the result. Conversely, declining demand results in more rivalry as companies fight to maintain revenues and market share. Demand declines when consumers are leaving the marketplace or when each consumer is buying less. In that situation, a company can grow only by taking market share away from other companies. Thus, declining demand constitutes a major threat, for it increases the extent of rivalry between established companies. Moreover, as we saw in the Opening Case, a slowdown in the rate of growth of demand can also create problems.

Exit Barriers Exit barriers are economic, strategic, and emotional factors that keep companies in an industry even when returns are low. If exit barriers are high, companies can become locked into an unprofitable industry where overall demand is static or declining. Excess productive capacity can result. In turn, excess capacity tends to lead to intensified price competition, with companies cutting prices in an attempt to obtain the orders needed to utilize their idle capacity.[10] Common exit barriers include the following:

1. Investments in plant and equipment that have no alternative uses and cannot be sold off. If the company wishes to leave the industry, it has to write off the book value of these assets.

2. High fixed costs of exit, such as severance pay to workers who are being made redundant.

3. Emotional attachments to an industry, as when a company is unwilling to exit from its original industry for sentimental reasons.

4. Economic dependence on the industry, as when a company is not diversified and so relies on the industry for its income.

The experience of the steel industry illustrates the adverse competitive effects of high exit barriers.[11] A combination of declining demand and new low-cost sources of supply created overcapacity in the global steel industry during the late 1980s. U.S. companies, with their high-cost structure, were on the sharp end of this decline. Demand for U.S. steel fell from a 1977 peak of 160 million tons to 70 million tons in 1986. The outcome was excess capacity amounting to an estimated 45 million tons in 1987, or 40 percent of total productive capacity. In order to try to utilize this capacity, many steel companies slashed their prices. As a consequence of the resulting price war, industry profits were low, and several of the majors, including LTV Steel and Bethlehem Steel, faced bankruptcy.

Since the steel industry was characterized by excess capacity for most of the 1980s, why did companies not reduce that capacity? The answer is that many tried to, but the costs of exit slowed this process and prolonged the associated price war. For example, in 1983 USX shut down 16 percent of its raw steel-making capacity at a cost of $1.2 billion. USX had to write off the book value of these assets; they could

3.2

STRATEGY *in* ACTION

The Great European Soap War

The European retail detergents market, like the global detergents market, is dominated by the products of just two companies, Unilever, the Anglo-Dutch concern, and the American consumer products giant, Procter & Gamble (P&G). Both companies sell a broad product line of detergents to consumers; both spend heavily on advertising, promotions, and brand positioning; and both de-emphasize price-based competition. The net result is that historically both companies have benefited from a relatively benign competitive environment, which has enabled them to earn higher profit margins than would be the case in a more price-competitive industry.

This cozy situation was rudely shattered in early 1994 after the Pan-European launch of a new detergent by Unilever. The product in question was Omo Power, which Unilever promoted as the biggest technical advance in fabric detergents in fifteen years. According to Unilever, Omo Power contained a powerful cleansing agent that washed clothes cleaner than any other product on the market. Consumers seemed to agree; sales of Omo Power surged in every country in which it was introduced during the first few months of 1994. P&G was alarmed by this development. The introduction of Omo Power seemed to violate a tacit understanding between the two companies that they would share technical information with each other. Moreover, Unilever was gaining market share at P&G's expense for the first time in two decades.

P&G's initial response was to try and discover what the secret ingredient in Omo Power might be. After extensive laboratory studies, P&G discovered that Unilever had used crystals of manganese. This surprised P&G, for although manganese could speed the bleaching process, P&G also knew from its own research that manganese attacked fabrics, which was why P&G had abandoned work on manganese ten years earlier. After submitting Omo Power to its own tests, P&G found that clothes washed repeatedly in the powder did indeed develop holes. Armed with this information, P&G decided to counterattack. Top

executives from P&G visited top management at Unilever and stated bluntly that Omo Power was fundamentally flawed and should be pulled off the market. Unilever executives chose to discount this private warning. After two years of market testing with no complaints from consumers, Unilever saw no need to withdraw the product and believed P&G was overstating the problem because it was losing market share. It was at this point that P&G broke with the industry tradition of not criticizing the products of competitors and launched a ruthless public relations campaign pointing out the flaws of Omo Power. P&G gave the press a set of color pictures showing clothes purportedly suffering the ill effects of Omo Power—including shots of some tattered boxer shorts that were duly reproduced by the press all over Europe.

Unilever initially tried to dismiss P&G's claims, but a growing number of independent research institutes backed up P&G's findings. After several months of increasingly bitter public recriminations between the two companies, Unilever was eventually forced to concede that there was a problem. Unilever repositioned Omo Power in the market place from a product with broad applicability to a niche product for use with white fabrics and low water temperatures (conditions that minimized the damage problems).

In the end, Unilever was forced to admit that its $300 million investment in Omo had been a washout. By the end of 1994, Unilever's market share had fallen back to the level the company had attained prior to the launching of Omo Power. Moreover, executives from both companies admitted that the rules of the game in the industry had changed as a result of the dispute. Gone was the cozy agreement of sharing technical information and forbearing from directly attacking the products of a competitor. Nonprice competition in the industry would now be much more difficult than before. P&G fully expected Unilever to try and get its revenge by attacking any new product launch that it might try.[9]

not be sold. In addition, it had to cover pensions and insurance for 15,400 terminated workers. Given such high exit costs, companies such as USX have remained locked into this unprofitable industry. The effect of impeded exit has been more intense price competition than might otherwise have been the case. Thus, high exit barriers, by slowing the speed with which companies leave the industry, threaten the profitability of all companies within the steel industry.

The Bargaining Power of Buyers

The third of Porter's five competitive forces is the bargaining power of buyers. A company's buyers may be the customers who ultimately consume its products (its end users), but they may also be the companies that distribute its products to end users, such as retailers and wholesalers. For example, while Unilever sells its soap powder to end users, the major buyers of its products are supermarket chains, which then resell the product to the end users. Buyers can be viewed as a competitive threat when they are in a position to demand lower prices from the company, or when they demand better service (which can increase operating costs). On the other hand, when buyers are weak, a company can raise its prices and earn greater profits. Whether buyers are able to make demands on a company depends on their power relative to that of the company. According to Porter, buyers are most powerful in the following circumstances:

1. When the supply industry is composed of many small companies and the buyers are few in number and large. These circumstances allow the buyers to dominate supply companies.

2. When the buyers purchase in large quantities. In such circumstances, buyers can use their purchasing power as leverage to bargain for price reductions.

3. When the supply industry depends on the buyers for a large percentage of its total orders.

4. When the buyers can switch orders between supply companies at a low cost, thereby playing off companies against each other to force down prices.

5. When it is economically feasible for the buyers to purchase the input from several companies at once.

6. When the buyers can use the threat to supply their own needs through vertical integration as a device for forcing down prices.

An example of an industry whose buyers are powerful is the auto component supply industry. The buyers here are the large automobile companies, such as General Motors, Ford, and Chrysler. The suppliers of auto components are numerous and typically small in scale. Their buyers, the auto manufacturers, are large in size and few in number. Chrysler, for example, does business with nearly 2,000 different component suppliers and normally contracts with a number of different companies to supply the same part. The auto majors have used their powerful position to play off suppliers against each other, forcing down the price they have to pay for component parts and demanding better quality. If a component supplier objects, then the auto major uses the threat of switching to another supplier as a bargaining tool.

Additionally, to keep component prices down, both Ford and General Motors have used the threat of manufacturing a component themselves rather than buying it from auto component suppliers.

Another issue is that the relative power of buyers and suppliers tends to change over time in response to changing industry conditions. For example, because of changes now taking place in the pharmaceutical and health care industries, major buyers of pharmaceuticals (hospitals and health maintenance organizations) are gaining power over the suppliers of pharmaceuticals and have been able to demand lower prices.

■ The Bargaining Power of Suppliers

The fourth of Porter's competitive forces is the bargaining power of suppliers. Suppliers can be viewed as a threat when they are able to force up the price that a company must pay for its inputs or reduce the quality of the inputs they supply, thereby depressing the company's profitability. On the other hand, if suppliers are weak, this gives a company the opportunity to force down prices and demand higher input quality. As with buyers, the ability of suppliers to make demands on a company depends on their power relative to that of the company. According to Porter, suppliers are most powerful in these circumstances:

1. When the product that suppliers sell has few substitutes and is important to the company.

2. When the company's industry is not an important customer to the suppliers. In such instances, the suppliers' health does not depend on the company's industry, and suppliers have little incentive to reduce prices or improve quality.

3. When suppliers' respective products are differentiated to such an extent that it is costly for a company to switch from one supplier to another. In such cases, the company depends on its suppliers and cannot play them off against each other.

4. When, to raise prices, suppliers can use the threat of vertically integrating forward into the industry and competing directly with the company.

5. When buying companies cannot use the threat of vertically integrating backward and supplying their own needs as a means of reducing input prices.

Manufacturers of personal computers exemplify an industry that depends on a very powerful supplier. In this case, the supplier is Intel, the world's largest manufacturer of microprocessors for personal computers (PCs). The industry standard for personal computers runs on Intel's X86 microprocessor family, such as the Pentium series microprocessors currently sold in most PCs. So PC manufacturers have little choice but to use an Intel microprocessor as the brains for their machines. Although several companies have tried to produce clones of Intel's microprocessors, their success has been limited, leaving Intel with about 85 percent of the market. This puts Intel in a very powerful position with regard to the PC manufacturers. The product it supplies has few substitutes and switching costs facing the buyers are high, which enables Intel to raise prices above the level that would prevail in a more competitive supply market.[12]

▉ Substitute Products

The final force in Porter's model is the threat of substitute products. Substitute products are the products of industries that serve similar consumer needs as the industry being analyzed. For example, companies in the coffee industry compete indirectly with those in the tea and soft-drink industries. All three industries serve consumer needs for drinks. The prices that companies in the coffee industry can charge are limited by the existence of substitutes such as tea and soft drinks. If the price of coffee rises too much relative to that of tea or soft drinks, then coffee drinkers will switch from coffee to those substitutes. This phenomenon occurred when unusually cold weather destroyed much of the Brazilian coffee crop in 1975–1976. The price of coffee rose to record highs, reflecting the shortage, and consumers began to switch to tea in large numbers.

The existence of close substitutes presents a strong competitive threat, limiting the price a company can charge and thus its profitability. However, if a company's products have few close substitutes (that is, if substitutes are a weak competitive force), then, other things being equal, the company has the opportunity to raise prices and earn additional profits. Consequently, its strategies should be designed to take advantage of this fact.

▉ A Sixth Force: Complementors

Andrew Grove, the former CEO of Intel, and a part-time teacher at Stanford's Graduate School of Business, has argued that Porter's five forces model ignores a sixth force—the power, vigor, and competence of complementors.[13] **Complementors** are companies that sell complements to the enterprise's own product offerings. For example, the complementors to Sony's popular home video game system, the Play Station, are the companies that produce and sell games that run on the Play Station. Grove's point is that without an adequate supply of complementary products, demand in the industry will be weak, and revenues and profits will be low. No one would purchase the Play Station if there were not enough games to play on it. For another example, consider the early automobile industry. When the automobile was first introduced at the beginning of the twentieth century, demand for the product was very limited. One reason for this was the lack of important complementary products, such as a network of paved roads and gas stations. An automobile was of limited use when there were few paved roads to drive on, and when gas stations were few and far between. As the supply of complementary products increased—as roads and gas stations started to spring up—so did the attractiveness of owning a car. With roads to drive on and an adequate supply of gas stations, owning a car became more practical, and so demand started to pick up. In turn, this created a demand for more roads and gas stations, setting up a self-reinforcing positive feedback loop.

Grove's argument has a strong foundation in economic theory. Most economic textbooks have long argued that *both* substitutes and complements influenced demand in an industry.[14] Moreover, recent research has emphasized the importance of complementary products in determining demand and profitability in many high-technology industries, such as the computer industry, in which Grove made his mark.[15] The basic point, therefore, is that when complements are an important determinant of demand in an industry, the health of the industry depends critically on there being an adequate supply of complementary products produced by complementors. It follows that if complementors are weak and lack attractive product offerings, this can be a threat for the industry (the converse holds true as well).

■ The Role of the Macroenvironment

So far we have treated industries as self-contained entities. In practice, they are embedded in a wider **macroenvironment:** the broader economic, technological, social, demographic, and political and legal environment (see Figure 3.2). Changes in the macroenvironment can have a direct impact on any one of the forces in Porter's model, thereby altering the relative strength of these forces and with it, the attractiveness of an industry. We briefly consider how each aspect of these macroenvironmental forces can affect an industry's competitive structure.

The Macroeconomic Environment   The state of the macroeconomic environment determines the general health and well-being of the economy. This in turn affects a company's ability to earn an adequate rate of return. The four most important factors in the macroeconomy are the growth rate of the economy, interest rates, currency exchange rates, and inflation rates.

Because it leads to an expansion in consumer expenditures, economic growth tends to produce a general easing of competitive pressures within an industry. This gives companies the opportunity to expand their operations and earn higher profits. Because economic decline leads to a reduction in consumer expenditures, it increases competitive pressures. Economic decline frequently causes price wars in mature industries.

FIGURE 3.2

The Role of the Macroenvironment

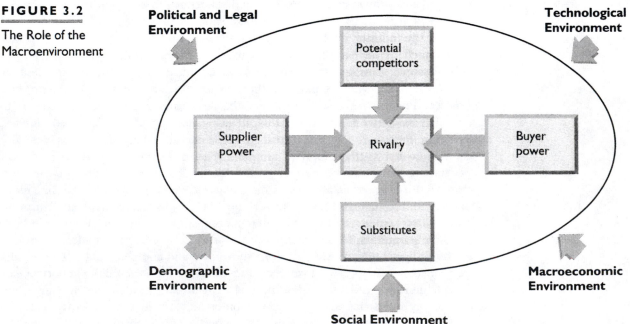

The level of interest rates can determine the level of demand for a company's products. Interest rates are important whenever consumers routinely borrow money to finance their purchase of these products. The most obvious example is the housing market, where the mortgage rate directly affects demand, but interest rates also have an impact on the sale of autos, appliances, and capital equipment, to give just a few examples. For companies in such industries, rising interest rates are a threat and falling rates an opportunity.

Currency exchange rates define the value of different national currencies against each other. Movement in currency exchange rates has a direct impact on the competitiveness of a company's products in the global marketplace. For example, when the value of the dollar is low compared with the value of other currencies, products made in the United States are relatively inexpensive and products made overseas are relatively expensive. A low or declining dollar reduces the threat from foreign competitors while creating opportunities for increased sales overseas. For example, the fall in the value of the dollar against the Japanese yen that occurred between 1985 and 1995, when the dollar/yen exchange rate declined from $1 = Y240 to $1 = Y85, sharply increased the price of imported Japanese cars, giving U.S. car manufacturers some degree of protection against the Japanese threat.

Inflation can destabilize the economy, producing slower economic growth, higher interest rates, and volatile currency movements. If inflation keeps increasing, investment planning becomes hazardous. The key characteristic of inflation is that it makes the future less predictable. In an inflationary environment, it may be impossible to predict with any accuracy the real value of returns that can be earned from a project five years hence. Such uncertainty makes companies less willing to invest. Their holding back in turn depresses economic activity and ultimately pushes the economy into a slump. Thus, high inflation is a threat to companies.

The Technological Environment Since World War II, the pace of technological change has accelerated,[16] unleashing a process that has been called a "perennial gale of creative destruction."[17] Technological change can make established products obsolete overnight, and at the same time it can create a host of new product possibilities. Thus, technological change is both creative and destructive—both an opportunity and a threat.

One of the most important impacts of technological change is that it can affect the height of barriers to entry and, as a result, radically reshape industry structure. This was clearly demonstrated in the Opening Case, when we saw how the spread of the Internet has lowered barriers to entry into the on-line stockbrokerage industry and produced a flood of new entrants and a more fragmented industry structure. In turn, these new entrants have driven down commission rates in the industry, just as theory would predict. In point of fact, the Internet represents a major technological change, and it appears to be in the process of unleashing a similar process of creative destruction across a wide range of industries. On-line retailers are springing up, selling everything from books and CDs to groceries and clothes, suggesting that the Internet has lowered entry barriers in the retail industry. The ability to buy airline tickets and book vacations on-line is a threat to established travel agents, while providing an opportunity for Internet-based start-ups that want to enter the travel industry. The rise of the Internet has also lowered barriers to entry into the news industry. For example, the providers of financial news now have to compete for advertising dollars and consumer attention with new Internet-based media organizations, which have sprung up in recent years, such as TheStreet.com, the Motley Fool, and Yahoo!'s financial section.

Another example of how technological change is reshaping an established industry can be found by considering the impact of biotechnology on the pharmaceutical industry. Although large companies such as Merck, Pfizer, and Eli Lilly have long dominated the pharmaceutical industry, a significant number of small biotechnology companies using recombinant DNA technology are threatening to change the competitive landscape. Between 1945 and 1990, only one new firm became a major player in the pharmaceutical industry, Syntex. Since 1990, a number of biotechnology companies have started to generate significant sales, including Amgen, Biogen, Genetech, Chiron, and Immunex. Moreover, there are now over 300 publicly traded companies in the United States developing novel medicines using biotechnology. The chance is that some of them will develop into significant companies in their own right, illustrating once again that technological change lowers entry barriers and allows new players to challenge the dominance of incumbents.

The Social Environment   Like technological change, social change creates opportunities and threats. One of the major social movements of the 1970s and 1980s was the trend toward greater health consciousness. Its impact has been immense, and companies that recognized the opportunities early have often reaped significant gains. Philip Morris, for example, capitalized on the growing health-consciousness trend when it acquired Miller Brewing and then redefined competition in the beer industry with its introduction of low-calorie beer (Miller Lite). Similarly, PepsiCo was able to gain market share from its rival, Coca-Cola, by introducing diet colas and fruit-based soft drinks first. At the same time the health trend has created a threat for many industries. The tobacco industry, for example, is now in decline as a direct result of greater consumer awareness of the health implications of smoking. Similarly, the sugar industry has seen sales decrease as consumers have decided to switch to artificial sweeteners.

The Demographic Environment   The changing composition of the population is another factor in the macroenvironment that can create both opportunities and threats. For example, as the baby-boom generation of the 1960s has aged, it has created a host of opportunities and threats. During the 1980s, many baby boomers were getting married and creating an upsurge in demand for the consumer appliances normally bought by couples marrying for the first time. Companies such as Whirlpool and General Electric capitalized on the resulting upsurge in demand for washing machines, dishwashers, spin dryers, and the like. The other side of the coin is that industries oriented toward the young, such as the toy industry, have seen their consumer base decline in recent years.

The Political and Legal Environment   Political and legal factors also have a major effect on the level of opportunities and threats in the environment. One of the most significant trends in recent years has been the move toward deregulation. By eliminating many legal restrictions, deregulation has lowered barriers to entry and led to intense competition in a number of industries. The deregulation of the airline industry in 1979 created the opportunity to establish low-fare carriers—an opportunity that Southwest Airlines, Value Jet, and others tried to capitalize on. At the same time, the increased intensity of competition created many threats, including, most notably, the threat of prolonged fare wars, which have thrown the airline industry into turmoil several times since 1979. The global telecommunications industry is now beginning to experience the same kind of turmoil following the deregulation of that industry in both the United States and the European Union.

STRATEGIC GROUPS WITHIN INDUSTRIES

■ The Concept of Strategic Groups

So far we have said little about how companies in an industry might differ from each other and what implications these differences might have for the opportunities and threats they face. In practice, companies in an industry often differ from each other with respect to factors such as the distribution channels they use, the market segments they serve, the quality of their products, technological leadership, customer service, pricing policy, advertising policy, and promotions. As a result of these differences, within most industries, it is possible to observe groups of companies in which each member follows the same basic strategy as other companies in the group, but a strategy that is *different* from that followed by companies in other groups. These groups of companies are known as **strategic groups**.[18]

Normally, a limited number of groups captures the essence of strategic differences between companies within an industry. For example, in the pharmaceutical industry, two main strategic groups stand out (see Figure 3.3).[19] One group, which includes such companies as Merck, Pfizer, and Eli Lilly, is characterized by heavy R&D spending and a focus on developing new proprietary blockbuster drugs. The companies in this *proprietary group* are pursuing a high-risk/high-return strategy. It is a high-risk strategy because basic drug research is difficult and expensive. Bringing a new drug to market can cost $100 million to $300 million in R&D money and a decade of research and clinical trials. The strategy is also a high-return one because a single successful drug can be patented, giving the innovator a seventeen-year monopoly on its production and sale. This lets the innovator charge a very high price for the patented drug, allowing the company to earn millions, if not billions, of dollars, over the lifetime of the patent.

The second strategic group might be characterized as the *generic drug* group. This group of companies, which includes Marion Labs, Carter Wallace, and ICN Pharmaceuticals, focuses on the manufacture of generic drugs—low-cost copies of drugs pioneered by companies in the proprietary group whose patents have now expired. The companies in this group are characterized by low R&D spending and an emphasis on price competition. They are pursuing a low-risk, low-return strategy. It is low risk because they are not investing millions of dollars in R&D. It is low return because they cannot charge high prices.

■ Implications of Strategic Groups

The concept of strategic groups has a number of implications for identifying threats and opportunities within an industry. First, a company's closest competitors are those in its strategic group—not those in other strategic groups. Since all the companies in a strategic group are pursuing similar strategies, consumers tend to view

FIGURE 3.3

Strategic Groups in the Pharmaceutical Industry

the products of such enterprises as direct substitutes for each other. Thus, a major threat to a company's profitability can come from within its own strategic group.

Second, different strategic groups can have a different standing with respect to each of the competitive forces. In other words, the risk of new entry by potential competitors, the degree of rivalry among companies within a group, the bargaining power of buyers, the bargaining power of suppliers, and the competitive force of substitute products can all vary in intensity among different strategic groups within the same industry.

For example, in the pharmaceutical industry, companies in the proprietary group have historically been in a very powerful position vis-à-vis buyers because their products are patented. Besides, rivalry within this group has been limited to competition to be the first to patent a new drug (so-called patent races). Price competition has been rare. Without price competition, companies in this group have been able to charge high prices and earn very high profits. In contrast, companies in the generic group have been in a much weaker position in regard to buyers since they lack patents for their products and since buyers can choose between very similar competing generic drugs. Moreover, price competition between the companies in this group has been quite intense, reflecting the lack of product differentiation. Thus, companies within this group have earned somewhat lower returns than companies in the proprietary group.

It follows that some strategic groups are more desirable than others, for they have a lower level of threats and greater opportunities. Managers must evaluate whether their company would be better off competing in a different strategic group. If the environment of another strategic group is more benign, then moving into that group can be regarded as an opportunity. Yet this opportunity is rarely without costs, mainly because of mobility barriers between groups. **Mobility barriers** are factors that inhibit the movement of companies between groups in an industry. They include both the barriers to entry into a group and the barriers to exit from a company's existing group. For example, Marion Labs would encounter mobility barriers if it attempted to enter the proprietary group in the pharmaceutical industry. These mobility barriers would arise from the fact that Marion lacks the R&D skills possessed by companies in the proprietary group, and building these skills would be an expensive proposition. Thus, a company contemplating entry into another strategic group must evaluate the height of mobility barriers before deciding whether the move is worthwhile.

Mobility barriers also imply that companies within a given group may be protected to a greater or lesser extent from the threat of entry by companies based in other strategic groups. If mobility barriers are low, the threat of entry from companies in other groups may be high, effectively limiting the prices companies can charge and the profits they can earn without attracting new competition. If mobility barriers are high, however, the threat of entry is low, and companies within the protected group have an opportunity to raise prices and earn higher returns without attracting entry.

LIMITATIONS OF THE FIVE FORCES AND STRATEGIC GROUP MODELS

The five forces and strategic group models provide useful ways of thinking about and analyzing the nature of competition within an industry to identify opportunities and threats. However, managers need to be aware of their shortcomings, for both models (1) present a static picture of competition that slights the role of innovation and (2) de-emphasize the significance of individual company differences while overemphasizing the importance of industry and strategic group structure as determinants of company profit rates.

■ Innovation and Industry Structure

Over any reasonable length of time, in many industries competition can be viewed as a process driven by innovation.[20] Companies that pioneer new products, processes, or strategies can often earn enormous profits. This prospect gives companies a strong incentive to seek innovative products, processes, and strategies. Consider, for example, the explosive growth of Apple Computer, Dell Computer, Toys 'R' Us, or Wal-Mart. In one way or another, all these companies were innovators. Apple pioneered the personal computer, Dell pioneered a whole new way of selling personal computers (by mail order), Toys 'R' Us pioneered a new way of selling toys (through large discount warehouse-type stores), and Wal-Mart pioneered the low-price discount superstore concept.

Successful innovation can revolutionize industry structure. In recent decades one of the most common consequences of innovation has been to lower the fixed costs of production, thereby reducing barriers to entry and allowing new, and smaller, enterprises to compete with large established organizations. Take the steel industry as an example. Two decades ago the industry was populated by large integrated steel companies such as U.S. Steel, LTV, and Bethlehem Steel. Dominated by a small number of large producers, the industry was a typical oligopoly, in which tacit price collusion was practiced. Then along came a series of efficient minimill producers such as Nucor and Chaparral Steel, which utilized a new technology—electric arc furnaces. Over the last twenty years, they have revolutionized the structure of the industry. What was once a consolidated industry is now much more fragmented and price competitive. The successor company to U.S. Steel, USX, now has only a 15 percent market share, down from 55 percent in the mid 1960s, and both Bethlehem and LTV have been through Chapter 11 bankruptcy proceedings. In contrast, as a group, the minimills now hold more than 30 percent of the market, up from 5 percent twenty years ago. Thus, the minimill innovation has reshaped the nature of competition in the steel industry.[21] A five forces model applied to the industry in 1970 would look very different from a five forces model applied in 1995.

In his more recent work, Michael Porter, the originator of the five forces and strategic group concepts, has explicitly recognized the role of innovation in revolutionizing industry structure. Porter now talks of innovations as "unfreezing" and "reshaping" industry structure. He argues that after a period of turbulence triggered by innovation the structure of an industry once more settles down into a fairly stable pattern. When the industry stabilizes in its new configuration, the five forces and strategic group concepts can once more be applied.[22] This view of the evolution of industry structure is often referred to as *punctuated equilibrium*.[23] The punctuated equilibrium view holds that long periods of equilibrium, when an industry's structure is stable, are punctuated by periods of rapid change when industry structure is revolutionized by innovation; there is an unfreezing and refreezing process

Figure 3.4 shows what punctuated equilibrium might look like for one key dimension of industry structure—competitive structure. From time t_0 to t_1 the competitive structure of the industry is a stable oligopoly, with a few companies sharing the market. At time t_1 a major new innovation is pioneered by either an existing company or a new entrant. The result is a period of turbulence between t_1 and t_2. After a while, however, the industry settles down into a new state of equilibrium, but now the competitive structure is far more fragmented. Note that the opposite could have happened: the industry could have become more consolidated, although this seems to be less common. In general, innovations seem to lower barriers to entry, allow more companies into the industry, and as a result lead to fragmentation rather than consolidation.

It is important to understand that during periods of rapid change, when industry structure is being revolutionized by innovation, value typically migrates to new business models.[24] In stockbrokerage, which we discussed in the Opening Case, value is currently migrating from the full-service broker model toward the on-line trading model. In the steel industry, the introduction of electric arc technology led to a migration of value from large integrated enterprises toward small minimills. In the book-selling industry, value may be beginning to migrate from "brick and mortar" booksellers toward on-line bookstores such as amazon.com (although it is still too early to state definitively how successful the on-line retail model will eventually be).

Because the five forces and strategic group models are static, they cannot adequately capture what occurs during periods of rapid change in the industry environment when value is migrating, but they are useful tools for analyzing industry

FIGURE 3.4

Punctuated Equilibrium
and Competitive
Structure

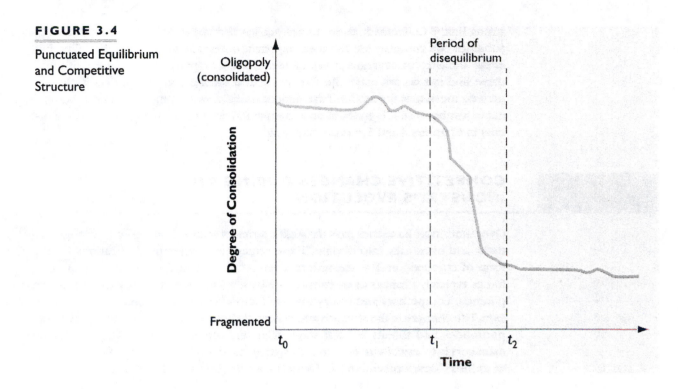

structure during periods of stability. Some scholars, though, question the validity of the punctuated equilibrium approach. Richard D'Avani has argued that many industries are **hypercompetitive**.[25] Hypercompetitive industries are characterized by permanent and ongoing innovation (the computer industry is often cited as an example of a hypercompetitive industry). The structure of such industries is constantly being revolutionized by innovation; there are no periods of equilibrium. When this is the case, some might argue that the five forces and strategic group models are of limited value since they represent no more than snapshots of a moving picture.

■ Industry Structure and Company Differences

The second criticism of the five forces and strategic group models is that they overemphasize the importance of industry structure as a determinant of company performance and underemphasize the importance of differences between companies within an industry or strategic group.[26] As we point out in the next chapter, there can be enormous variance in the profit rates of individual companies within an industry. Research by Richard Rumelt and others, for example, suggests that industry structure explains only about 10 percent of the variance in profit rates across companies.[27] The implication being that individual company differences explain much of the remainder. Other studies have put the explained variance closer to 20 percent, which is still not a large figure.[28] Similarly, a growing number of studies have found only very weak evidence of a link between strategic group membership and company profit rates, despite the fact that the strategic group model predicts a strong link.[29] Collectively, these studies suggest that the individual resources and capabilities of a company are far more important determinants of its profitability than is the industry or strategic group of which the company is a member. Although these findings do not make the five forces and strategic group models irrelevant, they do mean that the models have limited usefulness. A company will not be profitable just because it is based in an attractive industry or strategic group. As we discuss in Chapters 4 and 5, more is required.

COMPETITIVE CHANGES DURING AN INDUSTRY'S EVOLUTION

Over time, most industries pass through a series of stages, from growth through maturity and eventually into decline. These stages have different implications for the form of competition. The strength and nature of each of Porter's five competitive forces typically changes as an industry evolves.[30] This is particularly true regarding potential competitors and rivalry, and we focus on these two forces in our discussion. The changes in the strength and nature of these forces give rise to different opportunities and threats at each stage of an industry's evolution. The task facing managers is to *anticipate* how the strength of each force will change with the stage of industry development and to formulate strategies that take advantage of opportunities as they arise and that counter emerging threats.

The **industry life cycle model** is a useful tool for analyzing the effects of industry evolution on competitive forces. With it, we can identify five industry environments, each linked to a distinct stage of an industry's evolution: (1) an embryonic industry environment, (2) a growth industry environment, (3) a shakeout environment, (4) a mature industry environment, and (5) a declining industry environment (see Figure 3.5).

FIGURE 3.5

Stages of the Industry
Life Cycle

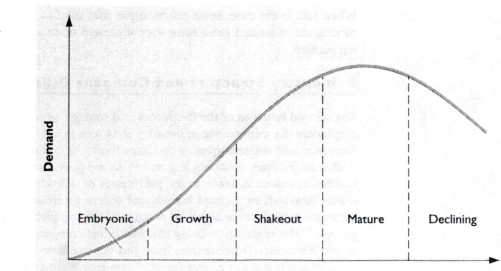

▨ Embryonic Industries

An *embryonic* industry is one that is just beginning to develop (for example, personal computers in 1980). Growth at this stage is slow because of such factors as buyers' unfamiliarity with the industry's product, high prices due to the inability of companies to reap any significant scale economies, and poorly developed distribution channels. Barriers to entry at this stage in an industry's evolution tend to be based on access to key technological know-how rather than cost economies or brand loyalty. If the core know-how required to compete in the industry is complex and difficult to grasp, barriers to entry can be quite high and incumbent companies will be protected from potential competitors. Rivalry in embryonic industries is based not so much on price as on educating customers, opening up distribution channels, and perfecting the design of the product. Such rivalry can be intense, and the company that is the first to solve design problems often has the opportunity to develop a significant market position. An embryonic industry may also be the creation of one company's innovative efforts, as happened with personal computers (Apple), vacuum cleaners (Hoover), and photocopiers (Xerox). In such circumstances, the company has a major opportunity to capitalize on the lack of rivalry and build up a strong hold on the market.

▨ Growth Industries

Once demand for the industry's product begins to take off, the industry develops the characteristics of a growth industry. In a *growth* industry, first-time demand is expanding rapidly as many new consumers enter the market. Typically, an industry grows when consumers become familiar with the product, when prices fall because experience and scale economies have been attained, and when distribution channels develop. The U.S. cellular telephone industry was in the growth stage for most of the 1990s. In 1990, there were only 5 million cellular subscribers in the nation. By 1998, however, this figure had increased to 70 million, and overall demand was still growing at a rate in excess of 25 percent per year. Similarly, in the United States the number of subscribers to on-line Internet services expanded from less than 1 million in 1990 to more than 60 million by the end of the decade.

Normally, the importance of control over technological knowledge as a barrier to entry has diminished by the time an industry enters its growth stage. Because few companies have yet achieved significant scale economies or differentiated their product sufficiently to guarantee brand loyalty, other entry barriers tend to be relatively low as well, particularly early in the growth stage. Thus, the threat from potential competitors is generally highest at this point. Paradoxically, however, high growth usually means that new entrants can be absorbed into an industry without a marked increase in competitive pressure.

During an industry's growth stage, rivalry tends to be relatively low. Rapid growth in demand enables companies to expand their revenues and profits without taking market share away from competitors. A company has the opportunity to expand its operations. In addition, a strategically aware company takes advantage of the relatively benign environment of the growth stage to prepare itself for the intense competition of the coming industry shakeout.

Industry Shakeout

Explosive growth of the type experienced by the cellular telephone or personal computer industries in the first half of the 1990s cannot be maintained indefinitely. Sooner or later the rate of growth slows, and the industry enters the shakeout stage. In the *shakeout* stage, demand approaches saturation levels. In a saturated market, there are few potential first-time buyers left. Most of the demand is limited to replacement demand.

As an industry enters the shakeout stage, rivalry between companies becomes intense. What typically happens is that companies that have become accustomed to rapid growth during an industry's growth phase continue to add capacity at rates consistent with past growth. Managers use historic growth rates to forecast future growth rates, and they plan expansions in productive capacity accordingly. As an industry approaches maturity, however, demand no longer grows at historic rates. The consequence is the emergence of excess productive capacity. This condition is illustrated in Figure 3.6, where the solid curve indicates the growth in demand over time and the broken curve indicates the growth in productive capacity over time. As you can see, past point t_1, demand growth becomes slower as the industry becomes mature. However, capacity continues to grow until time t_2. The gap between the solid and the broken lines signifies excess capacity. In an attempt to utilize this capacity, companies often cut prices. The result can be a price war, which drives many of the most inefficient companies into bankruptcy. This is itself enough to deter any new entry.

Mature Industries

The shakeout stage ends when the industry enters its *mature* stage. In a mature industry, the market is totally saturated and demand is limited to replacement de-

FIGURE 3.6

Growth in Demand and Capacity

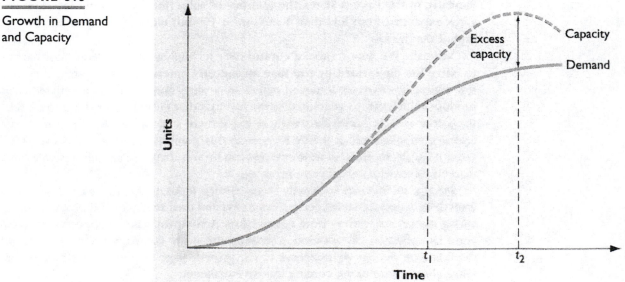

mand. During this stage, growth is low or zero. What little growth there is comes from population expansion bringing new consumers into the market.

As an industry enters maturity, barriers to entry increase and the threat of entry from potential competitors decreases. As growth slows during the shakeout, companies can no longer maintain historic growth rates merely by holding on to their market share. Competition for market share develops, driving down prices. Often the result is a price war, as happened in the airline industry during the 1988–1992 shakeout. To survive the shakeout, companies begin to focus both on cost minimization and on building brand loyalty. The airlines, for example, tried to cut operating costs by hiring nonunion labor and to build brand loyalty by introducing frequent-flyer programs. By the time an industry matures, the surviving companies are those that have brand loyalty and low-cost operations. Because both of these factors constitute a significant barrier to entry, the threat of entry by potential competitors is greatly diminished. High entry barriers in mature industries give companies the opportunity to increase prices and profits.

As a result of the shakeout, most industries in the maturity stage have consolidated and become oligopolies. In the airline industry, for example, because of the shakeout, the top five companies controlled 80 percent of the industry in 1995, up from only 50 percent in 1984. In mature industries, companies tend to recognize their interdependence and try to avoid price wars. Stable demand gives them the opportunity to enter into price-leadership agreements. The net effect is to reduce the threat of intense rivalry among established companies, thereby allowing greater profitability. However, as noted earlier, the stability of a mature industry is always threatened by further price wars. A general slump in economic activity can depress industry demand. As companies fight to maintain their revenues when demand flags, price-leadership agreements break down, rivalry increases, and prices and profits fall. The periodic price wars that occur in the airline industry seem to follow this pattern.

■ Declining Industries

Eventually, most industries enter a decline stage. In the *decline* stage, growth becomes negative for a variety of reasons, including technological substitution (for example, air travel for rail travel), social changes (greater health consciousness hitting tobacco sales), demographics (the declining birthrate hurting the market for baby and child products), and international competition (low-cost foreign competition pushing the U.S. steel industry into decline). Within a declining industry, the degree of rivalry among established companies usually increases. Depending on the speed of the decline and the height of exit barriers, competitive pressures can become as fierce as in the shakeout stage.[31] The main problem in a declining industry is that falling demand leads to the emergence of excess capacity. In trying to utilize this capacity, companies begin to cut prices, thus sparking a price war. As noted earlier, the U.S. steel industry experienced these problems because of the attempt of steel companies to utilize their excess capacity. The same problem occurred in the airline industry in the 1990–1992 period, as companies cut prices to ensure that they would not be flying with half-empty planes (that is, that they would not be operating with substantial excess capacity). Exit barriers play a part in adjusting excess capacity. The greater the exit barriers, the harder it is for companies to reduce capacity and the greater is the threat of severe price competition.

■ Variations on the Theme

It is important to remember that the industry life cycle model is a generalization. In practice, industry life cycles do not always follow the pattern illustrated in Figure 3.5. In some cases, growth is so rapid that the embryonic stage is skipped altogether. In other instances, industries fail to get past the embryonic stage. Industry growth can be revitalized after long periods of decline, either through innovations or through social changes. For example, the health boom brought the bicycle industry back to life after a long period of decline. The time span of the different stages can also vary significantly from industry to industry. Some industries can stay in maturity almost indefinitely if their products become basic necessities of life, as is the case for the automobile industry. Others skip the mature stage and go straight into decline. That is essentially what occurred in the vacuum tube industry. Vacuum tubes were replaced by transistors as a major component in electronic products while the industry was still in its growth stage. Still other industries may go through not one but several shakeouts before they enter full maturity.

NETWORK ECONOMICS AS A DETERMINANT OF INDUSTRY CONDITIONS

In recent years, there has been a growing realization that network economics are a primary determinant of competitive conditions in many high-technology industries, including computer hardware and software, consumer electronics, home video games, telecommunications, and Internet service providers.[32] **Network economics** arise in industries where the size of the "network" of *complementary* products is a primary determinant of demand for the industry's product. As argued earlier, the demand for automobiles early in the twentieth century was an increasing function of the *network* of paved roads and gas stations. Similarly, the demand for telephones is an increasing function of the number of other numbers that can be called with that phone; in other words, of the size of the telephone network (that is, the telephone network is the complementary product). When the first telephone service was introduced in New York City, only a hundred numbers could be called. The network was very small. There was only a limited number of wires and telephone switches. Consequently, the telephone was a relatively useless piece of equipment, nothing more than a technological curiosity. However, as more and more people got telephones and as the network of wires and switches expanded, the value of a telephone connection increased. This led to an increase in demand for telephone lines, which further increased the value of owning a telephone, setting up a positive feedback loop.

The same type of positive feedback loop is now at work in the Internet. The value of an Internet connection to individual users is an increasing function of the supply of useful information that they can access over the Internet and of the opportunity for engaging in commercial transactions through the medium of the Internet. The number of people with Internet connections drives forward the supply of such information and commercial services. The larger the number of people who are connected to the Internet, the greater is the opportunity for making money by supplying information and commercial services over the Internet. Thus, as more people connect to the Internet, this produces an increase in the supply of information and commercial services offered over the Internet. This increase, in turn, enhances the value of an Internet connection, which drives forward the demand for Internet connections, which leads to a further increase in the supply of information and services, and so on.

Why do network economics affect industry conditions? Well, for a start, once established, a positive feedback loop can help generate rapid demand growth, as we are now seeing in the Internet arena. The demand for Internet on-line services has been expanding at an exponential pace, primarily because a positive feedback loop is at work. Of course, such exponential surges in demand cannot go on forever, but while they are at work they make for very attractive industry conditions. Second, the operation of positive feedback loops can result in an industry becoming very concentrated and potential competitors being locked out by high switching costs. To understand this process, consider the history of the personal computer industry.

The value of a personal computer is an increasing function of the amount of software that is used on that computer and of the number of other complementary products that can be used with that computer, including printers, modems, and Internet connections. In other words, the value of a PC is an increasing function of the "network" of complementary products. In the late 1970s, a large number of different personal computers were on the market, and they used different operating systems and different microprocessors. Now the market is dominated by just one offering, the so-called Windows-Intel (or Wintel) standard. The only other viable product offering is that sold by Apple Computer, which has a small share of the market (in recent years, its share has never been more than 10 percent). The markets for personal computer operating systems and for microprocessors have become very concentrated, with Microsoft and Intel, respectively, dominating them. Moreover, high switching costs have raised entry barriers, making it extremely difficult for new enterprises to enter these markets.

This situation developed because IBM picked a Microsoft operating system (MS-DOS) and an Intel microprocessor to power its first personal computer, which was introduced in 1981. The IBM brand name had a lot of clout among businesses at the time, and demand for IBM PCs took off. As the *installed base* of IBM PCs grew, independent software developers faced a choice: whether to first write applications for the IBM PC or for competing products, such as that sold by Apple Computer. They were forced into making this choice because software written to run on one operating system and microprocessor will not run on another. As the sales of IBM PCs expanded, increasingly software developers wrote applications to run on an MS-DOS operating system powered by an Intel microprocessor, before turning their attention to applications for other computers, such as Apple's offering. Consequently, from early on, there was always more software available to run on the MS-DOS/Intel computers than on Apple computers. This increased the value of MS-DOS/Intel computers, relative to the alternatives, which led to a further increase in demand, and in turn, a more rapid increase in the supply of software to run on MS-DOS/Intel machines. In other words, the early lead gained by MS-DOS/Intel-based machines set up a positive feedback loop which resulted in the installed base of MS-DOS/Intel machines growing much faster than the installed base of alternative product offerings. This lead was sustained when Apple introduced its Macintosh operating system, which was arguably superior to Microsoft's MS-DOS offering, and continued when Microsoft replaced MS-DOS with Windows to create the Wintel standard (see Figure 3.7).

As a result of network economics, the markets for personal computer operating systems and microprocessors have become very concentrated. Microsoft and Intel

FIGURE 3.7

Positive Feedback in the Computer Industry

have tremendous bargaining power versus their suppliers and buyers, while switching costs have produced high barriers to entry. Because of these factors, as one might expect, Microsoft and Intel enjoy very high profit margins. Despite several attempts, new competitors have remained locked out of these profitable markets (see Strategy in Action 3.3 for an example). However, it would be wrong to assume that Microsoft and Intel are therefore immune to competition. If a new competitor should arise offering an operating system or microprocessor that is so superior that consumers are willing to bear switching costs, Microsoft and Intel could lose market share. The fact that this has not happened yet is partly a testament to the ability of Microsoft and Intel to improve continually the performance capabilities of the Windows operating systems and Intel's microprocessors.

In summary, a consideration of network economics leads to a number of important conclusions. First, in industries where network economics are important, positive feedback loops tend to operate. Once initiated, a positive feedback loop can lead to a rapid increase in demand. Second, markets where positive feedback loops operate tend to be winner-takes-all markets, with second- or third-string competitors being marginalized. This has occurred in the markets for computer operating systems and microprocessors. Third, enterprises that benefit from network economics tend to be in a powerful position relative to buyers and suppliers and tend to be protected from potential competitors by entry barriers arising from switching costs. From the perspective of an individual company, the trick is to find the right strategy that enables it to grow the installed base of its product rapidly in order to set up a positive feedback loop.

GLOBALIZATION AND INDUSTRY STRUCTURE

A fundamental change is occurring in the world economy.[34] We seem to be witnessing the globalization of production and of markets. With regard to the **globalization of production**, it has been observed that individual companies are increasingly dispersing parts of their production process to different locations around the globe to take advantage of national differences in the cost and quality of factors of production such as labor, energy, land, and capital. The objective is to lower costs and boost profits.

STRATEGY *in* ACTION

The Failure of Digital's Alpha Chip

In February 1992, Digital Equipment Corporation introduced the world's fastest microprocessor, the Alpha chip. Microprocessors are the brains of personal computers, workstations, and servers. The Alpha chip operated at more than twice the speed of Intel's best-selling microprocessors. Many at Digital had great hopes for the product, believing that it could ultimately grab a significant share of the booming market for microprocessors. By 1997, however, after Digital had spent $2.5 billion to develop the Alpha, the chip ranked dead last in market share, with an estimated 1 percent of the $18 billion microprocessor market. Intel's share stood at 92 percent.

The failure of the Alpha to gain market share despite its apparent performance advantage over existing microprocessors can be explained easily enough: there was never enough software to run on the Alpha. Hence, potential customers stayed away from investing in computers based on the Alpha chip. Digital was never able to get a positive feedback cycle going in which an increase in the supply of software configured to run on Alpha-based systems would have driven demand for Alpha-based computers, which would have meant that developers would have supplied more software for the Alpha, which would have further increased the demand for Alpha-based computers, and so on.

To be fair, Digital seemed to start off on the correct foot. In 1992, Microsoft agreed to adapt its next-generation operating system for corporate computers, Windows NT, so that it would run on the Alpha chip, in addition to Intel microprocessors. In return for this commitment from Microsoft, Digital agreed to make NT a central part of its own computer business. (Digital sold workstations, servers, and personal computers.) Following the agreement, Digital engineers devoted tremendous effort to fine-tuning the Alpha so that it would work with NT. However, when Digital engineers loaded tested versions of NT into their computers, it became clear that NT needed far too much computer memory to run on a typical PC, putting Alpha beyond the reach of the mass market Digital had been hoping for.

In the spring of 1995, Digital tried again to kick start demand for the Alpha. Under the terms of a revised agreement with Microsoft, Digital agreed to provide network installation services for Microsoft. For its part, Microsoft agreed to continue to write a version of NT for the Alpha chip and to pay Digital up to $100 million to help train Digital NT technicians. Moreover, in October of that year, Microsoft stopped writing versions of NT for the IBM Power PC chip and Motorola's MIPS microprocessor, leaving the Alpha and Intel's Pentium series as the only chips that could run Windows NT.

Despite these developments, sales of the Alpha chip were still slow to take off. The Intel-based system now had such a huge lead in the Windows NT business that few developers were willing to take the risk and customize their software applications to run on the Alpha version of Windows NT, as opposed to Intel-based machines. To make matters worse, Digital hurt its own prospects by continuing to attach a premium price to Alpha machines, which slowed demand growth. By late 1994, Digital engineers had found a way to deliver Alpha workstations for $4,995. However, some of Digital's senior management vetoed the move because they feared that it would damage the 50 percent gross margins that Digital enjoyed in the high-end computer markets, which at the time was one of the few bright spots in Digital's business. In the end, when Digital did introduce its Alpha-based workstations for Windows NT, they were priced at $7,995, significantly above the price of high-end Intel-based machines. For corporate customers, this made the decision to go with Intel machines for Windows NT obvious—they were cheaper and more software applications were available for the Intel versions.[33]

For example, Boeing's new commercial jet aircraft, the 777, involves 132,500 engineered parts, which are produced around the world by 545 different suppliers. Eight Japanese suppliers make parts of the fuselage, doors, and wings; a supplier in Singapore makes the doors for the nose landing gear; three suppliers in Italy manufacture wing flaps; and so on. Part of Boeing's rationale for outsourcing so much production to foreign suppliers is that these various suppliers are the best in the world at performing their particular activity. Therefore, the result of having foreign suppliers build specific parts is a better final product.[35]

As for the **globalization of markets**, it has been argued that we are moving away from an economic system in which national markets are distinct entities, isolated from each other by trade barriers and barriers of distance, time, and culture, and toward a system in which national markets are merging into one huge global marketplace. Increasingly, consumers around the world demand and use the same basic product offerings. Consequently, in many industries it is no longer meaningful to talk about the German market, the U.S. market, or the Japanese market—there is only the global market. The global acceptance of Coca-Cola, Citigroup credit cards, Levi's blue jeans, the Sony PlayStation, McDonald's hamburgers, Nokia wireless phones, and Microsoft's Windows operating system exemplifies this trend.[36]

The trend toward the globalization of production and markets has several important implications for competition within an industry. First, it is crucial for companies to recognize that an industry's boundaries do not stop at national borders. Because many industries are becoming global in scope, actual and potential competitors exist not only in a company's home market, but also in other national markets. Companies that scan just their home market can be caught unprepared by the entry of efficient foreign competitors. The globalization of markets and production all imply that companies around the globe are finding their home markets under attack from foreign competitors. To illustrate, in Japan, Merrill Lynch and Citicorp are making inroads against Japanese financial service institutions. In the United States, Fuji has been taking market share from Kodak and Finland's Nokia has taken the lead from Motorola in the market for wireless phone handsets (see Strategy in Action 3.4). In the European Union, the once dominant Dutch company, Philips, has seen its market share in the consumer electronics industry taken by Japan's JVC, Matsushita, and Sony.

Second, the shift from national to global markets during the last twenty years has intensified competitive rivalry in industry after industry. National markets that were once consolidated oligopolies, dominated by three or four companies and subjected to relatively little foreign competition, have been transformed into segments of fragmented global industries, where a large number of companies battle each other for market share in country after country. This rivalry has driven down profit rates and made it all the more critical for companies to maximize their efficiency, quality, customer responsiveness, and innovative ability. The painful restructuring and downsizing that has been going on at companies such as Motorola and Kodak is as much a response to the increased intensity of global competition as it is to anything else. However, not all global industries are fragmented. Many remain consolidated oligopolies, except that now they are consolidated global, rather than national, oligopolies.

Third, as competitive intensity has increased, so has the rate of innovation. Companies strive to gain an advantage over their competitors by pioneering new products, processes, and ways of doing business. The result has been to compress product life cycles and make it vital for companies to stay on the leading edge of technology. In regard to highly competitive global industries, where the rate of innovation is accelerating, the criticism that Porter's five forces model is too static may be particularly relevant.

Finally, even though globalization has increased both the threat of entry and the intensity of rivalry within many formerly protected national markets, it has also created enormous opportunities for companies based in those markets. The steady decline in trade barriers has opened up many once protected markets to companies based outside them. Thus, for example, in recent years, western European, Japanese, and U.S. companies have accelerated their investments in the nations of eastern Europe, Latin America, and Southeast Asia as they try to take advantage of growth opportunities in those areas.

THE NATION-STATE AND COMPETITIVE ADVANTAGE

Despite the globalization of production and markets, many of the most successful companies in certain industries are still clustered in a small number of countries. For example, many of the world's most successful biotechnology and computer companies are based in the United States, many of the world's most successful consumer electronics companies are based in Japan, and many of the world's most successful chemical and engineering companies are based in Germany. This suggests that the nation-state within which a company is based may have an important bearing on the competitive position of that company in the global marketplace.

Companies need to understand how national factors can affect competitive advantage, for then they will be able to identify (1) where their most significant competitors are likely to come from and (2) where they might want to locate certain productive activities. Thus, seeking to take advantage of U.S. expertise in biotechnology, many foreign companies have set up research facilities in U.S. locations such as San Diego, Boston, and Seattle, where U.S. biotechnology companies tend to be clustered. Similarly, in an attempt to take advantage of Japanese success in consumer electronics, many U.S. electronics companies have set up research and production facilities in Japan, often in conjunction with Japanese partners.

In a study of national competitive advantage, Porter identified four attributes of a nation-state that have an important impact on the global competitiveness of companies located within that nation:

- *Factor endowments:* a nation's position in factors of production such as skilled labor or the infrastructure necessary to compete in a given industry

- *Local demand conditions:* the nature of home demand for the industry's product or service

- *Competitiveness of related and supporting industries:* the presence or absence in a nation of supplier industries and related industries that are internationally competitive

- *Strategy, structure, and rivalry:* the conditions in the nation governing how companies are created, organized, and managed and the nature of domestic rivalry[37]

Porter speaks of these four attributes as constituting *the diamond* (see Figure 3.8). He argues that firms are most likely to succeed in industries or industry segments

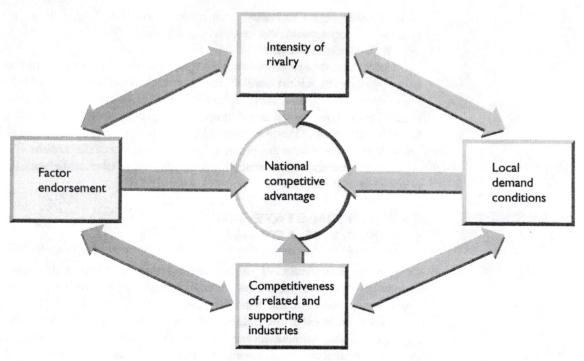

FIGURE 3.8

National Competitive
Advantage

where conditions with regard to the four attributes are favorable. He also argues that the diamond's attributes form a mutually reinforcing system in which the effect of one attribute is dependent on the state of others.

Factor Endowments

Porter follows basic economic theory in stressing that **factor conditions**—the cost and quality of factors of production—are a prime determinant of the competitive advantage that certain countries might have in certain industries. Factors of production include **basic factors,** such as land, labor, capital, and raw materials, and **advanced factors** such as technological know-how, that is, managerial sophistication and physical infrastructure (such as, roads, railways, and ports). The competitive advantage that the United States enjoys in biotechnology might be explained by the presence of certain advanced factors of production—technological know-how, for instance—in combination with some basic factors, which might be a pool of relatively low-cost venture capital that can be used to fund risky start-ups in industries such as biotechnology.

Local Demand Conditions

Porter emphasizes the role home demand plays in providing the impetus for "upgrading" competitive advantage. Companies are typically most sensitive to the needs of their closest customers. Hence, the characteristics of home demand are particularly important in shaping the attributes of domestically made products and in creating pressures for innovation and quality. Porter argues that a nation's companies gain competitive advantage if their domestic consumers are sophisticated and demanding. Sophisticated and demanding consumers pressure local companies to meet high standards of product quality and to produce innovative products. Porter notes that Japan's sophisticated and knowledgeable buyers of cameras helped stimulate the Japanese camera industry to improve product quality and to introduce innovative models. A similar example can be found in the cellular phone equipment industry, where sophisticated and demanding local customers in Scandinavia helped push Nokia of Finland and Ericsson of Sweden to invest in cellular phone technology long before demand for cellular phones took off in other developed nations. As a result, Nokia and Ericsson, together with Motorola, are today dominant players in the global cellular telephone equipment industry. The case of Nokia is reviewed in more depth in Strategy in Action 3.4.

Competitiveness of Related and Supporting Industries

The third broad attribute of national advantage in an industry is the presence in a country of suppliers or related industries that are internationally competitive. The benefits of investments in advanced factors of production by related and supporting industries can spill over into an industry, thereby helping it achieve a strong competitive position internationally. Swedish strength in fabricated steel products (for instance, ball bearings and cutting tools) has drawn on strengths in Sweden's specialty steel industry. Technological leadership in the U.S. semiconductor industry during the period up to the mid 1980s provided the basis for U.S. success in personal computers and several other technically advanced electronic products. Similarly, Switzerland's success in pharmaceuticals is closely linked to its previous international success in the technologically related dye industry. One consequence of this process is that successful industries within a country tend to be grouped into "clusters" of related industries. Indeed, this was one of the most pervasive findings of Porter's study. One such cluster is the German textile and apparel sector, which includes high-quality cotton, wool, synthetic fibers, sewing machine needles, and a wide range of textile machinery.

Strategy, Structure, and Rivalry

The fourth broad attribute of national competitive advantage in Porter's model is the strategy, structure, and rivalry of companies within a nation. Porter makes two important points here. His first is that different nations are characterized by different "management ideologies," which either help them or do not help them build national competitive advantage. For example, he notes the predominance of engineers on the top-management teams of German and Japanese companies. He attributes this to the companies' emphasis on improving manufacturing processes and product design. In contrast, Porter notes a predominance of people with finance backgrounds on the top-management teams of many U.S. companies. He links this to the lack of attention paid in many U.S. companies to improving manufacturing processes and product design, particularly during the 1970s and 80s. He also argues that the dominance of finance has led to a corresponding overemphasis on maximizing short-term financial returns. According to Porter, one consequence of these different management ideologies has been a relative loss of U.S. competitiveness in

Finland's Nokia

The wireless phone market is one of the great growth stories of the 1990s. Starting from a very low base in 1990, annual global sales of wireless phones surged to 163 million units in 1998, representing an increase of 51 percent over the prior year. By 2000, some 300 million people worldwide will probably be using wireless phones. Four companies currently dominate the global market for wireless handsets: Motorola, Nokia, Ericsson, and Qualcomm. In 1998, the global market leader was Nokia, which had a 23 percent share, followed by Motorola with 20 percent and Ericsson with 15 percent. In the United States, the world's largest market, Nokia's dominance was even greater. The company had a 30 percent share of the U.S. market in 1998, compared with 23 percent for Motorola (which used to dominate the market), 11 percent for Ericsson, and 10 percent for Qualcomm.

Nokia's roots are in Finland, not normally a country that jumps to mind when we talk about leading-edge technology companies. Back in the 1980s, Nokia was a rambling Finnish conglomerate whose activities embraced tire manufacturing, paper production, consumer electronics and telecommunications equipment. How has this former conglomerate emerged to take a global leadership position in wireless handsets? Much of the answer lies in the history, geography, and political economy of Finland and its Nordic neighbors.

The story starts in 1981. It was then that the Nordic nations got together to create the world's first international wireless telephone network. Sparsely populated and inhospitably cold, they had good reason to become pioneers; it cost far too much to lay down a traditional wire line telephone service. Yet the very conditions causing the difficulty made telecommunications all the more valuable there; people driving through the Arctic winter and owners of remote northern houses needed a telephone to summon help if things went wrong. As a result, Sweden, Norway, and Finland became the first nations in the world to take wireless telecommunications seriously. They found, for example, that while it cost up to $800 per subscriber to bring a traditional wire line service to remote locations in the far north, the same locations could be linked by wireless cellular for only $500 per person.

Consequently, 12 percent of people in Scandinavia owned cellular phones by 1994, compared with less than 6 percent in the United States, the world's second most developed market. This lead continued during the decade. It is estimated that by 2000 more than 50 percent of Finland's phone users will have a wireless phone, compared with 25 percent in the United States, and the figure may reach 100 percent by 2010.

Nokia, a long-time telecommunications equipment supplier, was well positioned to take advantage of this development from the start, but there were also other forces at work in Finland that helped Nokia gain a competitive edge. Unlike virtually every other developed country, Finland has never had a national telephone monopoly. Instead, telephone service has long been provided by fifty or so autonomous local telephone companies, whose elected boards set prices by referendum (which, naturally, results in low prices). This army of independent and cost-conscious telephone service providers prevented Nokia from taking anything for granted in its home country. With typical Finnish pragmatism, its customers were willing to buy from the lowest-cost supplier, whether that was Nokia, Ericsson, Motorola, or someone else. This situation contrasted sharply with that prevailing in most developed nations up until the late 1980s and early 1990s, where domestic telephone monopolies typically purchased equipment from a dominant local supplier or made it themselves. Nokia responded to this competitive pressure by doing everything possible to drive down its manufacturing costs while staying at the leading edge of wireless technology.

The consequences of these forces are clear: the once obscure Finnish firm is now a global leader in the wireless market. Moreover, Nokia has emerged as the leader in digital wireless technology, which is the wave of the future. In no small part, Nokia has the lead because Scandinavia started switching over to digital technology five years before the rest of the world. In addition, spurred on by its cost-conscious customers, Nokia now has the lowest cost structure of any wireless handset equipment manufacturer in the world, and as a result, it is a more profitable enterprise than its global competitors.[39]

those engineering-based industries where manufacturing processes and product design issues are all-important (such as automobiles).

Porter's second point is that there is a strong association between vigorous domestic rivalry and the creation and persistence of competitive advantage in an industry. Vigorous domestic rivalry induces companies to look for ways to improve efficiency, which in turn makes them better international competitors. Domestic rivalry creates pressures to innovate, to improve quality, to reduce costs, and to invest in upgrading advanced factors. All this helps create world-class competitors. As an illustration, Porter cites the case of Japan:

> Nowhere is the role of domestic rivalry more evident than in Japan, where it is all-out warfare in which many companies fail to achieve profitability. With goals that stress market share, Japanese companies engage in a continuing struggle to outdo each other. Shares fluctuate markedly. The process is prominently covered in the business press. Elaborate rankings measure which companies are most popular with university graduates. The rate of new product and process development is breathtaking.[38]

A similar point about the stimulating effects of strong domestic competition can be made with regard to the rise of Nokia of Finland to global preeminence in the market for cellular telephone equipment (see Strategy in Action 3.4).

In sum, Porter's argument is that the degree to which a nation is likely to achieve international success in a certain industry is a function of the combined impact of factor endowments, domestic demand conditions, related and supporting industries, and domestic rivalry. He argues that for this "diamond" to have a positive impact on competitive performance usually requires the presence of all four components (although there are some exceptions). Porter also contends that government can influence each of the four components of the diamond either positively or negatively. It can affect factor endowments through subsidies, policies toward capital markets, policies toward education, and the like, and it can shape domestic demand through local product standards or with regulations that mandate or influence buyer needs. Government policy can also influence supporting and related industries through regulation, and influence rivalry through such devices as capital market regulation, tax policy, and antitrust laws.

As an example of Porter's theory, consider the U.S. computer hardware industry (personal computers, workstations, minicomputers, and mainframes). The existence of a world-class industry in the United States can be explained by the presence of advanced factors of production in the form of technological know-how; an intense rivalry among myriad competing computer companies; a strong local demand for computers (more personal computers have been sold in the United States than in the rest of the world combined); and internationally competitive supporting industries, such as the computer software and microprocessor industries.

Perhaps the most important implication of Porter's framework is its message about the attractiveness of certain locations for performing certain productive activities. For instance, many Japanese computer companies have moved much of their R&D activity to the United States so that they can benefit from the international competitiveness of the United States in this industry. Most U.S. financial service companies have substantial operations in London so that they can take advantage of London's central position in the world financial services industry. And many international textile companies have design operations in Italy so that they can take advantage of Italian style and design know-how. In all these cases, companies are trying to build a competitive advantage by establishing critical productive activities in the optimal location, as defined by the various elements highlighted in Porter's framework. This is an issue we discuss in depth in Chapter 8.

SUMMARY OF CHAPTER

This chapter details a framework that managers can use to analyze the external environment of their company, enabling them to identify opportunities and threats. The following major points are made in the chapter:

- For a company to succeed, either its strategy must fit the environment in which the company operates, or the company must be able to re-shape this environment to its advantage through its choice of strategy. Companies typically fail when their strategy no longer fits the environment in which they operate.

- The main technique used to analyze competition in the industry environment is the five forces model. The five forces are (1) the risk of new entry by potential competitors, (2) the extent of rivalry among established firms, (3) the bargaining power of buyers, (4) the bargaining power of suppliers, and (5) the threat of substitute products. The stronger each force, the more competitive is the industry and the lower is the rate of return that can be earned.

- The risk of entry by potential competitors is a function of the height of barriers to entry. The higher the barriers to entry, the lower is the risk of entry and the greater are the profits that can be earned in the industry.

- The extent of rivalry among established companies is a function of an industry's competitive structure, demand conditions, and barriers to exit. Strong demand conditions moderate the competition among established companies and create opportunities for expansion. When demand is weak, intensive competition can develop, particularly in consolidated industries with high exit barriers.

- Buyers are most powerful when a company depends on them for business, but they themselves are not dependent on the company. In such circumstances, buyers are a threat.

- Suppliers are most powerful when a company depends on them for business but they themselves are not dependent on the company. In such circumstances, suppliers are a threat.

- Substitute products are the products of companies serving consumer needs that are similar to the needs served by the industry being analyzed. The greater the similarity of the substitute products, the lower is the price that companies can charge without losing customers to the substitutes.

- Some argue that there is a sixth competitive force of some significance—the power, vigor and competence of complementors. Powerful and vigorous complementors may have a strong positive impact on demand in an industry.

- Most industries are composed of strategic groups. Strategic groups are groups of companies pursuing the same or a similar strategy. Companies in different strategic groups pursue different strategies.

- The members of a company's strategic group constitute its immediate competitors. Since different strategic groups are characterized by different opportunities and threats, it may pay a company to switch strategic groups. The feasibility of doing so is a function of the height of mobility barriers.

- The five forces and strategic group models have been criticized for presenting a static picture of competition that de-emphasizes the role of innovation. Innovation can revolutionize industry structure and completely change the strength of different competitive forces.

- The five forces and strategic group models have been criticized for de-emphasizing the importance of individual company differences. A company will not be profitable just because it is based in an attractive industry or strategic group; much more is required.

- Industries go through a well-defined life cycle, from an embryonic stage, through growth, shake-out, and maturity, and eventually into decline. Each stage has different implications for the competitive structure of the industry, and each stage gives rise to its own set of opportunities and threats.

- In many high-technology industries, network economics are important and positive feedback loops tend to operate. Once initiated, a positive feedback loop can lead to a rapid increase in demand. Markets where positive feedback loops operate tend to be "winner takes all" markets. Enterprises that benefit from network economics tend to be in a powerful position relative to buyers and suppliers and tend to be protected from potential competitors by entry barriers arising from switching costs

- A fundamental change is occurring in the world economy: the globalization of production and of markets. The consequences of this change include more intense rivalry, more rapid innovation, and shorter product life cycles.

- There is a link between the national environment and the competitive advantage of a company in the global economy.

DISCUSSION QUESTIONS

1. Under what environmental conditions are price wars most likely to occur in an industry? What are the implications of price wars for a company? How should a company try to deal with the threat of a price war?

2. Discuss Porter's five forces model with reference to what you know about the U.S. airline industry. What does the model tell you about the level of competition in this industry?

3. Explain what impact network effects might have on demand and industry structure in the market for wireless handsets.

4. Identify a growth industry, a mature industry, and a declining industry. For each industry, identify the following: (a) the number and size distribution of companies; (b) the nature of barriers to entry; (c) the height of barriers to entry; and (d) the extent of product differentiation. What do these factors tell you about the nature of competition in each industry? What are the implications for the company in terms of opportunities and threats?

5. Assess the impact of macroenvironmental factors on the likely level of enrollment at your university over the next decade. What are the implications of these factors for the job security and salary level of your professors?

Practicing Strategic Management

SMALL-GROUP EXERCISE
Competing with Microsoft

Break up into groups of three to five people, and discuss the following scenario:

You are a group of managers and software engineers at a small start-up. You have developed a revolutionary new operating system for personal computers. This operating system offers distinct advantages over Microsoft's Windows operating system. It takes up less memory space on the hard drive of a personal computer. It takes full advantage of the power of the personal computer's microprocessor, and in theory can run software applications much faster than Windows. It is much easier to install and use than Windows. And it responds to voice instructions with an accuracy of 99.9 percent, in addition to input from a keyboard or mouse. The operating system is the only product offering that your company has produced.

1. Analyze the competitive structure of the market for personal computer operating systems. On the basis of this analysis, identify what factors might inhibit adoption of your operating system by consumers.

2. Can you think of a strategy that your company might pursue, either alone or in conjunction with other enterprises, in order to beat Microsoft? What will it take to successfully execute that strategy?

STRATEGIC MANAGEMENT PROJECT
Module 3

This module requires you to analyze the industry environment in which your company is based. Using the information you have at your disposal, perform the following tasks and answer the questions:

1. Apply the five forces model to the industry in which your company is based. What does this model tell you about the nature of competition in the industry?

2. Are there any changes taking place in the macroenvironment that might have an impact, either positive or negative, on the industry in which your company is based? If so, what are these changes and how will they affect the industry?

3. Identify any strategic groups that might exist in the industry. How does the intensity of competition differ across the strategic groups you have identified?

4. How dynamic is the industry in which your company is based? Is there any evidence that innovation is reshaping competition or has done so in the recent past?

5. In what stage of its life cycle is the industry in which your company is based? What are the implications of this for the intensity of competition, both now and in the future?

6. Is your company based in an industry that is becoming more global? If so, what are the implications of this change for competitive intensity?

7. Analyze the impact of national context as it pertains to the industry in which your company is based. Does national context help or hinder your company in achieving a competitive advantage in the global market place?

ARTICLE FILE 3

Find an example of an industry that has become more competitive in recent years. Identify the reasons for the increase in competitive pressure.

EXPLORING THE WEB
Visiting Boeing and Airbus

Visit the Web sites of Boeing (http://www.boeing.com) and of Airbus Industrie (http://www.airbus.com). Go to the news features of both sites and read through the press releases issued by both companies. Also look at the annual reports and company profile (or history features) contained on both sites. With this material as your guide, perform the following:

1. Use Porter's five forces model to analyze the nature of competition in the global commercial jet aircraft market.

2. Assess the likely outlook for competition during the next ten years in this market. Try to establish whether new entry into this industry is likely, whether demand will grow or shrink, how powerful buyers are likely to become, and what the impli-

cations of all this may be for the nature of competition ten years from now.

General Task   Search the Web for information that allows you to assess the *current* state of competition in the market for personal computers. Use that information to perform an analysis of the structure of the market in the United States. (Hint: Try visiting the Web sites of personal computer companies. Also visit Electronic Business Today at http://www.ebtmag.com).

Boom and Bust in the Market for DRAMs

FOR MUCH OF THE FIRST HALF OF THE 1990s, the semiconductor industry seemed like one of the most extraordinary moneymaking machines ever invented. In no case has this been more true than in the market for dynamic random access memories (DRAMs), the memory devices used in personal computers (PCs), which account for about one-third of all semiconductor sales. In 1993, the global market for DRAMs was valued at $13.6 billion. In 1994, it increased to $23.1 billion, and in 1995 it surged to $55 billion. This rapid increase in demand for DRAMs was due to the confluence of a number of favorable factors.

First, stimulated by price cutting in the PC market, worldwide sales of personal computers grew at an annual average compound rate of 30 percent over the 1990–1995 period. Second, as more and more users of PCs switched to graphics-based software, such as Microsoft's Windows 95 operating system, the memory component of PCs increased. (Running graphics programs on a PC requires a large amount of memory.) Between 1991 and 1995, the average amount of DRAM contained in each PC sold increased from 2 megabytes to 12 megabytes. Third, other applications for DRAMs—particularly in telecommunications equipment and cellular phone handsets—also grew rapidly. For example, global shipments of cellular phones increased from 5 million to 50 million between 1991 and 1995.

As demand for DRAMs was surging during the 1990–1995 period, the supply was constrained. One reason for the shortage was the reluctance of many semiconductor companies to invest in new semiconductor fabricating plants. By 1995, a new fabrication facility could cost anywhere from $1 billion to $2.5 billion and take eighteen months to construct. Such enormous fixed costs made many companies wary of investing in the plants, particularly since demand conditions could change significantly in the eighteen months required to bring the new facility on line. Managers in this industry still remember the 1985–1987 period when a combination of slowing demand and massive capacity expansions by Japanese semiconductor companies led to an excess supply of DRAMs, plunging prices, and significant financial losses for most of the world's DRAM manufacturers. Indeed, it was during this period that a number of U.S. companies exited the DRAM market, including Intel, the company that invented the DRAM.

The combination of surging global demand for DRAMs and the constrained supply caused DRAM prices to rise dramatically between 1993 and 1995. In 1993, the average selling price for DRAM was $8.89 per megabyte, in 1994 it was $11.69, and by the middle of 1995 it was $14. This situation, however, benefited Micron Technology of Boise, Idaho—one of only two U.S. firms that remained in the DRAM market after the debacle of 1985–1987 (the other was Texas Instruments). In 1990, Micron had sales of under $300 million and was barely breaking even. Riding the industry wave, by 1994 the company had revenues of $1.63 billion and net income of $400 million. In 1995, its revenues rose to $2.95 billion and the net income to $844 million. Micron's gross profit margin for 1995 was 55 percent—an almost unheard of figure for a DRAM company—compared with 23 percent in 1990. Nor was Micron alone in achieving such impressive profit performance. By 1995, almost every DRAM company in the world was making record profits.

The huge profits became a signal for incumbent companies to expand their capacity and for new companies to enter the semiconductor industry. Starting in late 1994, more and more companies announced their intentions to invest in semiconductor fabrication plants. Micron Technology, too, jumped on the capacity expansion bandwagon; in June 1995, it unveiled plans to invest $2.5 billion in a new fabrication facility in Lehi, Utah, which was scheduled to begin production at the end of 1996. When Micron made its announcement, almost 100 new semiconductor fabrication facilities were being constructed around the world, many of them scheduled to come on stream in 1995 and 1996. Moreover, by the end of 1995, plans to build another 100 facilities had been announced.

In the fall of 1995, the other shoe dropped. After four years of rapid growth, there was a sudden slowdown in the growth rate of personal computer sales, particularly in the huge North American market. This slowdown occurred just as the new DRAM capacity was becoming operational. To make matters worse, throughout 1995 manufacturers of personal computers had been building up their inventories of DRAMs, both as a hedge against future price increases and to ensure an adequate supply of DRAMs for what they thought would be a very busy Christmas season. When the expected surge in Christmas sales of PCs failed to materialize, PC manufacturers found themselves holding too much inventory. They responded by drastically cutting back on their orders for DRAMs. The result: DRAM sales volume and prices slumped. Between late 1995 and March 1996, DRAM prices fell from $14 to $7 per megabyte. The consequences included falling profit margins for DRAM companies.

Reflecting the widespread perception that excess demand and rising prices had been replaced in short order by excess supply and plunging prices, the Philadelphia Semi-Conductor Index, a measure of the share price of American semiconductor companies, fell by 45 percent between September 1995 and March 1996. In February 1996, Micron Technology responded to this situation by dramatically slowing down the construction schedule for its Lehi facility, pushing out the start date for volume manufacturing another two to five years. Nor was Micron alone. By the spring of 1996, companies around the world were also announcing that they had put their capacity expansion plans on hold.[40]

Case Discussion Questions

1. Analyze the competitive structure of the DRAM market.

2. Using this analysis, explain why the industry has been characterized by boom and bust cycles.

3. If you were a company such as Micron Technology, what strategy might you adopt to deal more effectively with the boom-and-bust nature of the industry?

End Notes

1. C. Gasparino and R. Buckman, "Horning In: Facing Internet Threat, Merrill to Offer Trading Online for Low Fee," *Wall Street Journal*, June 1, 1999, p. A1; "Bears or Bulls, More and More People Are Trading Shares Online," *Economist*, October 17, 1998; L. N. Spiro and E. C. Baig, "Who Needs a Broker?" *Business Week*, February 22, 1999, p. 113.

2. M. E. Porter, *Competitive Strategy* (New York: Free Press, 1980).

3. Charles W. L. Hill has acted as an outside consultant to Tacoma City Light and evaluated the strategy on its behalf.

4. J. E. Bain, *Barriers to New Competition* (Cambridge, Mass: Harvard University Press, 1956). For a review of the modern literature on barriers to entry, see R. J. Gilbert, "Mobility Barriers and the Value of Incumbency," in R. Schmalensee and R. D. Willig, *Handbook of Industrial Organization*, (Amsterdam: North Holland, 1989), I.

5. A detailed discussion of switching costs and lock-in can be found in C. Shapiro and H. R. Varian, *Information Rules: A Strategic Guide to the Network Economy* (Boston, Mass: Harvard Business School Press, 1999).

6. Most of this information on barriers to entry can be found in the industrial organization economics literature. See especially Bain, *Barriers to New Competition;* M. Mann, "Seller Concentration, Barriers to Entry and Rates of Return in 30 Industries," *Review of Economics and Statistics,* 48 (1966), 296–307; W. S. Comanor and T. A. Wilson, "Advertising, Market Structure and Performance," *Review of Economics and Statistics,* 49 (1967), 423–440; and Gilbert, "Mobility Barriers and The Value of Incumbency"; K. Cool, L. H. Roller, and B. Leleux, "The Relative Impact of Actual and Potential Rivalry on Firm Profitability in the Pharmaceutical Industry," *Strategic Management Journal*, 20 (1999), 1–14.

7. "Only Here for the Biru," *Economist*, May 14, 1994, pp. 69–71; T. Craig, "The Japanese Beer Industry," in C. W. L. Hill and G. R. Jones, *Strategic Management: An Integrated Approach* (Boston: Houghton Mifflin, 1995); "Japan's Beer Wars," *Economist*, February 28, 1998, p. 68; A. Harney, "Japan's Favorite Beer Could Face Losing Its Sparkle," *Financial Times*, March 24, 1999, p. 27.

8. For a discussion of tacit agreements, see T. C. Schelling, *The Strategy of Conflict* (Cambridge, Mass.: Harvard University Press, 1960).

9. R. Oram, "Washing Whiter Proves a Murky Business," *Financial Times*, December 21, 1994, p. 6.

10. P. Ghemawat, *Commitment: The Dynamics of Strategy* (Boston, Harvard Business School Press, 1991).

11. For details, see D. F. Barnett, and R. W. Crandall, 1986. "*Up from the Ashes*," (Washington D.C.: Brookings Institution, 1986); and F. Koelbel, "Strategies for Restructuring the Steel Industry," *Metal Producing, 33* (December 1986), pp. 28–33.

12. D. Kirkpatrick, "Why Compaq Is Mad at Intel," *Fortune*, October 31, 1994, pp. 171–178.

13. A. S. Grove, *Only the Paranoid Survive* (New York: Doubleday, 1996).

14. In standard microeconomic theory, the concept used for assessing the strength of substitutes and complements is the cross elasticity of demand.

15. For details and further references, see C. W. L. Hill, "Establishing a Standard: Competitive Strategy and Technology Standards in Winner Take All Industries," *Academy of Management Executive*, 11, (1997), 7–25; and C. Shapiro and H. R. Varian, *Information Rules: A Strategic Guide to the Network Economy* (Boston: Harvard Business School Press, 1999).

16. See M. Gort and J. Klepper, "Time Paths in the Diffusion of Product Innovations," *Economic Journal* (September 1982), 630–653. Looking at the history of forty-six different products, Gort and Klepper found that the length of time before other companies entered the markets created by a few inventive companies declined from an average of 14.4 years for products introduced before 1930 to 4.9 years for those introduced after 1949.

17. The phrase was originally coined by J. Schumpeter, *Capitalism, Socialism and Democracy* (London: Macmillan, 1950), p. 68.

18. The development of strategic-group theory has been a strong theme in the strategy literature. Important contributions include the following: R. E. Caves and M. E. Porter, "From Entry Barriers to Mobility Barriers," *Quarterly Journal of Economics* (May 1977), 241–262; K. R. Harrigan, "An Application of Clustering for Strategic Group Analysis," *Strategic Management Journal*, 6 (1985), 55–73; K. J. Hatten and D. E. Schendel, "Heterogeneity Within an Industry: Firm Conduct in the U.S. Brewing Industry, 1952–71," *Journal of Industrial Economics, 26* (1977), 97–113; M. E. Porter, "The Structure Within Industries and Companies' Performance," *The Review of Economics and Statistics, 61* (1979), 214–227. For an example of more recent work, see K. Cool and D. Schendel, "Performance Differences Among Strategic Group Members," *Strategic Management Journal*, 9 (1988), 207–233; and C. S. Galbraith, G. B. Merrill, and G. Morgan, "Bilateral Strategic Groups," *Strategic Management Journal*, 15 (1994), 613–626.

19. For details on the strategic group structure in the pharmaceutical industry, see K. Cool and I. Dierickx, "Rivalry, Strategic Groups, and Firm Profitability," *Strategic Management Journal*, 14 (1993), 47–59.

20. This perspective is associated with the Austrian school of economics. The perspective goes back to Schumpeter. For a recent summary of this school and its implications for strategy, see R. Jacobson, "The Austrian School of Strategy," *Academy of Management Review*, 17 (1992), 782–807; and C. W. L. Hill and D. Deeds, "The Importance of Industry Structure for the Determination of Industry Profitability, A Neo-Austrian Approach," *Journal of Management Studies*, 33 (1996), 429–451.

21. Barnett and Crandall, *Up from the Ashes.*

22. M. E. Porter, *The Competitive Advantage of Nations* (New York, Free Press, 1990).

23. The term *punctuated equilibrium* is borrowed from evolutionary biology. For a detailed explanation of the concept see M. L. Tushman, W. H. Newman, and E. Romanelli, "Convergence and Upheaval: Managing the Unsteady Pace of Organizational Evolution," *California Management Review*, 29 (1985), 29–44; and C. J. G. Gersick, "Revolutionary Change Theories: A Multilevel Exploration of the Punctuated Equilibrium Paradigm," *Academy of Management Review*, 16: (1991), 10–36.

24. A. J. Slywotzky, *Value Migration: How To Think Several Moves Ahead of the Competition* (Boston: Harvard Business School Press, 1996).

25. R. D'Avani, *Hypercompetition* (New York: Free Press, 1994).

26. Hill and Deeds, "The Importance of Industry Structure," 429–451.

27. R. P. Rumelt, "How Much Does Industry Matter?" *Strategic Management Journal*, 12 (1991), 167–185. See also A. J. Mauri and M. P. Michaels, "Firm and Industry Effects Within Strategic Management: An Empirical Examination," *Strategic Management Journal*, 19 (1998), 211–219.

28. See R. Schmalensee, "Inter-Industry Studies of Structure and Performance," in R. Schmalensee, and R. D. Willig, *Handbook of Industrial Organization*, Vol 1 (Amsterdam: North Holland, 1989). Similar results were found by A. N. McGahan and M. E. Porter, "How Much Does Industry Matter, Really?" *Strategic Management Journal*, 18 (1997), 15–30.

29. For example, see K. Cool and D. Schendel, "Strategic Group Formation and Performance: The Case of the U.S. Pharmaceutical Industry 1932–1992," *Management Science* (September 1987), 1102–1124.

30. C. W. Hofer has argued that life cycle considerations may be the most important contingency when formulating business strategy; see C. W. Hofer, "Toward a Contingency Theory of Business Strategy," *Academy of Management Journal*, 18 (1975), 784–810. There is also empirical evidence to support this view. See C. R. Anderson and C. P. Zeithaml, "Stages of the Product Life Cycle, Business Strategy, and Business Performance," *Academy of Management Journal*, 27 (1984), 5–24; and D. C. Hambrick and D. Lei, "Towards an Empirical Prioritization of Contingency Variables for Business Strategy," *Academy of Management Journal*, 28 (1985), 763–788. Also see G. Miles, C. C. Snow, and M. P. Sharfman, "Industry Variety and Performance," *Strategic Management Journal*, 14 (1993), 163–177.

31. The characteristics of declining industries have been summarized by K. R. Harrigan, "Strategy Formulation in Declining Industries," *Academy of Management Review*, 5 (1980), 599–604.

32. For details, see C. W. L. Hill, "Establishing a Standard," 7–25; Shapiro and Varian, *Information Rules*; B. Arthur, "Increasing Returns and the New World of Business," *Harvard Business Review* (July–August 1996), 100–109.

33. P. C. Judge and A. Reinhardt, "Why the Fastest Chip Didn't Win," *Business Week*, April 28, 1997, pp. 92–96.

34. P. Dicken, *Global Shift* (New York: Guilford Press, 1992).

35. I. Metthee, "Playing a Large Part," *Seattle-Post Intelligence*, April 9, 1994, p. 13.

36. T. Levitt, "The Globalization of Markets," *Harvard Business Review* (May–June 1983), 92–102.

37. M. E. Porter, *The Competitive Advantage of Nations* (New York: Free Press, 1990). See also R. Grant, "Porter's Competitive Advantage of Nations: An Assessment," *Strategic Management Journal*, 7 (1991), 535–548.

38. Porter, *The Competitive Advantage of Nations*, p. 121.

39. "Lessons from the Frozen North," *Economist*, October 8, 1994, pp. 76–77; G. Edmondson, "Grabbing Markets from the Giants," *Business Week*, Special Issue: 21st Century Capitalism, 1995, p. 156; Q. Hardy, "Bypassing the Bells—A Wireless World," *Wall Street Journal*, September 21, 1998, p. R16; Q. Hardy and G. Naik, "Nokia Takes the Lead as Wireless Makers Sell 162.9 Million Phones in 1998," *Wall Street Journal*, February 8, 1999, p. A1.

40. The World Wide Web page for Micron Technology (http://www.micron.com); "When the Chips Are Down," *Economist*, March 23, 1996, pp. 19–21; L. Kehoe, "U.S. Chip Makers Seek to Dispel the Gloom," *Financial Times*, April 20, 1996, p. 20; "Remind Me How to Make Money," *Economist*, August 26, 1995, pp. 55–56; Standard & Poor's Industry Surveys, *Electronics*, August 3, 1995.

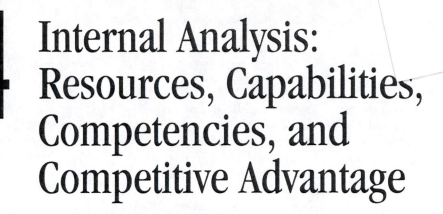

4 Internal Analysis: Resources, Capabilities, Competencies, and Competitive Advantage

OPENING CASE STUDY

Cisco Systems

CISCO SYSTEMS is one of the great success stories of recent years. Two Stanford University computer scientists, Leonard Bosack and Sandra Lerner, founded the company in 1984. In the early 1980s, Stanford University had accumulated many separate computer networks—each using different machines and different electronic languages to communicate among themselves. The problem was that these networks could not talk to each other. Bosack and Lerner, who were married at the time, were the managers of separate networks. They worked on the problem of hooking these networks together, partly, so legend has it, in order to be able to send each other E-mail messages. Their solution was a specialized computer known as a router, which was able to connect different computer systems. Realizing that this device might have commercial value, they established Cisco and shipped their first product in 1987. The company went public in 1990, with annual sales of around $70 million. Soon afterward, Cisco's sales started to increase exponentially as routers became a critical component of the rapidly expanding Internet. By 2000, Cisco had evolved into the dominant supplier of network equipment for the Internet—including routers, switches, and hubs—with annual sales in excess of $14 billion, no debt, a return on equity of around 24 percent and a return on assets of around 20 percent.

Cisco's rapid sales growth and high profitability owe much to its product innovation, which has continued at a fast pace since the company went public, but they are also due to the company's aggressive adoption of an e-business infrastructure. Here, too, Cisco has been an innovator. This infrastructure has enabled the company to reap major efficiency gains, while providing its customers with superior point-of-sales service and after-sales service and support. Cisco was one of the first companies to move much of its sales effort onto the Internet. The process began in 1996, when Cisco realized that its traditional sales infrastructure could not keep up with increasing demand. Rather than hire additional personnel to manage customer accounts, the company began to experiment with on-line sales. It developed a computer program to walk customers through the process of ordering equipment on-line. A critical feature of this program helps customers order exactly the right mix of equipment, thereby avoiding any ordering mistakes, such as the ordering of incompatible equipment. In 1997, the company sold $500 million worth of equipment on-line. By 1999, this figure had ballooned to $10 billion, or 80 percent of Cisco's total sales, making the company one of the most aggressive adopters of an on-line sales approach in the world.

Customers seem to love the automated order processing system, primarily because it minimizes ordering mistakes and allows quicker execution of orders. For example, at Sprint, which is a major customer, it used to take sixty days from the signing of a contract to complete a networking project. Now it takes thirty-five to forty-five days, primarily because of the efficiency of Cisco's on-line ordering system. Moreover, Sprint has been able to cut its order-processing staff from 21 to 6, significantly saving costs. As for Cisco, the company has just 300 service agents handling all of its customer accounts, compared with the 900 it would need if sales were not handled on-line. The difference represents an annual saving of $20 million.

Cisco has also placed its customer support functions on-line. All routine customer service functions are now handled on-line by a computer program that can translate a customer's fuzzy inquiry into a standard description of a familiar problem; then it provides the four most likely explanations on screen, so that the customer might avoid blind alleys and not waste time. Since the company implemented the system in 1996, its sales have quadrupled, while its engineering support staff has merely doubled to 800. Without automated sales support, Cisco calculates that it would need at least 1,000 additional service engineers, which would cost around $75 million. Cisco has also moved to distributing all support software over the Internet, rather than transferring it to disks and mailing it to customers. This has saved Cisco another $250 million per year in annual operating costs.[1]

OVERVIEW

In Chapter 3, we discuss the elements of the external environment that determine an industry's attractiveness, and we examine how industry structure explains why some industries are more profitable than others. However, industry structure is not the only force that affects company profits. Within any given industry some companies are more profitable than others. For example, in the global auto industry, Toyota has consistently outperformed General Motors for most of the last twenty years. In the steel industry, Nucor has consistently outperformed U.S. Steel. In the U.S. retail clothing industry, The Gap has consistently outperformed JC Penney's, while in the Internet network equipment market, Cisco Systems has consistently outperformed competitors such as Bay Networks and 3Com. The question, therefore, is why within a particular industry do some companies outperform others? What is the basis of their competitive advantage?

Cisco provides some clues as to the sources of **competitive advantage**, that is, a company's ability to outperform its competitors. In the Opening Case, we saw how Cisco's competitive advantage stems partly from product innovation—after all, the company invented the router, one of the key pieces of equipment required to make the Internet work. Moreover, although the Opening Case does not dwell on this fact, Cisco has continued to remain at the leading edge of product innovation in the market for networking equipment. But there is more to Cisco's success than its excellent track record with regard to product innovation. As explained in the Opening Case, Cisco's aggressive approach to moving sales and customer service on-line has yielded huge dividends in terms of efficiency gains and customer satisfaction. Put differently, Cisco's process innovations in the area of on-line sales and customer service have also had a positive impact on its competitive advantage.

As you will see in this chapter, *innovation*, *efficiency*, and *customer responsiveness* can be regarded as three of the main building blocks of competitive advantage. *Quality* is a fourth building block. Cisco has a competitive advantage because it has skills in product and process innovation, because it is efficient, and because its on-line, or e-business, infrastructure has made it more responsive to customer needs. It would also not be surprising to find that Cisco's product quality is excellent. It is not surprising, then, that Cisco has become one of the great success stories of recent years.

In this chapter and the next, we look inside an organization at the strengths and weaknesses that determine its efficiency, innovative capability, product quality, and customer responsiveness. We explore how the strengths of an organization are grounded in its resources, capabilities, and competencies, and we discuss how these help a company attain a competitive advantage based on superior efficiency, innovation, quality, and customer responsiveness. We also discuss three critical questions. First, once it is obtained, what factors influence the durability of competitive advantage? Second, why do successful companies lose their competitive advantage? Third, how can companies avoid competitive failure and sustain their competitive advantage over time? When you have finished this chapter, you will have a good understanding of the nature of competitive advantage. This understanding will help you make better strategic decisions as a manager.

COMPETITIVE ADVANTAGE: VALUE CREATION, LOW COST, AND DIFFERENTIATION

We say that a company has a *competitive advantage* when its profit rate is higher than the average for its industry, and that it has a *sustained competitive advantage* when it is able to maintain this high profit rate over a number of years. In the U. S. department store industry, for example, Wal-Mart has had a sustained competitive advantage that has persisted for decades. This has been translated into a high profit rate (for details, see Strategy in Action 4.1). Two basic conditions determine a company's profit rate and hence whether it has a competitive advantage: the amount of value customers place on the company's goods or services, and the company's costs of production. In general, the more value customers place on a company's products, the higher the price the company can charge for those products. Note, however, that the price a company charges for a good or service is typically less than the value placed on that good or service by the customer because the customer captures some of that value in the form of what economists call a consumer surplus.[2] The customer gains this surplus because the company is competing with other companies for the customer's business, and so must charge a lower price than it

STRATEGY *in* ACTION

4.1

Competitive Advantage in the U.S. Department Store Industry

Figure 4.1 graphs the return on capital employed (ROK) earned by four companies active in the U.S. department stores industry between 1989 and 1998.[3] Their profitability is compared with the average profitability for the entire U.S. department store sector over the same time period. Figure 4.1 clearly illustrates that Wal-Mart and to a lesser degree, Nordstrom, had a sustained competitive advantage over the entire period. In contrast, the Hudson Bay company and Kmart were at a sustained competitive disadvantage most of the period. Among other things, the competitive advantage of Wal-Mart has been based on efficient logistics, high employee productivity, and excellent customer service. Moreover, Wal-Mart has led the industry in its *innovative* use of advanced information systems to manage everything, from its inventory and product mix to its pricing strategy. This process innovation has enabled Wal-Mart to reap substantial operating efficiencies while allowing the company to respond to differences in consumer demand across stores. Put differently, Wal-Mart excels on at least three of the building blocks of competitive advantage: innovation, efficiency, and customer responsiveness. Thus, it is not surprising that the company has consistently outperformed its peers.

Nordstrom too, has consistently outperformed its peers. This company's competitive advantage stems from the combination of a high-quality product offering linked with excellence in customer service, which has enabled the company to build a sustained competitive advantage on the basis of *quality* and *customer responsiveness*. In particular, Nordstrom is legendary for the attention that its salespeople devote to individual customers. For example, they will devote considerable time to assist "fashion-challenged" men to pick a stylish and matching combination of suit, shirts, shoes, and tie from the selection in a store. This differentiating factor has enabled Nordstrom to charge a high price for the products it sells.

In contrast, Kmart and Hudson Bay have been unable to build a strong competitive advantage, and both have underperformed the industry for years. Although Kmart has focused on the same discount niche that Wal-Mart has dominated, it lacks Wal-Mart's efficient operations and has a higher cost structure. Moreover, Kmart has generally followed Wal-Mart's lead in the adoption of information technology. Kmart has not been an innovator. As for Hudson Bay, this full-service department store chain has failed to build a significant differentiating feature that might enable it to mimic Nordstrom and charge a higher price for delivering excellent customer service. Indeed, both the product mix and customer service offered by Hudson Bay have left much to be desired, while operating margins have been further squeezed by operating inefficiencies and a high cost structure.

FIGURE 4.1

Return on Capital Employed for Selected U.S. Department Stores, 1989–1998

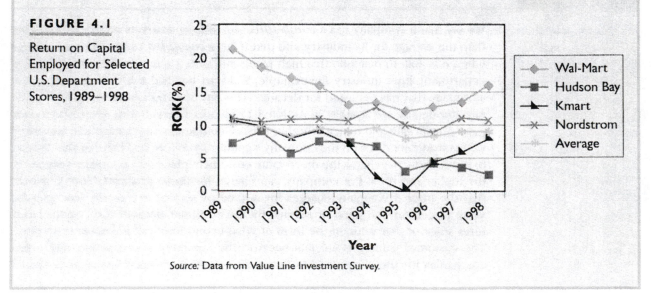

Source: Data from Value Line Investment Survey.

could as a monopoly supplier. Moreover, it is normally impossible to segment the market to such a degree that the company can charge each customer a price that reflects that individual's assessment of the value of a product—which economists refer to as a customer's reservation price. For these reasons, the price that gets charged tends to be less than the value placed on the product by many customers.

These concepts are illustrated in Figure 4.2. There you can see that the value of a product to a consumer may be V, the price that the company can charge for that product given competitive pressures may be P, and the costs of producing that product are C. The company's profit margin is equal to $P - C$, while the consumer surplus is equal to $V - P$. The company makes a profit so long as $P > C$, and its profit rate will be greater the lower C is *relative* to P. Bear in mind that the difference between V and P is in part determined by the intensity of competitive pressure in the marketplace. The lower the intensity of competitive pressure, the higher the price that can be charged relative to V.[4]

Note also that the value created by a company is measured by the difference between V and C $(V - C)$. A company creates value by converting inputs that cost C into a product on which consumers place a value of V. A company can create more value for its customers either by lowering C, or by making the product more attractive through superior design, functionality, quality, and the like, so that consumers place a greater value on it (V increases) and, consequently, are willing to pay a high price (P increases). This discussion suggests that a company has high profits, and thus a competitive advantage, when it creates more value for its customers than do rivals. Put differently, *the concept of value creation lies at the heart of competitive advantage.*[5]

For a more concrete example, consider the case of the personal computer industry. In the mid 1990s, Compaq Computer was selling its top-of-the-line personal computers for about $2,600 each ($P$), while all of the costs associated with producing these computers (C)—including material costs, administrative costs, manufacturing costs, marketing costs, R&D costs, and capital costs—amounted to $2,300 per computer, giving Compaq a net profit margin (net of all costs) of $300 per computer. In contrast, one of its competitors, AST, was able to charge only $2,300 for its equivalent personal computer, while the cost of producing these machines was $2,400, giving AST a net loss of $100 per computer.

This comparison shows how a company's profit rate is jointly determined by the price it can charge for its products and by its cost structure. Compaq made

FIGURE 4.2

Value Creation

$V - P$

$P - C$

V = Value to consumer
P = Price
C = Costs of production
$V - P$ = Consumer surplus
$P - C$ = Profit margin

more profit per computer than AST in the mid 1990s because it could charge a higher price for its machines *and* because it had a lower cost structure. Compaq's lower cost structure came primarily from manufacturing efficiencies that AST lacked. As for its higher price, Compaq could command a higher price for its computers because consumers placed a higher value on a Compaq machine than on an AST machine, and therefore they were willing to pay more for a Compaq computer. Why did consumers place more value on Compaq machines? Primarily because they perceived Compaq products to be of a superior quality, functionality, and design relative to AST products. Put differently, Compaq had succeeded in differentiating its computers from those of AST (and various other producers) in the eyes of consumers. Thus, Compaq's competitive advantage in the mid 1990s came from a combination of low costs and differentiation. As a consequence of its superior cost and differentiation position, Compaq created more value for consumers than AST ($V - C$ was greater for Compaq than for AST). So one could say that Compaq's competitive advantage over AST was based on superior value creation.

We should note that superior value creation does not necessarily require a company to have the lowest cost structure in an industry or to create the most valuable product in the eyes of consumers, but it does require that the gap between perceived value (V) and costs of production (C) be greater than the gap attained by competitors. For example, as described in Strategy in Action 4.1, Nordstrom has had a sustained competitive advantage in the American department store industry. Although Nordstrom has a higher cost structure than many of its competitors, it was able to create more value because it successfully differentiated its service offering in the eyes of consumers so that consumers assigned a higher V to products purchased at Nordstrom. This perception of superior value was based on Nordstrom's obsession with customer service. It allowed Nordstrom to charge a higher price (P) for the products it sold than many competing full-service department stores. The higher price translated into a greater profit margin ($P - C$) for Nordstrom, as shown in Figure 4.1.

Michael Porter has argued that *low cost* and *differentiation* are two basic strategies for creating value and attaining a competitive advantage in an industry.[6] According to Porter, competitive advantage (along with higher profits) goes to those companies that can create superior value, and the way to create superior value is to drive down the cost structure of the business and/or differentiate the product in some way so that consumers value it more and are prepared to pay a premium price. But how can a company drive down its cost structure and differentiate its product offering from that of competitors so that it can create superior value? We tackle this question in both this chapter and the next one. In Chapter 6, we shall return to Porter's notions of low cost and differentiation strategies, when we examine his idea in more depth.

THE GENERIC BUILDING BLOCKS OF COMPETITIVE ADVANTAGE

As we have seen, four factors build competitive advantage: efficiency, quality, innovation, and customer responsiveness. They are the generic building blocks of competitive advantage that any company can adopt, regardless of its industry or the products

FIGURE 4.3

Generic Building Blocks
of Competitive
Advantage

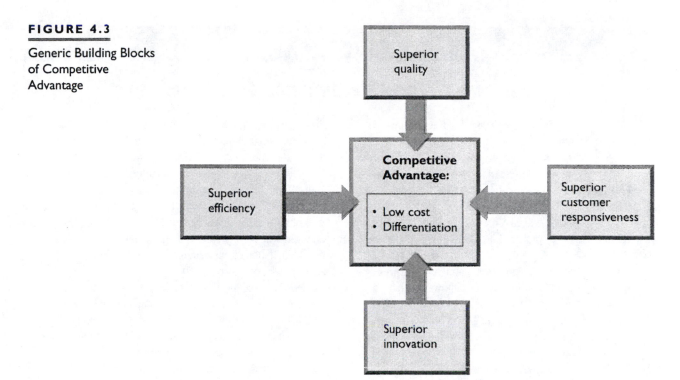

or services it produces (Figure 4.3). Although we discuss them separately below, they are highly interrelated. For example, superior quality can lead to superior efficiency, while innovation can enhance efficiency, quality, and customer responsiveness.

■ Efficiency

In one sense, a business is simply a device for transforming inputs into outputs. Inputs are basic factors of production such as labor, land, capital, management, and technological know-how. Outputs are the goods and services that the business produces. The simplest measure of efficiency is the quantity of inputs that it takes to produce a given output; that is, Efficiency = outputs/inputs. The more efficient a company, the fewer the inputs required to produce a given output. For example, if it takes General Motors thirty hours of employee time to assemble a car and it takes Ford twenty-five hours, we can say that Ford is more efficient than GM. Moreover, so long as other things are equal, such as wage rates, we can assume from these data that Ford will have a lower cost structure than GM. Thus, efficiency helps a company attain a low-cost competitive advantage. In the Opening Case, you saw how Cisco attained superior efficiency by pioneering the migration of sales and customer service functions to an on-line delivery model.

The most important component of efficiency for many companies is employee productivity, which is usually measured by output per employee. Holding all else constant, the company with the highest employee productivity in an industry will typically have the lowest costs of production. In other words, that company will have a cost-based competitive advantage. Strategy in Action 4.2 looks at the level of employee productivity attained by volume manufacturers of automobiles based in

Productivity in the Automobile Industry

Every year since 1980, Harbor Associates, a consulting company founded by former Chrysler executive James Harbor, has issued a report on the level of productivity in assembly plants of U.S.-based volume manufacturers of automobiles. Until 1993, the report focused on just the big three U.S. companies, General Motors, Ford, and Chrysler (now DaimlerChrysler), but now it also includes data on the U.S.-based assembly operations of Nissan and Toyota, both of which have a significant manufacturing presence in this country. The following table shows the number of hours of labor it took to assemble a vehicle at each of these companies from 1988 to 1998. On this measure, Nissan and Toyota are the most efficient volume producers in the United States, whereas Ford is close behind, and General Motors is the least efficient.

The higher labor productivity of Nissan, Toyota, and Ford is attributed to their lean production systems, which are based on a large number of productivity-enhancing management techniques. For example, all three companies make extensive use of self-managing work teams. Each team is given the responsibility for performing a major assembly task, and the teams are also set challenging productivity and quality goals. At the same time, the teams are empowered to find ways to improve their productivity and quality control and are rewarded through the use of incentive pay if they exceed their productivity or quality goals. While GM and DaimlerChrysler have also tried to introduce self-managing teams into the workplace, diffusion of the technique has been held back by a long history of adversarial labor relations at these companies, which has made it difficult for management and labor to cooperate to introduce new concepts.

However, DaimlerChrysler in particular claims that the data given above present an incomplete picture of productivity, primarily because it ignores that company's low product-development costs. According to DaimlerChrysler, these are a source of superior productivity not recognized in the Harbor Report. Until the early 1990s, it took DaimlerChrysler at least four years and 1,400 design engineers to design a new car, or 5,600 engineer years. The Chrysler Neon, however, was designed in just thirty-three months and required only 740 design engineers, which translates into 2,035 engineer years, a more than 50 percent improvement in productivity and a saving in design costs of $45 million. DaimlerChrysler estimates

the United States. These data suggest that in their assembly operations Japanese manufactures still enjoy a productivity-based competitive advantage relative to their U.S. counterparts but that the gap has closed significantly since the late 1980s. Moreover, it would seem that DaimlerChrysler in particular has realized huge productivity gains in its product design process, which, when added to its assembly process, may make the company the most efficient volume manufacturer in the United States.

The interesting issue, of course, is how to achieve superior productivity. Later chapters examine in detail how a company can achieve high productivity (and quality, innovation, and customer responsiveness). For now, we just note that to achieve high productivity a company must adopt the appropriate strategy, structure, and control systems.

■ Quality

Quality products are goods and services that are reliable in the sense that they do the job they were designed for and do it well. This concept applies whether we are talking about a Toyota automobile, clothes designed and sold by The Gap, the cus-that the design for its next major car project can be completed in two years by just 540 design engineers. James Harbor, the author of the Harbor Report, agrees that DaimlerChrysler's superior design capabilities are an important source of superior productivity. In his 1995 report, he concluded that when design costs are added to assembly costs, Chrysler emerged as the most productive automobile company in the United States.

How has DaimlerChrysler done this? Primarily by forming teams of design engineers, component suppliers, manufacturing personnel, and marketing staff to oversee the design process. These teams make sure that there is very tight integration in the design process among suppliers, engineering, manufacturing, and marketing. Cars are now designed for ease of manufacturing, and with input up front from marketing, while suppliers are brought into the process early on to ensure that their design for component parts interfaces well with Chrysler's design for the finished car. As a result, the amount of redesign work required has been dramatically reduced, and the design cycle time of four to six years has been decreased to under three years.[7]

Hours of labor required to assemble a vehicle

Company	1988	1994	1998
General Motors	39.02	30.26	30.32
DaimlerChrysler	36.64	27.8	32.15
Ford	26.0	25.0	22.85
Toyota	Not Available	19.30	21.20
Nissan	Not Available	18.3	17.07

tomer service department of Citibank, or the ability of an airline to have its planes arrive on time. The impact of high product quality on competitive advantage is twofold.[8] First, providing high-quality products increases the value of those products in the eyes of consumers. In turn, this enhanced perception of value allows the company to charge a higher price for its products. In the automobile industry, for example, companies such as Toyota not only have had a productivity-based cost advantage, but they have also been able to charge a higher price for their cars because of the higher quality of their products. Thus, compared with a company like General Motors, Toyota has had both lower costs and the ability to charge higher prices. As a result, historically Toyota has operated with a bigger profit margin than GM.

The second impact of high quality on competitive advantage comes from the greater efficiency and the lower unit costs it brings. Less employee time is wasted making defective products or providing substandard services and less time has to be spent fixing mistakes, which translates into higher employee productivity and lower unit costs. Thus, high product quality not only lets a company charge higher prices for its product, but also lowers costs (see Figure 4.4).

The importance of quality in building competitive advantage has increased dramatically during the last decade. Indeed, so crucial is the emphasis placed on quality

FIGURE 4.4

The Impact of Quality on Profits

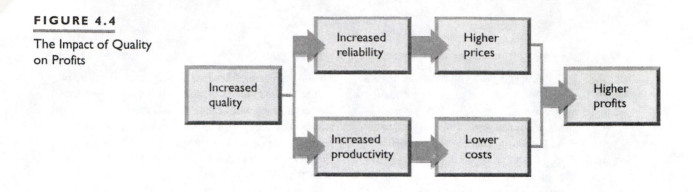

by many companies that achieving high product quality can no longer be viewed as just one way of gaining a competitive advantage. In many industries, it has become an absolute imperative for survival. Strategy in Action 4.3, which discusses the turn-around of Continental Airlines, illustrates the importance of quality in a service environment.

■ Innovation

Innovation can be defined as anything new or novel about the way a company operates or the products it produces. Innovation includes advances in the kinds of products, production processes, management systems, organizational structures, and strategies developed by a company. All of the following can be viewed as *innovations*: Intel's development of the microprocessor; the discounting strategy of Toys 'R' Us in the retail toy business; Toyota's lean production system for manufacturing automobiles; Cisco's development of the router and pioneering approach to on-line selling and customer service; and Wal-Mart's pioneering efforts to use information systems to manage its logistics, product mix, and product pricing. Successful innovation is about developing new products and/or managing the enterprise in a novel way that creates value for consumers.[10]

Innovation is perhaps the single most important building block of competitive advantage. In the long run, competition can be viewed as a process driven by innovation. Although not all innovations succeed, those that do can be a major source of competitive advantage because, by definition, they give a company something **unique**—something its competitors lack (until they imitate the innovation). Uniqueness lets a company differentiate itself from its rivals and charge a premium price for its product, or reduce its unit costs far below those of competitors.

As with efficiency and quality, we explore the issue of innovation more fully later in the book. A few examples can highlight the importance of innovation as the bedrock of competitive advantage. Consider Xerox's development of the photocopier, Cisco's development of the router, Intel's development of new microprocessors, Hewlett-Packard's development of the laser printer, Nike's development of high-tech athletic shoes, Bausch & Lomb's development of contact lenses, or Sony's development of the Walkman. All these product innovations helped build a competitive advantage for the pioneering companies. In each case, the company, by virtue of being the sole supplier of a new product, could charge a premium price. By the time competitors succeeded in imitating the innovator, the innovating com-

4.3 STRATEGY in ACTION

Continental Airlines Goes from Worst to First

When Gordon Bethune left Boeing to become the CEO of Continental Airlines in 1994, the company was the worst performing and least profitable of all major U.S. airlines. One of the main problems was the lack of reliability. In 1994, Continental planes arrived on time only 61 percent of the time, placing the company dead last in the influential Air Customer Satisfaction Study, produced by J.D. Power & Associates. To make matters worse, airline travelers ranked on-time performance as the most important factor when deciding which airline to fly on. Reliability was the primary metric passengers used to determine an airline's quality.

Bethune soon came to the conclusion that the prior management had cut costs so far that the service had suffered. In his words, "our service was lousy and nobody knew when a plane might land. We were unpredictable and unreliable, and when you are an airline, where does that leave you? It leaves you with a lot of empty planes. We had a lousy product, and nobody particularly wanted to buy it." Bethune's solution: he told Continental employees that if the airline's on-time performance improved, every employee would receive a $65 bonus. The total cost to the airline was $2.6 million. Bethune was proposing to improve performance by spending more money. It worked. When the program was launched in January 1995, 71 percent of the planes landed on time. By year-end, the figure was up to 80 percent, and Continental had risen to fifth in its on-time performance. For 1996, Bethune announced that the airline had to finish third or higher for employees to get the bonus, which he increased to $100. The airline finished second. It has not dropped out of the top three since then.

To support the drive toward greater reliability, Bethune also reorganized the way employees were managed. Out went the employee manual, to be replaced by a new set of guidelines, which gave front-line employees significant decision-making power to fix customer problems. For example, if a flight is canceled, a customer service agent might have to decide which passengers should receive priority to get on the next flight. Under the old system, the employee would have had to refer to the rule book, and if that did not provide an answer, ask a higher-level manager. This inflexible approach led to significant frustration among both passengers and employees. The new system allows customer service agents to fix problems as they see fit. According to Bethune, concentrating decision-making power in the hands of employees gave them the ability to solve customer problems in creative ways, which has had a dramatic impact on customers' perception of the quality of service they get at Continental.[9]

pany had built up such strong brand loyalty and supporting management processes that its position proved difficult for imitators to attack. Sony is still known for its Walkman, Hewlett-Packard for its laser printers, and Intel for its microprocessors.

■ Customer Responsiveness

To achieve superior customer responsiveness, a company must be able to do a better job than competitors of identifying and satisfying the needs of its customers. Consumers will then place more value on its products, creating a differentiation-based competitive advantage. Improving the quality of a company's product offering is consistent with achieving responsiveness, as is developing new products with features that existing products lack. In other words, achieving superior quality and innovation are an integral part of achieving superior customer responsiveness.

Another factor that stands out in any discussion of customer responsiveness is the need to customize goods and services to the unique demands of individual customers or customer groups. For example, the proliferation of different types of soft drinks and beers in recent years can be viewed partly as a response to this trend. Automobile companies, too, have become more adept at customizing cars to the demands of individual customers. For instance, following the lead of Toyota, the Saturn division of General Motors builds cars to order for individual customers, letting them choose from a wide range of colors and options.

An aspect of customer responsiveness that has drawn increasing attention is **customer response time,** which is the time that it takes for a good to be delivered or a service to be performed.[11] For a manufacturer of machinery, response time is the time it takes to fill customer orders. For a bank, it is the time it takes to process a loan or the time that a customer must stand in line to wait for a free teller. For a supermarket, it is the time that customers must stand in checkout lines. Customer survey after customer survey has shown slow response time to be a major source of customer dissatisfaction.[12]

Besides quality, customization, and response time, other sources of enhanced customer responsiveness are superior design, superior service, and superior after-sales service and support. All these factors enhance customer responsiveness and allow a company to differentiate itself from its less responsive competitors. In turn, differentiation enables a company to build brand loyalty and to charge a premium price for its products. For example, consider how much more people are prepared to pay for next-day delivery of Express Mail, as opposed to delivery in three to four days. In 1996, a two-page letter sent by overnight Express Mail within the United States cost about $10, compared with 32 cents for regular mail. Thus, the price premium for express delivery (reduced response time) was $9.68, or a premium of 3,025 percent over the regular price.

■ Summary

Efficiency, quality, customer responsiveness, and innovation are all important elements in obtaining a competitive advantage. Superior efficiency enables a company to lower its costs; superior quality lets it both charge a higher price and lower its costs; superior customer responsiveness allows it to charge a higher price; and superior innovation can lead to higher prices or lower unit costs (Figure 4.5). Together, these four factors help a company create more value by lowering costs or differentiating its products from those of competitors, which enables the company to outperform its competitors.

BUSINESS FUNCTIONS, THE VALUE CHAIN, AND VALUE CREATION

In this section, we consider the role played by the different functions of a company—such as production, marketing, R&D, service, information systems, materials management, and human resources—in the value creation process. Specifically, we briefly review how the different functions of a company can help in the process of driving down costs and increasing the perception of value through differentiation. As a first step, consider the concept of the value chain, which is illustrated in Figure

FIGURE 4.5

The Impact of Efficiency, Quality, Customer Responsiveness, and Innovation on Unit Costs and Prices

4.6. [13] The term *value chain* refers to the idea that a company is a chain of activities for transforming inputs into outputs that customers value. The process of transforming inputs into outputs comprises a number of primary and support activities. Each activity adds value to the product.

Primary Activities

Primary activities have to do with the design, creation, and delivery of the product, as well as its marketing and its support and after-sales service. In the value chain illustrated in Figure 4.6, the primary activities are broken down into four functions: research and development, production, marketing and sales, and service.

Research and development (R&D) is concerned with the design of products and production processes. Although we think of R&D as being associated with the design of physical products and production processes in manufacturing enterprises, many service companies also undertake R&D. For example, banks compete with each other by developing new financial products and new ways of delivering those products to customers. On-line banking and smart debit cards are two recent examples of the fruits of new product development in the banking industry. Earlier examples of innovation in the banking industry included ATM machines, credit cards, and debit cards.

By superior product design, R&D can increase the functionality of products, which makes them more attractive to consumers. Alternatively, the work of R&D may result in more efficient production processes, thereby lowering production

FIGURE 4.6

The Value Chain

costs. Either way, the R&D function of an enterprise can create value. At Intel, for example, R&D creates value both by developing ever more powerful microprocessors, and by helping to pioneer ever more efficient manufacturing processes (in conjunction with equipment suppliers).

Production is concerned with the creation of a good or service. For physical products, when we talk about production we generally mean manufacturing. For services such as banking or retail operations, production typically takes place when the service is actually delivered to the customer (for example, when a bank originates a loan for a customer, it is engaged in production of the loan). The production function of a company creates value by performing its activities efficiently so that lower costs result. Thus, as suggested by the data contained in Strategy in Action 4.2, the efficient production operations of Nissan, Ford, and Toyota are helping those automobile companies to create more value relative to competitors such as General Motors. Production can also create value by performing its activities in a way that is consistent with high product quality, which leads to differentiation and lower costs—both of which increase the value created by a company.

There are several ways in which the **marketing and sales** functions of a company can help create value. Through brand positioning and advertising, the marketing function can increase the value that consumers perceive to be contained in a company's product. Insofar as these activities help create a favorable impression of the company's product in the minds of consumers, they increase value. For example, in the 1980s the French company Perrier did a wonderful job of persuading U.S. consumers that slightly carbonated bottled water was worth $1.50 per bottle, rather than a price closer to the 50 cents that it cost to physically collect, bottle, and distribute the water. Perrier's marketing function increased the value that consumers ascribed to the product.

Marketing and sales can also create value by discovering consumer needs and communicating them back to the R&D function of the company, which can then design products that better match those needs. For another example of value creation by the marketing function of an enterprise, see Strategy in Action 4.4, which examines how the sales force of Pfizer increased the perception of the value associated with one of that company's main pharmaceuticals, Zoloft.

The role of the **service** function of an enterprise is to provide after-sales service and support. This function can create a perception of superior value in the minds of consumers by solving customer problems and supporting customers after they have purchased the product. For example, Caterpillar, the U.S.-based manufacturer

---

4.4 STRATEGY *in* ACTION

Value Creation at Pfizer

The antidepressant drug Prozac, introduced by Eli Lilly in 1988, has been one of the most lucrative mental health drugs in history. In 1995, U.S. consumers alone filled almost 19 million prescriptions for Prozac, hoping to mitigate the effects of a wide range of mental disorders including chronic depression, bulimia, and obsessive disorders. Worldwide sales of the drug topped $2 billion in 1995, making it a gold mine for Lilly.

But Prozac's market position is now under attack from an aggressive marketing and sales campaign by rival pharmaceutical company Pfizer. In 1992, Pfizer introduced its own antidepressant, Zoloft. According to medical experts, the differences between Prozac and Zoloft are slight at best. Both drugs function in the same basic manner, by boosting serotonin, a brain chemical believed to be in short supply in many depressed people. Both drugs also have a similar list of possible side effects: Prozac's label mentions nausea, nervousness, anxiety, insomnia, and drowsiness, and Zoloft's lists nausea and other stomach problems, diarrhea, sexual dysfunction, and sleepiness. As one expert noted, "these drugs are so similar that you have to be kidding yourself if you think one drug is going to be consistently superior to the other in treating patients."

Despite the similarity between the two products, however, Pfizer has been gaining share from Lilly in the antidepressant market. By 1998, Zoloft accounted for 40 percent of the market, up from little more than zero in 1992. The main reason for the success of Zoloft seems to be an aggressive marketing and sales campaign by Pfizer, which has given physicians the impression that Zoloft is a safer drug. Pfizer salespeople bill their product as a kind of Prozac Lite: just as effective but without Prozac's occasional downside, anxiety. The reference to anxiety seems carefully designed to remind doctors of a spate of failed lawsuits alleging that Prozac caused suicides and violent acts. Pfizer's sales force has also logged more "face time" with physicians than Lilly's. According to Scott-Levin and Associates, in 1995 Zoloft sales representatives made 660,000 sales visits to doctors—70,000 more than the Prozac sales force logged. About three-quarters of the visits by Zoloft representatives were not to psychiatrists but to primary care physicians, who increasingly prescribe antidepressants but presumably are less familiar with their more subtle properties. Doctors also claim that Pfizer salespeople play up Prozac's clinical reputation that it is more agitating than Zoloft. They also emphasize that unlike Zoloft, Prozac remains in the bloodstream for weeks after a patient stops taking it, raising the possibility of adverse drug interaction if a patient switches to other medications.

The important point here is that Pfizer's marketing and sales force is altering physicians' perceptions of the relative value of Prozac and Zoloft. For Pfizer, the payoff has come in terms of rapidly increasing revenues and market share and, of course, a greater return on the company's investment in developing Zoloft.[14]

of heavy earthmoving equipment, can get spare parts to any point in the world within twenty-four hours, thereby minimizing the amount of downtime its customers have to suffer if their Caterpillar equipment malfunctions. This is an extremely valuable support capability in an industry where downtime is very expensive. It has helped to increase the value that customers associate with Caterpillar products, and thus the price that Caterpillar can charge for them.

■ Support Activities

The **support activities** of the value chain provide inputs that allow the primary activities to take place (see Figure 4.6). The **materials management** (or logistics) function controls the transmission of physical materials through the value chain, from procurement through production and into distribution. The efficiency with which this is carried out can significantly lower costs, thereby creating more value. Wal-Mart, the U.S. retailing giant, reportedly has the most efficient materials management setup in the retail industry. By tightly controlling the flow of goods from its suppliers through its stores and into the hands of consumers, Wal-Mart has eliminated the need to hold large inventories of goods. Lower inventories mean lower costs, and hence greater value creation.

Similarly, there are a number of ways in which the **human resource** function can help an enterprise create more value. The human resource function ensures that the company has the right mix of skilled people to perform its value creation activities effectively. It is also the job of the human resource function to ensure that people are adequately trained, motivated, and compensated to perform their value creation tasks.

Information systems refer to the (largely) electronic systems for managing inventory, tracking sales, pricing products, selling products, dealing with customer service inquires, and so on. Information systems, when coupled with the communications features of the Internet, are holding out the promise of being able to alter the efficiency and effectiveness with which a company manages its other value creation activities. In the Opening Case, we saw how Cisco has used Internet-based information systems to profoundly alter the way its marketing, sales, and service functions are performed, realizing substantial efficiency gains in the process. Wal-Mart is another company that has used information systems to alter the way it does business. Wal-Mart's materials management function is able to track the sale of individual items very closely. This has enabled Wal-Mart to optimize its product mix and pricing strategy. Wal-Mart is rarely left with unwanted merchandise on its hands, which reduces costs, and the company is able to provide the right mix of goods to consumers, which increases the perception of value that consumers associate with Wal-Mart.

The final support activity is the **company infrastructure**. This has a somewhat different character from the other support activities. By infrastructure we mean the companywide context within which all the other value creation activities take place. The infrastructure includes the organizational structure, control systems, and culture of the company. Since top management can exert considerable influence on these aspects of a company, top management should also be viewed as part of a company's infrastructure. Indeed, through strong leadership, top management can consciously shape a company's infrastructure, and through it, the performance of all other value creation activities within the company.

■ Cross-Functional Goals

Achieving superior efficiency, quality, innovation, and customer responsiveness requires strategies that embrace several distinct value creation activities. Indeed, these goals can be regarded as *goals that cut across the different value creation functions of a company*; they are goals whose attainment requires substantial cross-functional integration. In Chapter 11, we consider in greater detail how to achieve cross-functional integration.

DISTINCTIVE COMPETENCIES, RESOURCES, AND CAPABILITIES

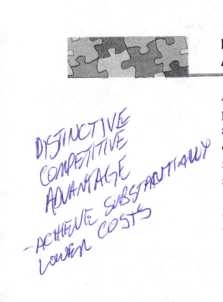

A **distinctive competency** is unique strength that allows a company to achieve superior efficiency, quality, innovation, or customer responsiveness and thereby to create superior value and attain a competitive advantage. A firm with a distinctive competency can differentiate its products or achieve substantially lower costs than its rivals. Consequently, it creates more value than its rivals and will earn a profit rate substantially above the industry average.

For example, it can be argued that Toyota has distinctive competencies in the development and operation of manufacturing processes. Toyota has pioneered a whole range of manufacturing techniques, such as just-in-time inventory systems, self-managing teams, and reduced setup times for complex equipment. These competencies have helped Toyota attain superior efficiency and product quality, which are the basis of its competitive advantage in the global automobile industry.[15]

■ Resources and Capabilities

The distinctive competencies of an organization arise from two complementary sources: its **resources** and **capabilities** (see Figure 4.7).[16] The financial, physical, human, technological, and organizational resources of the company can be divided into **tangible resources** (land, buildings, plant, and equipment) and **intangible resources** (brand names, reputation, patents, and technological or marketing know-how). To give rise to a distinctive competency, a company's resources must be both *unique* and *valuable*. A unique resource is one that no other company has. For example, Polaroid's distinctive competency in instant photography was based on a unique intangible resource: technological know-how in instant film processing protected from imitation by a thicket of patents. A resource is valuable if it in some way helps create strong demand for the company's products. Polaroid's technological know-how was valuable because it created strong demand for its photographic products.

Capabilities refer to a company's skills at coordinating its resources and putting them to productive use. These skills reside in an organization's routines; that is, in the way a company makes decisions and manages its internal processes in order to achieve organizational objectives. More generally, a company's capabilities are the product of its organizational structure and control systems. They specify how

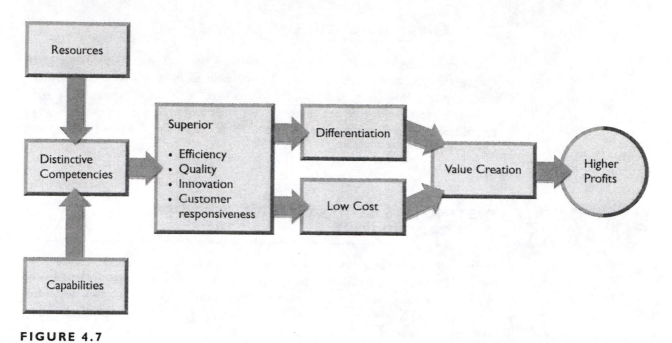

FIGURE 4.7

The Roots of
Competitive Advantage

and where decisions are made within a company, the kind of behaviors the company rewards, and the company's cultural norms and values. (We discuss in Chapters 11 and 12 how organizational structure and control systems help a company obtain capabilities.) It is important to keep in mind that capabilities are, by definition, intangible. They reside not so much in individuals as in the way individuals interact, cooperate, and make decisions within the context of an organization.[17]

The distinction between resources and capabilities is critical to understanding what generates a distinctive competency. A company may have unique and valuable resources, but unless it has the capability to use those resources effectively, it may not be able to create or sustain a distinctive competency. It is also important to recognize that a company may not need unique and valuable resources to establish a distinctive competency so long as it has capabilities that no competitor possesses. For example, the steel minimill operator Nucor is widely acknowledged to be the most cost-efficient steel maker in the United States. But Nucor's distinctive competency in low-cost steel making does not come from any unique and valuable resources. Nucor has the same resources (plant, equipment, skilled employees, and know-how) as many other minimill operators. What distinguishes Nucor is its unique capability to manage its resources in a highly productive way. Specifically, Nucor's structure, control systems, and culture promote efficiency at all levels of the company.

In sum, for a company to have a distinctive competency, it must at a minimum have either (1) a unique and valuable resource and the capabilities (skills) necessary to exploit that resource (as illustrated by Polaroid) or (2) a unique capability to manage common resources (as exemplified by Nucor). A company's distinctive competency is strongest when it possesses *both* unique and valuable resources and unique capabilities to manage those resources.

■ Strategy and Competitive Advantage

The primary objective of strategy is to achieve a competitive advantage. Attaining this goal demands a two-pronged effort. A company needs to pursue strategies that build on its existing resources and capabilities (its competencies), as well as strategies that build additional resources and capabilities (that is, develop new competencies) and thus enhance the company's long-run competitive position.[18] Figure 4.8 illustrates the relationship between a firm's strategies and its resources and capabilities. It is important to note that by *strategies* we mean *all* types of strategy—functional-level strategies, business-level strategies, corporate-level strategies, international strategies, or, more typically, some combination of them. We discuss the various strategies available to a company in detail throughout the next six chapters. What needs stressing here is that successful strategies often either build on a company's existing distinctive competencies or help a company develop new ones.

The history of The Walt Disney Company during the 1980s exemplifies the need to pursue strategies that build on a firm's resources and capabilities. In the early 1980s, Disney suffered a string of poor financial years. This culminated in a 1984 management shakeup, when Michael Eisner was appointed CEO. Four years later, Disney's sales had increased from $1.66 billion to $3.75 billion, its net profits from $98 million to $570 million, and its stock market valuation from $1.8 billion to $10.3 billion. What brought about this transformation was the company's deliberate attempt to exploit its existing resources and capabilities more aggressively. These resources and capabilities included Disney's enormous film library, its brand name, and its in-house filmmaking skills, particularly in animation. Under Eisner, many old Disney classics were rereleased, first in movie theaters, and then on video, earning the company millions in the process. Disney also started a cable television channel, the Disney Channel, to utilize this library and capitalize on the firm's brand name. In addition, under Eisner, the filmmaking arm of Disney flourished, first with a string of low-budget box-office hits under the Touchstone label and then with the reintroduction of the product that had originally made Disney famous, the full-length animated feature. Putting together its brand name and in-house animation capabilities, Disney produced three major box-office hits in four years: *The Little Mermaid, Beauty and the Beast,* and *Aladdin.*[19] In sum, Disney's transformation was based primarily on strategies that exploited the company's existing resource base.

FIGURE 4.8

The Relationship Between Strategies and Resources and Capabilities

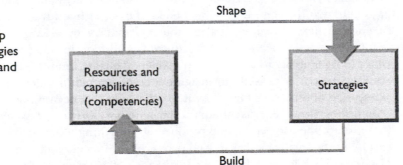

Other companies that have successfully exploited their resources and capabilities to create profitable opportunities include 3M and Honda. The former exploited its distinctive competency in sticky tape to create businesses as diverse as Post-it Notes, pressure-sensitive tapes, and coated abrasives. The latter exploited its distinctive competency in the design and manufacture of high-powered lightweight engines to move from motorcycles to cars, lawn mowers, and four-wheel off-road buggies. On the other hand, some of the most striking strategic failures have occurred at companies that have strayed too far from their distinctive competencies. For example, Exxon, which has distinctive competencies in oil exploration, extraction, and refining, spent much of the 1970s diversifying into areas such as office automation equipment, where it had no capabilities. The effort failed and Exxon sold off these diversified businesses during the 1980s.

As for the process of building resources and capabilities through strategies, consider Xerox. During the late 1970s, its market share in the photocopier business slumped by 50 percent because its main Japanese competitors, Canon and Ricoh, were paying close attention to their distinctive competencies, whereas Xerox was not. As a result, by the early 1980s, Canon and Ricoh were selling high-quality and technologically superior copiers at a price approximating that of Xerox. To recapture its lost market share, Xerox had to fundamentally rethink the way it did business. It launched a series of functional-level strategies designed to improve quality and product design, eliminate unnecessary inventory, and reduce new product development time (cycle time). The goal of these strategies was to develop the kind of resources and capabilities that had enabled Canon and Ricoh to take market share away from Xerox. Xerox was reasonably successful in this endeavor; its share of the U.S. copier market increased from a low of 10 percent in 1985 to 18 percent in 1991.[20] The company's renaissance stemmed from the successful implementation of functional-level strategies to build new distinctive competencies.

■ The Role of Luck

A number of scholars have argued that luck plays a critical role in determining competitive success and failure.[21] In its most extreme version, the luck argument devalues the importance of planned strategy. Instead, it states that in coping with uncertainty some companies just happened to stumble on the correct strategy. Put another way, they just happened to develop or possess the right kind of resources and capabilities by accident rather than by design.

Although luck may be the reason for a company's success in particular cases, it is an unconvincing explanation for the persistent success of a company. Recall our argument that the generic building blocks of competitive advantage are superior efficiency, quality, innovation, and customer responsiveness. Keep in mind also that competition is a process in which companies are continually trying to outdo each other in their ability to achieve high efficiency, quality, innovation, and customer responsiveness. It is possible to imagine a company getting lucky and coming into possession of resources that allow it to achieve excellence on one or more of these dimensions. However, it is difficult to imagine how *sustained* excellence on any of these four dimensions could be produced by anything other than conscious effort, that is, by strategy. Luck may indeed play a role in success, and Strategy in Action 4.5 discusses the role of luck in the early history of Microsoft. However, to argue that success is entirely a matter of luck is to strain credibility.

STRATEGY *in* ACTION

4.5

Microsoft's Luck

The product that launched Microsoft into its leadership position in the software industry was MS-DOS, the operating system for IBM and IBM-compatible PCs. The original DOS program, however, was not developed by Microsoft. Instead, it was developed by a company called Seattle Computer, where it was known as Q-DOS (which stood for "quick and dirty operating system"). When IBM was looking for an operating system to run its original PC, it made contact with a number of software companies, including Microsoft, asking them whether they could develop such a system. IBM did not, however, make contact with Seattle Computer. Bill Gates, a player in the emerging Seattle computer community, knew that Seattle Computer had already developed a disk operating system. Borrowing $50,000 from his father, a senior partner in a prominent Seattle law company, Gates went to see the CEO of Seattle Computer and offered to purchase the rights to the company's Q-DOS system. He did not, of course, reveal that

IBM was looking for a disk operating system. Since Seattle Computer was short of cash, the CEO quickly agreed. Gates then renamed the system MS-DOS, upgraded it somewhat, and licensed it to IBM. The rest, as they say, is history.

So was Microsoft lucky? Of course it was. It was lucky that Seattle Computer had not heard about IBM's request. It was lucky that IBM approached Microsoft. It was lucky that Gates knew about Seattle Computer's operating system. And it was lucky that Gates had a father wealthy enough to lend him $50,000 on short notice. On the other hand, to attribute all of Microsoft's subsequent success to luck would be wrong. While MS-DOS gave Microsoft a tremendous head start in the industry, it did not guarantee Microsoft continued worldwide success. To achieve that, Microsoft had to build the appropriate set of resources and capabilities required to produce a continual stream of innovative software, which is precisely what the company did with the cash generated from MS-DOS.[22]

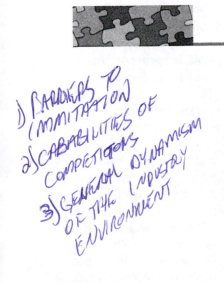

THE DURABILITY OF COMPETITIVE ADVANTAGE

The question that we now need to address is, How long will a competitive advantage last once it has been created? What is the durability of competitive advantage given that other companies are also seeking to develop distinctive competencies that will give them a competitive advantage? The answer depends on three factors: barriers to imitation, the capability of competitors, and the general dynamism of the industry environment.

▨ Barriers to Imitation

A company with a competitive advantage will earn higher than average profits. These profits send a signal to rivals that the company is in possession of some valuable distinctive competency that allows it to create superior value. Naturally, its competitors will try to identify and imitate that competency. Insofar as they are successful, they may ultimately surpass the company's superior profits.[23] How quickly will rivals imitate a company's distinctive competencies? This is an important question, because the speed of imitation has a bearing upon the durability of a company's competitive advantage. Other things being equal, the more rapidly competitors imitate a company's distinctive competencies, the less durable will be its competitive advantage and the more urgent the need to continually improve its competencies in order to stay one step ahead of the imitators. It is important to stress at the outset that ultimately almost any distinctive competency can be imitated by a competitor. The critical issue is *time*. The longer it takes competitors to imitate a distinctive competency, the greater the opportunity the company has to build a strong market position and reputation with consumers, which is then more difficult for competitors to attack. Moreover, the longer it takes to achieve an imitation, the greater is the opportunity for the imitated company to enhance its competency, or build other competencies, that will keep it ahead of the competition.

Barriers to imitation are a primary determinant of the speed of imitation. **Barriers to imitation** are factors that make it difficult for a competitor to copy a company's distinctive competencies. The greater the barriers to such imitation, the more sustainable is a company's competitive advantage.[24]

Imitating Resources   In general, the easiest distinctive competencies for prospective rivals to imitate tend to be those based on possession of unique and valuable tangible resources, such as buildings, plant, and equipment. Such resources are visible to competitors and can often be purchased on the open market. For example, if a company's competitive advantage is based on sole possession of efficient-scale manufacturing facilities, competitors may move fairly quickly to establish similar facilities. Although Ford gained a competitive advantage over General Motors in the 1920s by being the first to adopt an assembly line manufacturing technology to produce automobiles, General Motors quickly imitated that innovation. A similar process is occurring in the auto industry at present, as companies try to imitate Toyota's famous production system, which formed the basis for much of its competitive advantage during the 1970s and 1980s. GM's Saturn plant, for instance, is GM's attempt to replicate Toyota's production system.

Intangible resources can be more difficult to imitate. This is particularly true of brand names. Brand names are important because they symbolize a company's reputation. In the heavy earthmoving equipment industry, for example, the Caterpillar brand name is synonymous with high quality and superior after-sales service and support. Similarly, the St. Michael's brand name used by Marks & Spencer, Britain's largest retailer and one of the world's most profitable, symbolizes high-quality but reasonably priced clothing. Customers will often display a preference for the products of such companies because the brand name is an important guarantee of high quality. Although competitors might like to imitate well-established brand names, the law prohibits them from doing so.

Marketing and technological know-how are also important intangible resources. Unlike brand names, however, company-specific marketing and technological know-how can be relatively easy to imitate. In the case of marketing know-how, the movement of skilled marketing personnel between companies may facilitate the general dissemination of know-how. For example, in the 1970s, Ford was acknowledged as the best marketer among the big three U.S. auto companies. In 1979, it lost a lot of its marketing know-how to Chrysler when its most successful marketer, Lee Iacocca, joined Chrysler. Iacocca subsequently hired many of Ford's top marketing people to work with him at Chrysler. More generally, successful marketing strategies are relatively easy to imitate because they are so visible to competitors. Thus, Coca-Cola quickly imitated PepsiCo's Diet Pepsi brand with the introduction of its own brand, Diet Coke.

With regard to technological know-how, in theory the patent system should make technological know-how relatively immune to imitation. Patents give the inventor of a new product a twenty-year exclusive production agreement. Thus, for example, the biotechnology company Immunex discovered and patented a biological product that treats rheumatoid arthritis. Known as Enbrel, this product is capable of halting the disease-causing mechanism that leads to rheumatoid arthritis, whereas all prior treatments simply provided patients with some relief from the symptoms of the illness. Approved by the FDA in 1998, this product racked up sales of more than $400 million in its first year on the market and may ultimately generate revenues of $2 billion per year for Immunex. Despite the enormous market potential here, Immunex's patent stops potential competitors from introducing their own version of Enbrel. Many other inventions, however, are not as easily protected from imitation by the patent system as are biological products. In electrical and computer engineering, for instance, it is often possible to "invent around" patents. One study found that 60 percent of patented innovations were successfully invented around in four years.[26] This statistic suggests that, in general, distinctive competencies based on technological know-how can be relatively short-lived.

Imitating Capabilities   Imitating a company's capabilities tends to be more difficult than imitating its tangible and intangible resources, chiefly because a company's capabilities are often invisible to outsiders. Since capabilities are based on the way decisions are made and processes managed deep within a company, by definition it is hard for outsiders to discern them. Thus, for example, outsiders may have trouble identifying precisely why 3M is so successful at developing new products, why Nucor is such an efficient steel producer, or why Cisco is able to stay at the cutting edge of the market for network equipment.

On its own, the invisible nature of capabilities would not be enough to halt imitation. In theory, competitors could still gain insights into how a company operates by hiring people away from that company. However, a company's capabilities rarely reside in a single individual. Rather, they are the product of how numerous individuals interact within a unique organizational setting. It is possible that no one individual within a company may be familiar with the totality of a company's internal operating routines and procedures. In such cases, hiring people away from a successful company in order to imitate its key capabilities may not be helpful.

Consider a football team. Its success is the product not of any one individual but of the way individuals work together as a team and the unwritten or tacit understanding between them. Therefore, the transfer of a star player from a winning to a losing team may not be enough to improve the performance of the losing team. However, suppose you buy the whole team. This is what almost happened in 1993 to the German subsidiary of General Motors. It had to obtain an injunction from the German government to prevent Ignacio Lopez de Arriortua, the former GM vice president of operations and the new CEO of Volkswagen, from poaching forty of GM's managers by offering them very high salaries. His intent was to take all the managers who were expert in low-cost production to Volkswagen, which is desperately trying to reduce its costs to compete with the Japanese. Clearly, he was trying to imitate GM's new-found competency in efficiency by buying GM's capabilities through buying its managers.

To sum up, since resources are easier to imitate than capabilities, a distinctive competency based on a company's unique capabilities is probably more durable (less imitable) than one based on its resources. It is more likely to form the foundation for a long-run competitive advantage.

■ Capability of Competitors

According to work by Pankaj Ghemawat, a major determinant of the capability of competitors to rapidly imitate a company's competitive advantage is the nature of the competitors' prior strategic commitments.[26] By **strategic commitment**, Ghemawat means a company's commitment to a particular way of doing business—that is, to developing a particular set of resources and capabilities. Ghemawat's point is that once a company has made a strategic commitment it will find it difficult to respond to new competition if doing so requires a break with this commitment. Therefore, when competitors already have long-established commitments to a particular way of doing business, they may be slow to imitate an innovating company's competitive advantage. Its competitive advantage will thus be relatively durable.

The U.S. automobile industry offers an example. From 1945 to 1975, the industry was dominated by the stable oligopoly of General Motors, Ford, and Chrysler, all of whom geared their operations to the production of large cars—which was what American consumers demanded at the time. When the market shifted from large cars to small, fuel-efficient ones during the late 1970s, U.S. companies lacked the resources and capabilities required to produce these cars. Their prior commitments had built the wrong kind of skills for this new environment. As a result, foreign producers, and particularly the Japanese, stepped into the market breach by providing compact, fuel-efficient, high-quality, and low-cost cars. The failure of U.S. auto manufacturers to react quickly to the distinctive competency of Japanese auto companies gave the latter time to build a strong market position and brand loyalty, which subsequently proved difficult to attack.

Another determinant of the ability of competitors to respond to a company's competitive advantage is their **absorptive capacity**[27]—that is, the ability of an enterprise to identify, value, assimilate and utilize new knowledge. For example, in the 1960s and 1970s, Toyota developed a competitive advantage based on its innovation of lean production systems. Competitors such as General Motors were slow to imitate this innovation, primarily because they lacked the necessary absorptive capacity. General Motors was such a bureaucratic and inward-looking organization that it was very difficult for the company to identify, value, assimilate, and utilize the knowledge underlying lean production systems. Indeed, long after General Motors had identified and understood the importance of lean production systems, the company was still struggling to assimilate and utilize that new knowledge. Put differently, internal inertia can make it difficult for established competitors to respond to a rival whose competitive advantage is based on new products or internal processes—that is, on innovation.

Taken together, factors such as existing strategic commitments and low absorptive capacity limit the ability of established competitors to imitate the competitive advantage of a rival, particularly when that competitive advantage derives from in-

With regard to technological know-how, in theory the patent system should make technological know-how relatively immune to imitation. Patents give the inventor of a new product a twenty-year exclusive production agreement. Thus, for example, the biotechnology company Immunex discovered and patented a biological product that treats rheumatoid arthritis. Known as Enbrel, this product is capable of halting the disease-causing mechanism that leads to rheumatoid arthritis, whereas all prior treatments simply provided patients with some relief from the symptoms of the illness. Approved by the FDA in 1998, this product racked up sales of more than $400 million in its first year on the market and may ultimately generate revenues of $2 billion per year for Immunex. Despite the enormous market potential here, Immunex's patent stops potential competitors from introducing their own version of Enbrel. Many other inventions, however, are not as easily protected from imitation by the patent system as are biological products. In electrical and computer engineering, for instance, it is often possible to "invent around" patents. One study found that 60 percent of patented innovations were successfully invented around in four years.[26] This statistic suggests that, in general, distinctive competencies based on technological know-how can be relatively short-lived.

Imitating Capabilities Imitating a company's capabilities tends to be more difficult than imitating its tangible and intangible resources, chiefly because a company's capabilities are often invisible to outsiders. Since capabilities are based on the way decisions are made and processes managed deep within a company, by definition it is hard for outsiders to discern them. Thus, for example, outsiders may have trouble identifying precisely why 3M is so successful at developing new products, why Nucor is such an efficient steel producer, or why Cisco is able to stay at the cutting edge of the market for network equipment.

On its own, the invisible nature of capabilities would not be enough to halt imitation. In theory, competitors could still gain insights into how a company operates by hiring people away from that company. However, a company's capabilities rarely reside in a single individual. Rather, they are the product of how numerous individuals interact within a unique organizational setting. It is possible that no one individual within a company may be familiar with the totality of a company's internal operating routines and procedures. In such cases, hiring people away from a successful company in order to imitate its key capabilities may not be helpful.

Consider a football team. Its success is the product not of any one individual but of the way individuals work together as a team and the unwritten or tacit understanding between them. Therefore, the transfer of a star player from a winning to a losing team may not be enough to improve the performance of the losing team. However, suppose you buy the whole team. This is what almost happened in 1993 to the German subsidiary of General Motors. It had to obtain an injunction from the German government to prevent Ignacio Lopez de Arriortua, the former GM vice president of operations and the new CEO of Volkswagen, from poaching forty of GM's managers by offering them very high salaries. His intent was to take all the managers who were expert in low-cost production to Volkswagen, which is desperately trying to reduce its costs to compete with the Japanese. Clearly, he was trying to imitate GM's new-found competency in efficiency by buying GM's capabilities through buying its managers.

novative products or processes. This is why, when innovations reshape the rules of competition in an industry, value often migrates away from established competitors and toward new enterprises that are operating with new business models.

Industry Dynamism

A dynamic industry environment is one that is changing rapidly. We examined the factors that determine the dynamism and intensity of competition in an industry in Chapter 3 when we discussed the external environment. The most dynamic industries tend to be those with a very high rate of product innovation—for instance, the consumer electronics industry and the personal computer industry. In dynamic industries, the rapid rate of innovation means that product life cycles are shortening and that competitive advantage can be very transitory. A company that has a competitive advantage today may find its market position outflanked tomorrow by a rival's innovation.

In the personal computer industry, for example, the rapid increase in computing power during the last two decades has contributed to a high degree of innovation and a turbulent environment. Reflecting the persistence of innovation, in the late 1970s and early 1980s Apple Computer had an industrywide competitive advantage due to its innovation. In 1981, IBM seized the advantage with its introduction of its first personal computer. By the mid 1980s, however, IBM had lost its competitive advantage to high-power "clone" manufacturers such as Compaq, which had beaten IBM in the race to introduce a computer based on Intel's 386 chip. In turn, in the 1990s Compaq subsequently lost its competitive advantage to companies such as Dell and Gateway, which pioneered new low-cost ways of delivering computers to consumers utilizing the Internet as a direct selling device.

Summary

The durability of a company's competitive advantage depends on three factors: the height of barriers to imitation, the capability of competitors to imitate its innovation, and the general level of dynamism in the industry environment. When barriers to imitation are low, capable competitors abound, and the environment is very dynamic, with innovations being developed all the time, then competitive advantage is likely to be transitory. On the other hand, even within such industries, companies can achieve a more enduring competitive advantage if they are able to make investments that build barriers to imitation. During the 1980s, Apple Computer built a competitive advantage based on the combination of a proprietary disk operating system and an intangible product image (as noted earlier, intangible resources are difficult to imitate). The resulting brand loyalty enabled Apple to carve out a fairly secure niche in an industry where competitive advantage has otherwise proved to be very fleeting. However, by the mid 1990s, its strategy had been imitated, primarily due to the introduction of Microsoft's Windows operating system, which imitated most of the features that had enabled Apple to build brand loyalty. As a result, by 1996 Apple was in financial trouble, providing yet another example that no competitive advantage lasts forever. Ultimately, anything can be imitated. (Interestingly enough, though, Apple has shown remarkable resilience. In the late 1990s, it clawed its way back from the brink of bankruptcy to once again establish a viable position within its niche).

WHY DO COMPANIES FAIL?

In this section, we take the issue of why a company might lose its competitive advantage one step further and ask, Why do companies fail? We define a failing company as one whose profit rate is substantially lower than the average profit rate of its competitors. A company can lose its competitive advantage but still not fail. It may just earn average profits. Failure implies something more drastic. Failing companies typically earn low or negative profits; in other words, they are at a competitive disadvantage.

The question is particularly pertinent since some of the most successful companies of the twentieth century have at times seen their competitive position deteriorate. Companies such as IBM, General Motors, American Express, Digital Equipment, and Compaq Computer, all at one time held up as examples of managerial excellence, have gone through periods of poor financial performance, when they clearly lacked any competitive advantage. We explore three related reasons for failure: inertia, prior strategic commitments, and the Icarus paradox.

Inertia

The inertia argument says that companies find it difficult to change their strategies and structures in order to adapt to changing competitive conditions.[28] IBM is a classic example of this problem. For thirty years, it was viewed as the world's most successful computer company. Then, in the space of a few short years, its success turned into a disaster, with a loss of $5 billion in 1992 leading to layoffs of more than 100,000 employees. IBM's troubles were caused by a dramatic decline in the cost of computing power as a result of innovations in microprocessors. With the advent of powerful low-cost microprocessors, the locus of the computer market shifted from mainframes to small, low-priced personal computers. This left IBM's huge mainframe operations with a diminished market. Even though IBM had, and still has, a significant presence in the personal computer market, it had failed to shift the focus of its efforts away from mainframes and toward personal computers. This failure meant deep trouble for one of the most successful companies of the twentieth century (although IBM has now executed a successful turnaround, primarily by repositioning the company as a provider of e-commerce infrastructure and solutions).

Why do companies find it so difficult to adapt to new environmental conditions? One factor that seems to stand out is the role of an organization's capabilities in causing inertia. Earlier in the chapter, we argue that organizational capabilities can be a source of competitive advantage; their downside, however, is that they are difficult to change. Recall that capabilities are the way a company makes decisions and manages its processes. IBM always emphasized close coordination between different operating units and favored decision processes that stressed consensus among interdependent operating units as a prerequisite for a decision to go forward.[29] This capability was a source of advantage for IBM during the 1970s, when coordination among its worldwide operating units was necessary in order to develop, manufacture, and sell complex mainframes. But the slow-moving bureaucracy that it had spawned was a source of failure in the 1990s, when organizations had to adapt readily to rapid environmental change.

Capabilities are difficult to change because a certain distribution of power and influence is embedded within the established decision-making and management processes of an organization. Those who play key roles in a decision-making process clearly have more power. It follows that changing the established capabilities of an organization means changing its existing distribution of power and influence, and those whose power and influence would diminish resist such change. Proposals for change trigger turf battles. The power struggle and the political resistance associated with trying to alter the way in which an organization makes decisions and manages its process—that is, trying to change its capabilities—bring on inertia. This is not to say that companies cannot change. However, because change is so often resisted by those who feel threatened by it, in most cases change has to be induced by a crisis. By then the company may already be failing, as happened at IBM.

■ Prior Strategic Commitments

Ghemawat has argued that a company's prior strategic commitments not only limit its ability to imitate rivals, but may also cause competitive disadvantage.[30] IBM, for instance, had made major investments in the mainframe computer business. As a result, when the market shifted, it was stuck with significant resources that were specialized to that particular business. The company had manufacturing facilities geared to the production of mainframes, research organizations that were similarly specialized, and a mainframe sales force. Since these resources were not well suited to the newly emerging personal computer business, IBM's difficulties in the early 1990s were in a sense inevitable. Its prior strategic commitments locked IBM into a business that was shrinking. Shedding these resources was bound to cause hardship for all organization stakeholders.

■ The Icarus Paradox

In his book, Danny Miller has postulated that the roots of competitive failure can be found in what he termed the Icarus paradox.[31] Icarus is a figure in Greek mythology who used a pair of wings—made for him by his father—to escape from an island where he was being held prisoner. He flew so well that he went higher and higher, ever closer to the sun, until the heat of the sun melted the wax that held his wings together and he plunged to his death in the Aegean Sea. The paradox is that his greatest asset, his ability to fly, caused his demise. Miller argues that the same paradox applies to many once successful companies. According to Miller, many companies become so dazzled by their early success that they believe more of the same type of effort is the way to future success. As a result, however, a company can become so specialized and inner-directed that it loses sight of market realities and the fundamental requirements for achieving a competitive advantage. Sooner or later this leads to failure.

Miller identifies four major categories among the rising and falling companies. The "craftsmen," such as Texas Instruments and Digital Equipment Corporation

STRATEGY *in* ACTION

4.6

The Road to Ruin at DEC

DEC's original success was founded on the minicomputer, a cheaper more flexible version of its mainframe cousins that Ken Olson and his brilliant team of engineers invented in the 1960s. Olson and his staff improved their original minis until they could not be surpassed in quality and reliability. In the 1970s, their VAX series of minicomputers was widely regarded as the most reliable computers ever produced. DEC was rewarded by high profit rates and rapid growth. By 1990, DEC was number twenty-seven on the *Fortune 500* list of the largest corporations in America.

However, buoyed up by its own success, DEC turned into an engineering monoculture. Its engineers became idols; its marketing and accounting staff were barely tolerated. Component specifications and design standards were all that senior managers understood. Technological fine-tuning became such an obsession that the needs of customers for smaller, more economical, user-friendly

computers were ignored. For example, DEC's personal computers bombed because they were so out of touch with the needs of consumers. The company also failed to respond to the threat to its core market presented by the rise of computer workstations and client/server architecture. Indeed, Ken Olson was known for dismissing such new products. He once remarked, "We always say that customers are right, but they are not always right." That may be so, but DEC, blinded by its own early success, failed to remain responsive to its customers and to changing market conditions.

By the early 1990s, DEC was a company in deep trouble. Olson was forced out in July 1992, and the company lost billions of dollars between 1992 and 1995. It returned to profitability in 1996, primarily because of the success of a turnaround strategy aimed at re-orientating the company to serve precisely those areas that Olson had dismissed. In 1998, the company was acquired by Compaq Computer.[32]

(DEC) achieved early success through engineering excellence. But then the companies became so obsessed with engineering details that they lost sight of market realities. (The story of DEC's demise is summarized in Strategy in Action 4.6.) Then there are the "builders," for instance, Gulf & Western and ITT. Having built successful, moderately diversified companies, they then became so enchanted with diversification for its own sake that they continued to diversify far beyond the point at which it was profitable to do so. Miller's third group are the "pioneers," such as Wang Labs. Enamored of their own originally brilliant innovations they continued to search for additional brilliant innovations, but ended up producing novel but completely useless products. The final category comprises the "salesmen," exemplified by Procter & Gamble and Chrysler. They became so convinced of their ability to sell anything that they paid scant attention to product development and manufacturing excellence and as a result spawned a proliferation of bland, inferior products.

AVOIDING FAILURE AND SUSTAINING COMPETITIVE ADVANTAGE

How can a company avoid the traps that have snared so many once successful companies? How can it build a sustainable competitive advantage? We do not give a complete answer here as much of the remaining text deals with these issues. However, a number of key points can be made at this juncture.

Focus on the Building Blocks of Competitive Advantage

First, maintaining a competitive advantage requires a company to continue focusing on the four generic building blocks of competitive advantage—efficiency, quality, innovation, and customer responsiveness—and to develop distinctive competencies that contribute to superior performance in these areas. One of the messages of Miller's Icarus paradox is that many successful companies become unbalanced in their pursuit of distinctive competencies. DEC, for example, focused on engineering quality at the expense of almost everything else, including, most importantly, customer responsiveness. Other companies forget to focus on any distinctive competency. This was certainly the case at ITT, where an empire-building CEO, Harold Geneen, focused on diversification but lost sight of the need to focus on achieving excellence in efficiency, quality, innovation, and customer responsiveness at the level of business units within ITT.

Institute Continuous Improvement and Learning

The only constant in the world is change. Today's source of competitive advantage may soon be rapidly imitated by capable competitors, or it may be made obsolete by the innovations of a rival. In such a dynamic and fast-paced environment, the only way that a company can maintain a competitive advantage over time is to continually improve its efficiency, quality, innovation, and customer responsiveness. The way to do so is to recognize the importance of learning within the organization.[33] The most successful companies are not those that stand still, resting on their laurels. They are those that continually seek out ways of improving their operations and, in the process, are constantly upgrading the value of their distinctive competencies or creating new competencies. Companies such as General Electric and Toyota have a reputation for being learning organizations. What this means is that they are continually analyzing the processes that underlie their efficiency, quality, innovation, and customer responsiveness. Their objective is to learn from prior mistakes and to seek out ways to improve their processes over time. This has enabled Toyota, for example, to continually upgrade its employee productivity and product quality, allowing the company to stay one step ahead of imitators.

Track Best Industrial Practice and Use Benchmarking

One of the best ways to develop distinctive competencies that contribute to superior efficiency, quality, innovation, and customer responsiveness is to identify **best industrial practice** and to adopt it. Only by so doing will a company be able to build and maintain the resources and capabilities that underpin excellence in efficiency, quality, innovation, and customer responsiveness. What constitutes best industrial practice is an issue we discuss in some depth in Chapter 5. However, it requires tracking the practice of other companies, and perhaps the best way to do so is through **benchmarking**. This is the process of measuring the company against the products, practices, and services of some of its most efficient global competitors. For example, when Xerox was in trouble in the early 1980s, it decided to institute a policy of benchmarking as a means of identifying ways to improve the efficiency of its operations. Xerox benchmarked L.L. Bean for distribution procedures, Deere & Company for central computer operations, Procter & Gamble for marketing, and Florida Power & Light for total quality management processes. By the early 1990s, Xerox was benchmarking 240 functions against comparable areas in other companies. This process has been credited with helping Xerox dramatically improve the efficiency of its operations.[34]

■ Overcome Inertia

A further reason for failure is an inability to adapt to changing conditions because of organizational inertia. Overcoming the barriers to change within an organization is one of the key requirements for maintaining a competitive advantage, and we devote a whole chapter, Chapter 14, to this issue. Suffice it to say here that identifying barriers to change is an important first step. Once this step has been taken, implementing change requires good leadership, the judicious use of power, and appropriate changes in organizational structure and control systems. All these issues are discussed later in the book.

SUMMARY OF CHAPTER

The principal objective of this chapter is to identify the basis of competitive advantage by examining why, within a given industry, some companies outperform others. Competitive advantage is the product of at least one of the following: superior efficiency, superior quality, superior innovation, and superior customer responsiveness. Achieving superiority here requires that a company develop appropriate distinctive competencies, which in turn are a product of the kind of resources and capabilities that a company possesses. The chapter also examines issues related to the durability of competitive advantage. This durability is determined by the height of barriers to imitation, the capability of competitors to imitate a company's advantage, and the general level of environmental turbulence. Finally, the discussion of why companies fail and what they can do to avoid failure indicates that failure is due to factors such as organizational inertia, prior strategic commitments, and the Icarus paradox. Avoiding failure requires that a company constantly try to upgrade its distinctive competencies in accordance with best industrial practice and that it take steps to overcome organizational inertia. The main points made in this chapter can be summarized as follows:

✓ The source of a competitive advantage is superior value creation.

✓ To create superior value, a company must lower its costs, differentiate its product so that it can charge a higher price, or do both simultaneously.

✓ The four generic building blocks of competitive advantage are efficiency, quality, innovation, and customer responsiveness.

✓ Superior efficiency enables a company to lower its costs; superior quality allows it both to charge a higher price and to lower its costs; and superior customer service lets it charge a higher price. Superior innovation can lead to higher prices, particularly in the case of product innovations; or it can lead to lower unit costs, particularly in the case of process innovations.

✓ Distinctive competencies are the unique strengths of a company. Valuable distinctive competencies enable a company to earn a profit rate that is above the industry average.

✓ The distinctive competencies of an organization arise from its resources and capabilities.

✓ Resources refer to the financial, physical, human, technological, and organizational assets of a company.

✓ Capabilities refer to a company's skills at coordinating resources and putting them to productive use.

✓ In order to achieve a competitive advantage, companies need to pursue strategies that build on the existing resources and capabilities of an organization (its competencies), and they need to formulate strategies that build additional resources and capabilities (develop new competencies).

✓ The durability of a company's competitive advantage depends on the height of barriers to imitation, the capability of competitors, and environmental dynamism.

✓ Failing companies typically earn low or negative profits. Three factors seem to contribute to failure—organizational inertia in the face of environmental change, the nature of a company's prior strategic commitments, and the Icarus paradox.

✓ Avoiding failure requires a constant focus on the basic building blocks of competitive advantage, continuous improvement, identification and adoption of best industrial practice, and victory over inertia.

DISCUSSION QUESTIONS

1. What are the main implications of the material discussed in this chapter for strategy formulation?

2. When is a company's competitive advantage most likely to endure over time?

3. Which is more important in explaining the success and failure of companies, strategizing or luck?

Practicing Strategic Management

SMALL-GROUP EXERCISE
Analyzing Competitive Advantage

Break up into groups of three to five people. Drawing on the concepts introduced in this case, analyze the competitive position of your business school in the market for business education. Then answer the following questions:

1. Does your business school have a competitive advantage?

2. If so, on what is this advantage based and is this advantage sustainable?

3. If your school does not have a competitive advantage in the market for business education, identify the inhibiting factors that are holding it back.

4. How might the Internet change the way in which business education is delivered?

5. Does the Internet pose a threat to the competitive position of your school in the market for business education, or is it an opportunity for your school to enhance its competitive position? (Note: it can be both.)

ARTICLE FILE 4

Find an example of a company that has sustained its competitive advantage for more than ten years. Identify the source of the competitive advantage and describe why it has lasted so long.

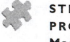

STRATEGIC MANAGEMENT PROJECT
Module 4

This module deals with the competitive position of your company. With the information you have at your disposal, perform the tasks and answer the questions listed:

1. Identify whether your company has a competitive advantage or disadvantage in its primary industry. (Its primary industry is the one in which it has the most sales.)

2. Evaluate your company against the four generic building blocks of competitive advantage: efficiency, quality, innovation, and customer responsiveness. How does this exercise help you understand the performance of your company relative to its competitors?

3. What are the distinctive competencies of your company?

4. What role have prior strategies played in shaping the distinctive competencies of your company? What role has luck played?

5. Do the strategies currently pursued by your company build on its distinctive competencies? Are they an attempt to build new competencies?

6. What are the barriers to imitating the distinctive competencies of your company?

7. Is there any evidence that your company finds it difficult to adapt to changing industry conditions? If so, why do you think this is the case?

EXPLORING THE WEB
Visiting Johnson & Johnson

Visit the Web site of Johnson & Johnson (http://www.jnj.com). Read through the material contained on the site, paying particular attention to the features on the company's history, its credo, innovations, and company news. On the basis of this information, answer the following questions:

1. Do you think that Johnson & Johnson has a distinctive competency?

2. What is the nature of this competency? How does it help the company attain a competitive advantage?

3. What are the resources and capabilities that underlie this competency? Where do these resources and capabilities come from?

4. How imitable is Johnson & Johnson's distinctive competency?

Search the Web for a company site that goes into depth about the history, products, and competitive position of that company. On the basis of the information you collect, answer the following questions.

1. Does the company have a distinctive competency?

2. What is the nature of this competency? How does it help the company attain a competitive advantage?

3. What are the resources and capabilities that underlie this competency? Where do these resources and capabilities come from?

4. How imitable is the company's distinctive competency?

CLOSING CASE

Marks & Spencer

MARKS & SPENCER (M&S) is a British retailing institution. Founded in 1884 by Michael Marks, a Polish Jew who had emigrated to England, the company has been a national chain since the early 1900s. By 1926, the company had a branch in every major town in the country and had become Britain's largest retailer, a position it still holds in 2000. Primarily a supplier of clothing and foodstuffs, M&S is one of the world's most profitable retailers. In 1999, M&S's 300 United Kingdom stores had sales of over 7 billion pounds sterling, accounted for 15 percent of all retail clothing sales in the United Kingdom and 5 percent of all food sales. According to the *Guinness Book of Records,* in 1991 the company's flagship store at Marble Arch in London had a turnover of $3,700 per square foot—more than any other department store in the world.

M&S provides a selective range of clothing and food items aimed at rapid turnover. The firm sells all its products under its own St. Michael's label. M&S offers high-quality products at moderate rather than low prices. This combination of high quality and reasonable price encourages customers to associate M&S with value for money, and the firm's ability to deliver this combination consistently over the years has built up enormous customer goodwill in Britain. So strong is M&S's reputation among British consumers that the company does no advertising in that market.

To achieve the combination of moderate prices and high quality, M&S works very closely with its suppliers, many of whom have been selling a major portion of their output to M&S for generations. The focus on quality is reinforced by M&S's practice of having its technical people work closely with suppliers on product design. Suppliers are more than willing to respond to the firm's demands, for they know that M&S is loyal to its suppliers and as it grows so do they. The sales volume generated by M&S's strategy of providing only a selective range of clothing and food enables M&S's suppliers to realize substantial economies of scale from large production runs. These cost savings are then passed on to M&S in the form of lower prices. In turn, M&S passes on part of the savings to the consumer.

Crucial to M&S's effectiveness is a clear focus on the customer. The tone is set by top management. Each senior manager makes a habit of wearing M&S clothes and eating M&S food. Thus, managers develop an understanding of what it is that customers want and like about M&S products; by staying close to the customer, they can improve the quality and design of the products they offer. The customer focus is reinforced at the store level by store managers who monitor sales volume and quickly identify lines that are selling and those that are not. Then store managers can transmit this information to suppliers, which have the capacity to quickly modify their production, increasing the output of lines that are selling well and reducing the output of lines that are not moving.

Another central feature of M&S is its pioneering approach to human relations. Long before it became fashionable to do so, M&S had developed a commitment to the well-being of its employees. M&S has always viewed itself as a family business with a broad responsibility for the welfare of its employees. It offers employees medical and pension plans that provide benefits that are well above the industry average. The company pays its employees at a rate that is also well above the industry average, and it makes a practice of promoting employees from within, rather than hiring from outside. Furthermore, there are a series of in-store amenities for employees, including subsidized cafeterias, medical services, recreation rooms, and hairdressing salons. The reward for M&S is the trust and loyalty of its employees and, ultimately, high employee productivity.

Just as vital is the company's commitment to simplifying its operating structure and strategic control systems.

M&S has a very flat hierarchy; there is little in the way of intervening management layers between store managers and top management. The firm utilizes just two profit margins, one for foodstuff and one for clothing. This practice reduces bureaucracy and frees its store managers from worrying about pricing issues. Instead, they are encouraged to focus on maximizing sales volume. A store's performance is assessed by its sales volume. Control is achieved partly through formal budgetary procedures and partly through an informal probing process, in which top management drops in unannounced at stores and quizzes managers there about the store. In a typical year, just about every store in Britain will receive at least one unan-

nounced visit from top management. This keeps store managers on their toes and constantly alert to the need to provide the kind of value-for-money products that customers have come to associate with M&S.[35]

Case Discussion Questions

1. What do you think is the source of Marks & Spencer's competitive advantage?

2. Marks & Spencer has managed to maintain its competitive advantage in British retailing for more than fifty years. Why, do you think, have rival firms found Marks & Spencer's competitive position so difficult to attack?

End Notes

1. "Cisco @ speed," *Economist*, June 26, 1999, Special report: Business and the Internet, p. 12; S. Tully, "How Cisco Mastered the Net," *Fortune*, August 17, 1997, p. 207–210; C. Kano, The Real King of the Internet, *Fortune*, September 7, 1998, 82–93.

2. The concept of consumer surplus is an important one in economics. For a more detailed exposition, see D. Besanko, D. Dranove, and M. Shanley. *Economics of Strategy* (New York: John Wiley, 1996).

3. The data is taken from the Value Line Investment Survey. The average ROK is the average of all 17 department stores followed continuously by Value Line over this time period.

4. However, $P = V$ only in the special case where the company has a perfect monopoly and where it can charge each customer a unique price that reflects the value of the product to that customer (i.e., where perfect price discrimination is possible). More generally, except in the limiting case of perfect price discrimination, even a monopolist will see most consumers capture some of the value of a product in the form of a consumer surplus.

5. This point is central to the work of Michael Porter. See M. E. Porter, *Competitive Advantage* (New York: Free Press, 1985). See also Chapter 4 in P. Ghemawat, *Commitment: The Dynamic of Strategy* (New York: Free Press, 1991).

6. M. E. Porter, *Competitive Strategy* (New York: Free Press, 1980).

7. D. Lavin, "Chrysler Is Now Low-Cost Producer in the Automobile Industry," *Wall Street Journal*, June 23, 1994, p. B5; N. Templin, "The Auto Trade Fight," *Wall Street Journal*, May 18, 1995, p. A6; W. M. Bulkeley, "Pushing the Pace," *Wall Street Journal*, December 23, 1994, p. A1; D. Levin. "GM Would Have to Cut 20,000 Workers to Match Ford," *Wall Street Journal*, June 24, 1994, p. C22; The Harbor Report. Harbor & Associates, 1999.

8. See D. Garvin, "What Does Product Quality Really Mean," *Sloan Management Review*, 26 (Fall 1984), 25–44; P. B. Crosby, *Quality Is Free* (Mentor, 1980); and A. Gabor, *The Man Who Discovered Quality* (Times Books, 1990).

9. G. Bethune, "From Worst to First," *Fortune*, May 25, 1998, pp. 185–190.

10. W. Chan Kim and R. Mauborgne, "Value Innovation: The Strategic Logic of High Growth," *Harvard Business Review* (January–February 1997), 102–115.

11. G. Stalk and T. M. Hout, *Competing Against Time* (New York: Free Press, 1990).

12. Ibid

13. M. E. Porter, *Competitive Advantage*.

14. R. Langreth, "High Anxiety: Rivals Threaten Prozac's Reign," *Wall Street Journal*, May 9, 1996, pp. B1–B2.

15. M. Cusumano, *The Japanese Automobile Industry* (Cambridge, Mass.: Harvard University Press, 1989).

16. The material in this section relies on the so-called resource-based view of the firm. For summaries of this perspective, see J. B. Barney, "Firm Resources and Sustained Competitive Advantage," *Journal of Management*, 17 (1991), 99–120; J. T. Mahoney and J. R. Pandian, "The Resource-Based View Within the Conversation of Strategic Management," *Strategic Management Journal*, 13 (1992), 63–380; R. Amit and P. J. H. Schoemaker, "Strategic Assets and Organizational Rent," *Strategic Management Journal*, 14 (1993), 33–46; M. A. Peteraf, "The Cornerstones of Competitive Advantage: A Resource-Based View," *Strategic Management Journal*, 14 (1993), 179–191; and B. Wernerfelt, "A Resource Based View of the Firm," *Strategic Management Journal*, 5 (1994), 171–180.

17. For a discussion of organizational capabilities, see R. R. Nelson and S. Winter, *An Evolutionary Theory of Economic Change* (Cambridge, Mass.: Belknap Press, 1982).

18. R. M. Grant, *Contemporary Strategic Analysis* (Cambridge, Mass.: Blackwell, 1991). See also Chan Kim and Mauborgne, "Value Innovation," pp. 102–115.

19. "Disney's Magic," *Business Week*, March 9, 1987; "Michael Eisner's Hit Parade," *Business Week* , February 1, 1988.

20. D. Kearns, "Leadership Through Quality," *Academy of Management Executive*, 4 (1990), 86–89; J. Sheridan, "America's Best Plants," *Industry Week*, October 15, 1990, pp. 27–40.

21. The classic statement of this position was made by A. A. Alchain, "Uncertainty, Evolution, and Economic Theory," *Journal of Political Economy*, 84 (1950), 488–500.

22. S. Manes and P. Andrews, *Gates* (New York: Simon & Schuster, 1993).

23. This is the nature of the competitive process. For more details see C. W. L. Hill and D. Deeds, "The Importance of Industry Structure for the Determination of Firm Profitability: A Neo-Austrian Perspective," *Journal of Management Studies*, 33, 1996, p. 429–452.

24. Like resources and capabilities, the concept of barriers to imitation is also grounded in the resource-based view of the firm. For details, see R. Reed and R. J. DeFillippi, "Causal Ambiguity, Barriers to Imitation, and Sustainable Competitive Advantage," *Academy of Management Review*, 15 (1990), 88–102.

25. E. Mansfield, "How Economists See R&D," *Harvard Business Review* (November–December 1981), 98–106.

26. P. Ghemawat, *Commitment: The Dynamic of Strategy* (New York: Free Press, 1991).

27. W. M. Cohen and D. A. Levinthal, "Absorptive Capacity: a New Perspective on Learning and Innovation," *Administrative Science Quarterly*, 35 (1990), 128–152.

28. M. T. Hannah and J. Freeman, "Structural Inertia and Organizational Change," *American Sociological Review*, 49 (1984), 149–164.

29. See "IBM Corporation," *Harvard Business School Case* No. 180-034, 1985.

30. Ghemawat, *Commitment*.

31. D. Miller, *The Icarus Paradox* (New York: HarperBusiness, 1990).

32. Ibid. Also P. D. Llosa, "We Must Know What We Are Doing," *Fortune*, November 14, 1994, p. 68.

33. P. M. Senge, *The Fifth Discipline: The Art and Practice of the Learning Organization* (New York: Doubleday, 1990).

34. D. Kearns, "Leadership Through Quality," pp. 86–89.

35. J. Thornhill, "A European Spark for Marks," *Financial Times*, July 13, 1992, p. 8; Marks & Spencer, Ltd. (A)," *Harvard Business School Case* No. 91–392–089, 1991; J. Marcom, "Blue Blazers and Guacamole," *Forbes*, November 25, 1991, pp. 64–68; M. Evans, "Marks & Spencer Battles On," *Financial Post*, December 11, 1989, p. 32.

5 Building Competitive Advantage Through Functional-Level Strategy

OPENING CASE

LEVI STRAUSS is an American icon. For two generations, it has dressed the world in its fabled blue jeans. In recent years, however, Levi's luster has begun to fade even more rapidly than the blue dye on an old pair of 501s. The fast-moving fashion world seems to be leaving Levi's behind. In 1998, for example, Levi's sales declined by 13 percent, to $6 billion, while its share of the domestic blue jeans market fell from 16.3 percent in 1997 to 14.8 percent. Levi's problems have two sources. First, a combination of good design and savvy marketing has helped competitors such as The Gap take share from Levi's. Second, Levi's jeans are just too expensive. Unlike most of its competitors, which have moved the bulk of their manufacturing to Asia or central America, Levi continues to have a significant manufacturing presence in the United States. But the high cost of labor in the United States means that Levi has to charge higher prices to recoup its costs, and consumers just don't seem willing to pay a premium price for Levi's jeans anymore.

Levi's Original Spin

Levi's solution to this problems has been twofold. First, the company announced that it would close eleven of its twenty-two U.S. plants, laying off 5,900 domestic employees, and move manufacturing to low-cost locations. Second, in an attempt to keep its remaining eleven U.S. plants humming, the company announced that it would step up its Original Spin program to supply jeans that are custom-made for individual consumers. Levi's thinking is that if it can customize its jeans for each individual's body shape—and no two people are identical—it will be able to charge a premium price and therefore cover the costs of continuing to have a substantial manufacturing presence in the United States.

At the core of the Original Spin program is an attempt to use Web-based technology and computer-controlled production equipment to implement a strategy of mass customization that has as its goal a desire to give each customer a better-fitting pair of jeans in the customer's preferred style. The idea is that, with the help of a sales associate, customers will create the jeans they want by picking from six colors, three basic models, five different leg openings, and two types of fly. Their waist, rear, and inseam will be measured, and then they will try on a pair of plain "test-drive" jeans to make sure that they like the fit. If they do, the order will be punched into a Web-based computer terminal linked to the stitching machines in a Levi Strauss factory. Customers can even give the jeans a name—for example, "Rebel" for a pair of black jeans. At the factory, computer-controlled tools precision-cut the jeans and stitch an individual bar code inside. The jeans are then sewn and washed, identified by the code, and shipped to the customer's home. The whole process takes no more than two to three weeks. The bar code tag stores the measurements for simple reordering.

Today, a fully stocked Levi's store carries approximately 130 pairs of ready-to-wear jeans. With the Original Spin program, the number of choices available will leap to 750. Sanjay Choudhuri, Levi's director of mass customization, feels that 750 is about the right number of choices. Unlimited choice would create inefficiencies at the manufacturing plant. Levi's strategy is to offer enough choice to give the customer the illusion of infinite variety, yet make it feasible to produce the jeans with little or no additional cost penalty. Levi hopes to charge a premium price—about 20 percent higher—for this service. However, in the company's view, the real benefit of the program is that it changes the nature of the relationship between Levi Strauss and its customers from an anonymous relationship in which the customer walks out of the store with a pair of off-the-shelf jeans, to one in which Levi Strauss aims to become each customer's personal jeans adviser. If the program works, Levi might extend it to embrace several other apparel offerings, such as its Dockers line of pants for men. It may also roll out the program in international markets.

Further down the road, Levi might use a device that will scan the entire body. The machine, developed by an independent company, projects 300,000 pinpoints of light from head to toe and then photographs the body from six angles to produce a kind of three-dimensional portrait. These data result in a custom pattern that can be transmitted to a production plant to manufacture jeans, shirts, or any other item of clothing. Within five years, body-scanning equipment may be available in Levi stores.[1]

OVERVIEW

In Chapter 4, we discuss the central role played by efficiency, quality, innovation, and customer responsiveness in building and maintaining a competitive advantage. In this chapter, we consider what managers can do at the level of functions, or operations, within a company to attain superior efficiency, quality, innovation, and customer responsiveness. Functional-level strategies are strategies directed at improving the effectiveness of basic operations within a company, such as production, marketing, materials management, research and development, and human resources. Even though these strategies may be focused on a given function, as often as not they embrace two or more functions and require close cooperation among functions to attain companywide efficiency, quality, innovation, and customer responsiveness goals.

For example, the Opening Case describes how Levi Strauss is utilizing Web-based technology and computer-controlled equipment to pursue a strategy of mass customization. If successful, this innovative program will change the nature of Levi's relationship with its customers. By customizing its basic product offering to the idiosyncratic body shapes and tastes of individual customers, Levi aims to build a reputation for customer responsiveness, to gain share from its competitors, and to charge a premium price for its products.

To explore the issue of functional-level strategies further, in this chapter we look at how companies can increase their efficiency, quality, innovation, and customer responsiveness. Although in some cases we will focus on the contribution of a given function—such as production or marketing—toward attaining these goals, we will also emphasize the importance of strategies and policies that cut across functions. By the time you have finished this chapter, you should have a much clearer understanding of the actions that managers can take at the operating level to attain superior efficiency, quality, innovation, and customer responsiveness.

ACHIEVING SUPERIOR EFFICIENCY

A company is a device for transforming inputs into outputs. Inputs are basic factors of production such as labor, land, capital, management, technological know-how, and so on. Outputs are the goods and services that a company produces. The simplest measure of efficiency is the quantity of inputs that it takes to produce a given output; that is, Efficiency = outputs/inputs. The more efficient a company is, the fewer the inputs required to produce a given output and, therefore, the lower its cost structure. Put another way, an efficient company has higher productivity than its rivals and, therefore, lower costs.

We review here the various steps that companies can take at the functional level to boost their efficiency and thus lower their unit costs. After considering the primary functions of production and marketing, we move on to examine the various support functions of the enterprise. We must stress, however, that achieving superior quality plays a major role in achieving superior efficiency. We delay discussion of how to achieve superior quality until the next section.

▓ Production and Efficiency: Economies of Scale

Economies of scale are unit-cost reductions associated with a large scale of output. One source of economies of scale is the ability to spread fixed costs over a large production volume. Fixed costs are costs that must be incurred to produce a product regardless of the level of output; they include the costs of purchasing machinery, the costs of setting up machinery for individual production runs, the costs of facilities, and the costs of advertising and R&D. For example, it is costing Microsoft approximately $1 billion to develop the next version of its Windows operating system, Windows 2000. Microsoft can realize substantial scale economies by spreading the fixed costs associated with developing a new operating system over the enormous unit-sales volume it expects for this operating system (90 percent of the world's personal computers use a Microsoft operating system). In Microsoft's case, these scale economies are even more significant due to the trivial incremental (or marginal) cost of producing additional copies of Windows 2000 (once the master copy has been produced, additional CDs containing the operating system can be produced for just a few cents).

Many high-technology companies face a similar cost structure: high fixed costs and trivial marginal costs. It costs telecommunications companies billions of dollars in infrastructure to build out their networks, but almost nothing to transmit additional signals down those networks. It costs Intel approximately $5 billion to build a new fabrication facility to produce microprocessors, but only a few cents to produce each chip. It can cost pharmaceutical companies as much as $500 million to develop a new drug, but only a few cents to produce additional units of that drug. For all of these companies, the key to their efficiency and profitability is to increase sales rapidly enough so that fixed costs can be spread out over a large unit volume, and substantial scale economies can be realized.

Another source of scale economies is the ability of companies producing in large volumes to achieve a greater division of labor and specialization. Specialization, in turn, is said to have a favorable impact on productivity, mainly because it enables employees to become very skilled at performing a particular task. The classic example of such economies is Ford's Model T automobile. The world's first mass-produced car, the Model T Ford was introduced in 1923. Until then, Ford had made cars using an expensive hand-built "craft production" method. By introducing mass-production techniques, the company achieved greater division of labor (that is, it split assembly into small, repeatable tasks) and specialization, which boosted employee productivity. Ford was also able to spread the fixed costs of developing an automobile and setting up production machinery over a large volume of output. As a result of these economies, the cost of manufacturing a car at Ford fell from $3,000 to less than $900 (in 1958 dollars).

Nor are scale economies relevant just to manufacturing enterprises such as Ford and Du Pont. Many service companies also benefit from realizing substantial scale economies. An example is given in Strategy in Action 5.1, which looks at the economies of scale realized from the merger between two large New York banks, Chemical Bank and Chase Manhattan Bank.

Some experts argue that after a certain minimum efficient scale (MES) of output is reached there are few, if any, additional scale economies to be had from expanding volume.[3] (**Minimum efficient scale** is the minimum plant size necessary to gain significant economies of scale.) In other words, as shown in Figure 5.1, the long-run unit-cost curve of a company is L-shaped. At outputs beyond MES in Figure 5.1, additional cost reductions are hard to come by. Another point worth bearing in mind is that diseconomies of scale can arise when large enterprises build up a substantial corporate bureaucracy, which increases corporate overhead without reducing unit costs.

Production and Efficiency: Learning Effects

Learning effects are cost savings that come from learning by doing. Labor, for example, learns by repetition how best to carry out a task. In other words, labor productivity increases over time, and unit costs fall as individuals learn the most efficient way to perform a particular task. Equally important, in new manufacturing facilities management typically learns over time how best to run the new operation. Hence, production costs decline because of increasing labor productivity and management efficiency.

Learning effects tend to be more significant when a technologically complex task is repeated, since there is more to learn. Thus, learning effects will be more significant in an assembly process involving 1,000 complex steps than in an assembly process involving 100 simple steps. Although learning effects are normally associated with the manufacturing process, as with economies of scale there are reasons for believing that they are just as important in many service industries. For example, one famous study of learning in the context of the health care industry found that

5.1   STRATEGY *in* ACTION

Chemical and Chase Banks Merge to Realize Scale Economies

In August 1995, two of the world's largest banks, Chemical Bank and Chase Manhattan Bank, both of New York, announced their intention to merge. The merger was officially completed on March 31, 1996. The combined bank, which goes under the Chase name, has more than $300 billion in assets, making it the largest bank in the United States and the fourth largest in the world. The new Chase is capitalized at $20 billion and is number one or two in the United States in numerous segments of the banking business, including loan syndication, trading of derivatives, currency and securities trading, global custody services, luxury auto financing, New York City retail banking, and mortgaging services.

The prime reason given for the merger was anticipated cost savings of more than $1.7 billion per year, primarily through the realization of economies of scale. The newly merged bank had good reason for thinking that these kinds of cost savings were possible. In a 1991 merger between Chemical and Manufacturers Hanover, another New York–based bank, cost savings of $750 million per year were realized by eliminating duplicated assets, such as physical facilities, information systems, and personnel.

The cost savings in the Chase-Chemical combination had several sources. First, significant economies of scale were possible by combining the 600 retail branches of the original banks. Closing excess branches and consolidating its retail business into a smaller number of branches allowed the new bank to significantly increase the capacity utilization of its retail banking network. The combined bank was able to generate the same volume of retail business from fewer branches. The fixed costs associated with retail branches—including rents, personnel, equipment, and utility costs—dropped, which translated into a substantial reduction in the unit cost required to serve the average customer.

Another source of scale-based cost savings arose from the combination of a whole array of back-office functions. For example, the combined bank now has to operate only one computer network instead of two. By getting greater utilization out of a fixed computer infrastructure—mainframe computers, servers, and the associated software—the combined bank was able to further drive down its fixed cost structure. Combining management functions also brought substantial savings. For example, the new Chase bank has doubled the number of auto loans and mortgage originations it issues, but because of office automation it can manage the increased volume with less than twice the management staff. This saving implies a big reduction in fixed costs and a corresponding fall in the unit costs of servicing the average auto loan or mortgage customer.[2]

more experienced medical providers posted significantly lower mortality rates for a number of common surgical procedures, suggesting that learning effects are at work in surgery.[4] The authors of this study used the evidence to argue for the establishment of regional referral centers for the provision of highly specialized medical care. These centers would perform many specific surgical procedures (for instance, heart surgery), replacing local facilities with lower volumes and presumably higher mortality rates.

In terms of the long-run average cost curve of a company, while economies of scale imply a movement along the curve (say from A to B in Figure 5.2), the realization of learning effects implies a downward shift of the entire curve (B to C in Figure 5.2) as both labor and management become more efficient over time at performing their tasks at each and every level of output. No matter how complex the task, however, learning effects typically die out after a limited period of time. Indeed, it has been suggested that they are really important only during the start-up period of a new process and cease after two or three years.[5]

FIGURE 5.1

A Typical Long-Run
Unit-Cost Curve

FIGURE 5.2

Economies of Scale and
Learning Effects

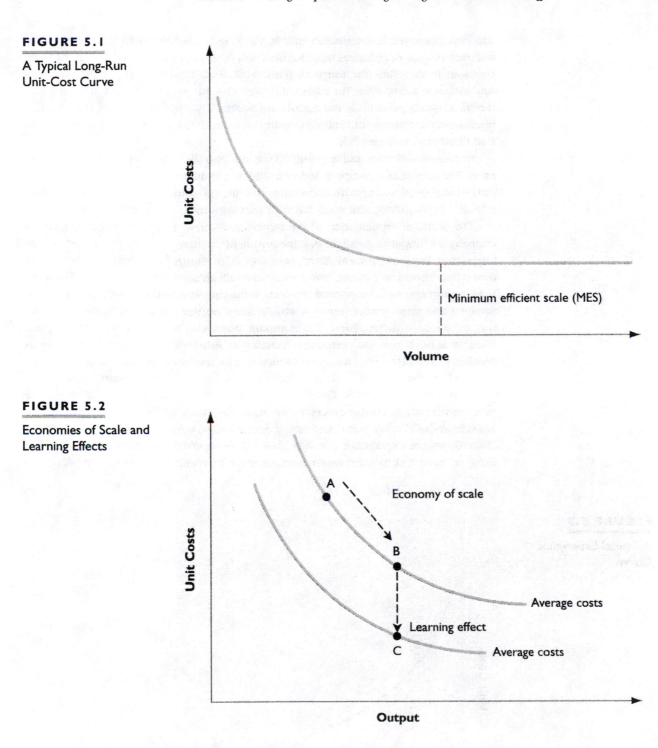

▓ Production and Efficiency: The Experience Curve

The experience curve refers to the systematic unit-cost reductions that have been observed to occur over the life of a product.[6] According to the experience curve concept, unit manufacturing costs for a product typically decline by some characteristic amount each time accumulated output of the product is doubled (accumulated output is the total output of a product since its introduction). The relationship was first observed in the aircraft industry, where it was found that each time accumulated output of airframes was doubled, unit costs declined to 80 percent of their previous level.[7] Thus, the fourth airframe typically cost only 80 percent of the second airframe to produce, the eighth airframe only 80 percent of the fourth, the sixteenth only 80 percent of the eighth, and so on. The outcome of this process is a relationship between unit manufacturing costs and accumulated output similar to that illustrated in Figure 5.3.

Economies of scale and learning effects underlie the experience curve phenomenon. Put simply, as a company increases the accumulated volume of its output over time, it is able to realize both economies of scale (as volume increases) and learning effects. Consequently, unit costs fall with increases in accumulated output.

The strategic significance of the experience curve is clear. It suggests that increasing a company's product volume and market share will also bring cost advantages over the competition. Thus, company A in Figure 5.3, because it is further down the experience curve, has a clear cost advantage over company B. The concept is perhaps most important in those industries where the production process involves the mass production of a standardized output (for example, the manufacture of semiconductor chips). If a company wishes to become more efficient, and thereby attain a low-cost position, it must try to ride down the experience curve as quickly as possible. This means constructing efficient scale manufacturing facilities even before the company has the demand and aggressively pursuing cost reductions from learning effects. The company might also need to adopt an aggressive marketing strategy, cutting prices to the bone and stressing heavy sales promotions in order to build up demand, and hence accumulated volume, as quickly as possible. Once down the experience curve, because of its superior efficiency, the company is likely to have a significant cost advantage over its competitors. For example, it has

FIGURE 5.3

A Typical Experience Curve

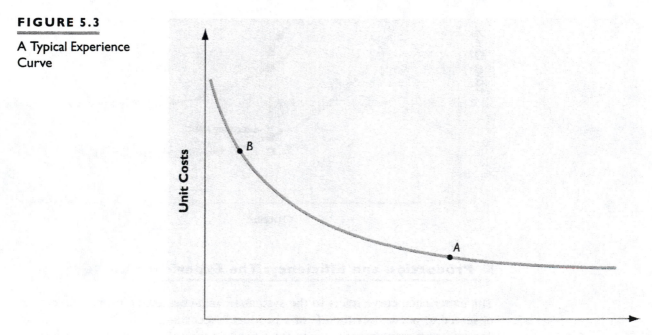

STRATEGY in ACTION

5.2

Too Much Experience at Texas Instruments

T exas Instruments (TI) was an early user of the experience curve concept. TI was a technological innovator, first in silicon transistors and then in semiconductors. The company discovered that with every doubling of accumulated production volume of a transistor or semiconductor, unit costs declined to 73 percent of their previous level. Building on this insight, whenever TI first produced a new transistor or semiconductor it would slash the price of the product to stimulate demand. The goal was to drive up the accumulated volume of production and so drive down costs through the realization of experience curve economies. As a result, during the 1960s and 1970s, TI hammered its competitors in transistors; then it moved on to prevail in semiconductors, and ultimately in hand-held calculators and digital watches. Indeed, for the twenty years up until 1982, TI enjoyed rapid growth, with sales quadrupling between 1977 and 1981 alone.

However, after 1982 things began to go wrong for TI. The company's single-minded focus on cost reductions,

an outgrowth of its strategic reliance on the experience curve, left it with a poor understanding of consumer needs and market trends. Competitors such as Casio and Hewlett-Packard began to make major inroads into TI's hand-held calculator business by focusing on additional features that consumers demanded rather than on cost and price. TI was slow to react to this trend and lost substantial market share as a result. In the late 1970s, TI also decided to focus on semiconductors for watches and calculators, where it had gained substantial cost economies based on the experience curve, rather than develop metal-oxide semiconductors for computer memories and advanced semiconductors. As it turned out, however, with the growth in minicomputers and personal computers in the early 1980s, the market shifted toward high-power metal-oxide semiconductors. Consequently, TI soon found itself outflanked by Intel and Motorola. In sum, TI's focus on realizing experience curve economies initially benefited the company, but then it seems to have contributed toward a myopia that was to cost the company dearly.[9]

been argued that the early success of Texas Instruments was based on exploiting the experience curve (see Strategy in Action 5.2 for details); that Intel uses such tactics to ride down the experience curve and gain a competitive advantage over its rivals in the market for microprocessors; and that one reason Matsushita came to dominate the global market for VHS videotape recorders is that it based its strategy on the experience curve.[8]

However, the company farthest down the experience curve must not become complacent about its cost advantage. As Strategy in Action 5.2 points out, an obsession with the experience curve at Texas Instruments may have harmed the company. More generally, there are three reasons why companies should not become complacent about their efficiency-based cost advantages derived from experience effects. First, since neither learning effects nor economies of scale go on forever, the experience curve is likely to bottom out at some point; indeed, it must do so by definition. When this occurs, further unit-cost reductions from learning effects and economies of scale will be hard to come by. Thus, in time, other companies can catch up with the cost leader. Once this happens, a number of low-cost companies can have cost parity with each other. In such circumstances, a sustainable competitive advantage must rely on other strategic factors besides the minimization of production costs by utilizing existing technologies—factors such as better customer responsiveness, product quality, or innovation.

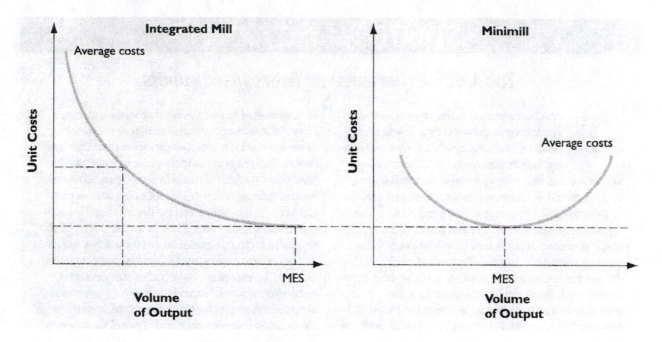

FIGURE 5.4

Unit Production Costs in an Integrated Steel Mill and a Minimill

Second, cost advantages gained from experience effects can be made obsolete by the development of new technologies. For example, the price of television picture tubes followed the experience curve pattern from the introduction of television in the late 1940s until 1963. The average unit price dropped from $34 to $8 (in 1958 dollars) in that time. The advent of color television interrupted the experience curve. Manufacturing picture tubes for color televisions required a new manufacturing technology, and the price for color TV tubes shot up to $51 by 1966. Then the experience curve reasserted itself. The price dropped to $48 in 1968, $37 in 1970, and $36 in 1972.[10] In short, technological change can alter the rules of the game, requiring that former low-cost companies take steps to reestablish their competitive edge.

A further reason for avoiding complacency is that high volume does not necessarily give a company a cost advantage. Some technologies have different cost functions. For example, the steel industry has two alternative manufacturing technologies: an integrated technology, which relies on the basic oxygen furnace, and a minimill technology, which depends on the electric arc furnace. As illustrated in Figure 5.4, the minimum efficient scale (MES) of the electric arc furnace is located at relatively low volumes, whereas the MES of the basic oxygen furnace is located at relatively high volumes. Even when both operations are producing at their most efficient output levels, steel companies with basic oxygen furnaces do not have a cost advantage over minimills.

Consequently, the pursuit of experience economies by an integrated company using basic oxygen technology may not bring the kind of cost advantages that a naive reading of the experience curve phenomenon would lead the company to expect. Indeed, there have been significant periods of time during which integrated companies have not been able to get enough orders to run at optimum capacity. Hence their production costs have been considerably higher than those of minimills.[11] More generally, as we discuss next, in many industries new flexible manufacturing technologies hold out the promise of allowing small manufacturers to produce at unit costs comparable to those of large assembly line operations.

■ Production and Efficiency: Flexible Manufacturing and Mass Customization

Central to the concept of economies of scale is the idea that the best way to achieve high efficiency, and hence low unit costs, is through the mass production of a standardized output. The tradeoff implicit in this idea is between unit costs and product variety. Producing greater product variety from a factory implies shorter production runs, which in turn imply an inability to realize economies of scale. That is, wide product variety makes it difficult for a company to increase its production efficiency and thus reduce its unit costs. According to this logic, the way to increase efficiency and drive down unit costs is to limit product variety and produce a standardized product in large volumes (see Figure 5.5a).

This view of production efficiency has been challenged by the rise of flexible manufacturing technologies. The term *flexible manufacturing technology*—or *lean production*, as it is often called—covers a range of manufacturing technologies designed to (1) reduce setup times for complex equipment, (2) increase the utilization of individual machines through better scheduling, and (3) improve quality control at all stages of the manufacturing process.[12] Flexible manufacturing technologies allow the company to produce a wider variety of end products at a unit cost that at one time could be achieved only through the mass production of a standardized output (see Figure 5.5b). Indeed, recent research suggests that the adoption of flexible manufacturing technologies may actually increase efficiency and lower unit costs relative to what can be achieved by the mass production of a standardized output, while at the same time enabling the company to customize its product offering to a much greater extent than was once thought possible. The term *mass customization* has been coined to describe the ability of companies to use flexible manufacturing technology to reconcile two goals that were once thought to be incompatible: low cost and product customization.[13]

Flexible manufacturing technologies vary in their sophistication and complexity. One of the most famous examples of a flexible manufacturing technology, Toyota's production system, is relatively unsophisticated, but it has been credited with making Toyota the most efficient auto company in the global industry. Toyota's flexible manufacturing system is profiled in Strategy in Action 5.3. **Flexible machine cells** are another common flexible manufacturing technology. A flexible machine cell is a grouping of various types of machinery, a common materials handler, and a centralized cell controller (computer). Each cell normally contains four to six machines capable of performing a variety of operations. The typical cell is dedicated to the production of a family of parts or products. The settings on machines are computer controlled, which allows each cell to switch quickly between the production of different parts or products.

Improved capacity utilization and reductions in work-in-progress (that is, stockpiles of partly finished products) and in waste are major efficiency benefits of flexible machine cells. Improved capacity utilization arises from the reduction in setup times and from the computer-controlled coordination of production flow between

FIGURE 5.5

The Tradeoff Between
Costs and Product
Variety

machines, which eliminates bottlenecks. The tight coordination between machines also reduces work-in-progress. Reductions in waste are due to the ability of computer-controlled machinery to identify ways to transform inputs into outputs while producing a minimum of unusable waste material. Given all these factors, whereas free standing machines might be in use 50 percent of the time, the same machines when grouped into a cell can be used more than 80 percent of the time and produce the same end product with half the waste. This increases efficiency and results in lower costs.

The efficiency benefits of installing flexible manufacturing technology can be dramatic. W.L. Gore, a privately owned company that manufactures a wide range of products from high-tech computer cables to its famous Gore-Tex fabric, has adopted flexible cells in several of its forty-six factories. In its cable-making facilities, the effect has been to cut the time taken to make computer cables by 50 percent, to reduce stock by 33 percent, and to shrink the space taken up by the plant by 25 percent. Similarly, Compaq Computer, the manufacturer of personal computers, replaced three of the sixteen assembly lines in its Houston factory with twenty-one cells. As a result, employee productivity rose by 25 percent, and the cost of converting the three assembly lines to cells was recouped in six months. Lexmark, a producer of computer printers, has also converted 80 percent of its 2,700-employee factory in Lexington, Kentucky, to flexible manufacturing cells, and it too has seen productivity increase by around 25 percent.[14]

Besides improving efficiency and lowering costs, flexible manufacturing technologies also enable companies to customize products to the unique demands of small consumer groups—at a cost that at one time could be achieved only by mass-producing a standardized output. Thus, they help a company achieve mass cus-

5.3 STRATEGY *in* ACTION

Toyota's Lean Production System

Toyota's flexible manufacturing system was developed by one of the company's engineers, Ohno Taiichi. After working at Toyota for five years and visiting Ford's U.S. plants, Ohno became convinced that the mass-production philosophy for making cars was flawed. He saw numerous problems, including three major drawbacks. First, long production runs created massive inventories, which had to be stored in large warehouses. This was expensive, both because of the cost of warehousing, and because inventories tied up capital in unproductive uses. Second, if the initial machine settings were wrong, long production runs resulted in the production of a large number of defects (that is, waste). Third, the mass production system was unable to accommodate consumer preferences for product diversity.

Ohno looked for ways to make shorter production runs economical. He developed a number of techniques designed to reduce setup times for production equipment (a major source of fixed costs). By using a system of levers and pulleys, he was able to reduce the time required to change dies on stamping equipment from a full day in 1950 to three minutes by 1971. This made small production runs economical, which in turn allowed Toyota to respond better to consumer demands for product diversity. Small production runs also eliminated the need to hold large inventories, thereby reducing warehousing costs. Furthermore, small product runs and the lack of inventory meant that defective parts were produced only in small numbers and entered the assembly process immediately. This reduced waste and made it easier to trace defects to their source and fix the problem. In sum, Ohno's innovations enabled Toyota to produce a more diverse product range at a lower unit cost than was possible with conventional mass production.[15]

---

tomization, which increases its customer responsiveness. The Opening Case on Levi Strauss provides a good example of this. By linking flexible manufacturing technology with the power of the Web, Levi has been able to customize jeans to an individual's measurements and tastes.

Marketing and Efficiency

The marketing strategy that a company adopts can have a major impact upon the efficiency and cost structure of an enterprise. **Marketing strategy** refers to the position that a company takes with regard to pricing, promotion, advertising, product design, and distribution. It can play a major role in boosting a company's efficiency. Some of the steps leading to greater efficiency are fairly obvious. For example, we have already discussed how riding down the experience curve to gain a low-cost position can be facilitated by aggressive pricing, promotions, and advertising—all of which are the task of the marketing function. However, there are other aspects of marketing strategy that have a less obvious, though not less significant, impact on efficiency. One important aspect is the relationship between customer defection rates and unit costs.[16]

Customer defection rates are the percentage of a company's customers that defect every year to competitors. Defection rates are determined by customer loyalty, which in turn is a function of the ability of a company to satisfy its customers. Because acquiring a new customer entails certain one-time fixed costs for advertising, promotions, and the like, there is a direct relationship between defection rates and costs. The longer a company holds on to a customer, the greater is the volume of customer-generated unit sales that can be set against these fixed costs, and the lower the average unit cost of each sale. Thus, lowering customer defection rates allows a company to achieve substantial cost economies. This is illustrated in Figure 5.6, which shows that high defection rates imply high average unit costs (and vice versa).

One consequence of the relationship summarized in Figure 5.6 is a relationship, illustrated in Figure 5.7, between the length of time that a customer stays with the company and profit per customer. Because of the fixed costs of acquiring new customers, serving customers who stay with the company only for a short time before switching to competitors can often yield a negative profit. However, the longer a customer stays with the company, the more the fixed costs of acquiring that customer can be spread out over repeat purchases, which boosts the profit per customer. Thus, as shown in Figure 5.7, there is a positive relationship between the length of time that a customer stays with a company and profit per customer.

For an example of this phenomenon, consider the credit card business.[17] In 1990, most credit card companies spent an average of $51 to recruit a customer and set up a new account. These costs came from the advertising required to attract new customers, from credit checks required for each customer, and from the mechanics of setting up an account and issuing a card. These one-time fixed costs can be recouped only if a customer stays with the company for at least two years. Moreover, when customers stay a second year, they tend to increase their use of the credit card, which raises the volume of revenues generated by each customer over time. As a result, the average profit per customer in the credit card business increases from minus $51 in year 1 (that is, a loss of $51) to $44 in year 3 and $55 in year 6.

Another economic benefit of long-time customer loyalty is the free advertising that customers provide for a company. Loyal customers do a lot of talking, and they

FIGURE 5.6

The Relationship Between Average Unit Costs and Customer Defection Rates

FIGURE 5.7

The Relationship
Between Customer
Loyalty and Profit per
Customer

can dramatically increase the volume of business through referrals. A striking example of this is the clothing and food retailer Marks & Spencer, which is Britain's largest and most profitable retailer. Its success is built on a well-earned reputation for providing its customers with high-quality goods at a reasonable price. The company has generated such customer loyalty that it does not need to do much advertising in Britain—a major source of cost saving.

The key message, then, is that reducing customer defection rates and building customer loyalty can be a major source of cost saving. Because it leads to lower unit costs, reducing customer defection rates by just 5 percent can increase profits per customer anywhere from 25 percent to 85 percent, depending on the industry. For example, a 5 percent reduction in customer defection rates leads to the following increases in profits per customer over the average customer life: a 75 percent increase in profit per customer in the credit card business; a 50 percent increase in profit per customer in the insurance brokerage industry; a 45 percent increase in profit per customer in the industrial laundry business; and a 35 percent increase in profit per customer in the computer software industry.[18]

How can a company reduce customer defection rates? It can do so by building brand loyalty, which in turn requires that the company be responsive to the needs of its customers. We consider the issue of customer responsiveness later in the chapter. For now, note that a central component of developing a strategy to reduce defection rates is to spot customers who do defect, find out why they defected, and act on that information so that other customers do not defect for similar reasons in the future. To take these measures, the marketing function must have information systems capable of tracking customer defections.

▪ Materials Management, JIT, and Efficiency

The contribution of materials management to boosting the efficiency of a company can be just as dramatic as the contribution of production and marketing. **Materials management** encompasses the activities necessary to get materials to a production facility (including the costs if purchasing material inputs), through the production process, and out through a distribution system to the end user.[19] The potential for reducing costs through more efficient materials management is enormous. In the average manufacturing enterprise, the materials and transportation costs account for 50 percent to 70 percent of revenues. Even a small reduction in these costs can have a substantial impact on profitability. According to one estimate, for a company with revenues of $1 million, a return on investment rate of 5 percent, and materials management costs that amount to 50 percent of sales revenues (including purchasing costs), increasing total profits by $15,000 would require either a 30 percent increase in sales revenues or a 3 percent reduction in materials costs.[20] In a saturated market, it would be much easier to reduce materials costs by 3 percent than to increase sales revenues by 30 percent.

Improving the efficiency of the materials management function typically requires the adoption of just-in-time (JIT) inventory systems. The basic philosophy behind JIT is to economize on inventory holding costs by having materials arrive at a manufacturing plant just in time to enter the production process, and not before. The major cost saving comes from increasing inventory turnover, which reduces inventory holding costs, such as warehousing and storage costs. For example, Wal-Mart uses JIT systems to replenish the stock in its stores at least twice a week. Many stores receive daily deliveries. The typical competitor—Kmart or Sears—replenishes its stock every two weeks. Compared with these competitors, Wal-Mart can maintain the same service levels with one-fourth the inventory investment, which is a major source of cost saving. Thus, faster inventory turnover has helped Wal-Mart achieve an efficiency-based competitive advantage in the retailing industry.[21]

The drawback of JIT systems is that they leave a firm without a buffer stock of inventory. Although buffer stocks of inventory are expensive to store, they can help tide a firm over shortages on inputs brought about by disruption among suppliers (for instance, a labor dispute at a key supplier). Buffer stocks can also help a firm respond quickly to increases in demand. However, there are ways around these limitations. For example, to reduce the risks linked to dependence on just one supplier for an important input, it might pay the firm to source inputs from multiple suppliers.

▪ R&D Strategy and Efficiency

The role of superior research and development in helping a company achieve greater efficiency is twofold. First, the R&D function can boost efficiency by designing products that are easy to manufacture. By cutting down on the number of parts that make up a product, R&D can dramatically decrease the required assembly time, which translates into higher employee productivity and lower unit costs. For example, after Texas Instruments redesigned an infrared sighting mechanism that it supplies to the Pentagon, the company found that it had reduced the number of parts from 47 to 12, the number of assembly steps from 56 to 13, the time spent fabricating metal from 757 minutes per unit to 219 minutes per unit, and unit assembly time from 129 minutes to 20 minutes. The result was a substantial decline in production costs. Design for manufacturing requires close coordination between the production and R&D functions of the company, of course. Cross-functional teams that contain production and R&D personnel, so that they can work on the problem jointly, best achieve such coordination.

The second way in which the R&D function can help a company achieve greater efficiency is by pioneering process innovations. A process innovation is an innovation in the way production processes operate that improves their efficiency. Process innovations have often been a major source of competitive advantage. In the automobile industry, Toyota's competitive advantage is based partly on the company's invention of new flexible manufacturing processes, which dramatically reduced setup times. This process innovation enabled Toyota to obtain efficiency gains associated with flexible manufacturing systems years ahead of its competitors.

■ Human Resource Strategy and Efficiency

Employee productivity is one of the key determinants of an enterprise's efficiency and cost structure. The more productive the employees, the lower will be the unit costs. The challenge for a company's human resource function is to devise ways to increase employee productivity. It has three main choices: training employees, organizing the work force into self-managing teams, and linking pay to performance.

Employee Training   Individuals are a major input into the production process. A company that employs individuals with higher skills is likely to be more efficient than one employing less skilled personnel. Individuals who are more skilled can perform tasks faster and more accurately and are more likely to learn the complex tasks associated with many modern production methods than individuals with lesser skills. Training can upgrade employee skill levels, bringing the firm productivity-related efficiency gains.[22]

Self-Managing Teams   Self-managing teams are a relatively recent phenomenon. Few companies used them until the mid 1980s, but since then they have spread rapidly. The growth of flexible manufacturing cells, which group workers into teams, has undoubtedly facilitated the spread of self-managing teams among manufacturing enterprises. The typical team comprises five to fifteen employees who produce an entire product or undertake an entire task. Team members learn all team tasks and rotate from job to job. A more flexible work force is one result. Team members can fill in for absent coworkers. Teams also take over managerial duties such as work and vacation scheduling, ordering materials, and hiring new members. The greater responsibility thrust on team members and the empowerment it implies are seen as motivators. (Empowerment is the process of giving lower-level employees decision-making power.) People often respond well to being given greater autonomy and responsibility. Performance bonuses linked to team production and quality targets work as an additional motivator.

The net effect of introducing self-managing teams is reportedly an increase in productivity of 30 percent or more and a substantial increase in product quality. Further cost savings arise from eliminating supervisors and creating a flatter organizational hierarchy. In manufacturing enterprises, perhaps the most potent combination is that of self-managing teams and flexible manufacturing cells. The two seem designed for each other. For example, after the introduction of flexible manufacturing technology and work practices based on self-managing teams in 1988, a General

Electric plant in Salisbury, North Carolina, increased productivity by 250 percent compared with GE plants that produced the same products in 1984.[23] Still, teams are no panacea; in manufacturing enterprises, self-managing teams may fail to live up to their potential unless they are integrated with flexible manufacturing technology. More generally, teams thrust a lot of management responsibilities on team members, and helping the members to cope with these responsibilities often requires substantial training—a fact that many companies often forget in their rush to drive down costs, with the result that the teams don't work out as well as planned.[24]

Pay for Performance   People work for money, so it is hardly surprising that linking pay to performance can help increase employee productivity. However, the issue is not quite so simple as just introducing incentive pay systems; it is also important to define what kind of performance is to be rewarded and how. Some of the most efficient companies in the world, mindful that cooperation among employees is necessary to realize productivity gains, do not link pay to individual performance. Instead they link pay to group or team performance. For example, at Nucor, which is widely viewed as one of the most efficient steel makers in the world, the work force is divided into teams of thirty or so. Bonus pay, which can amount to 30 percent of base pay, is linked to the ability of the team to meet productivity and quality goals. This link creates a strong incentive for individuals to cooperate with each other in pursuit of team goals; that is, it facilitates teamwork.

▓ Information Systems, the Internet, and Efficiency

With the rapid spread of computers, the explosive growth of the Internet and corporate Intranets (internal corporate computer networks based on Internet standards), and the spread of high-bandwidth communication conduits from fiber optics to digital wireless technology, the information system functions of enterprises are moving to center stage in the quest for operating efficiencies.[25] The impact of information systems on productivity is wide ranging and potentially affects all other activities of an enterprise. For example, in the Opening Case of Chapter 4, we saw how Cisco Systems has been able to realize significant cost savings by moving its ordering and customer service functions on-line. The company has just 300 service agents handling all its customer accounts, compared with the 900 it would need if sales were not handled on-line. The difference represents an annual saving of $20 million. Moreover, without automated customer service functions, Cisco calculates that it would need at least 1,000 additional service engineers, which would cost around $75 million.[26]

Dell Computer is famous for having been the first to implement on-line selling in the personal computer industry and now sells some 40 percent of its computers on-line. Dell has also put much of its customer service functions on-line, replacing telephone calls to customer service representatives. Each week some 200,000 people access Dell's troubleshooting tips on-line. Each of these hits at Dell's Web site saves the company a potential $15, which is the average cost of a technical support call. If just 10 percent of these people were to call Dell using a telephone, it would cost the company $15.6 million per year.[27]

More generally, what companies like Cisco and Dell are doing is using Web-based information systems to reduce the costs of coordination between the company and its customers, and the company and its suppliers. By using Web-based programs to automate customer and supplier interactions, a company can substantially reduce the number of people required to manage these interfaces, thereby decreasing costs and increasing productivity. Nor is this trend limited to high-technology companies such as Cisco or Dell Computer. Banks and financial service companies are finding that they can substantially reduce costs by moving customer accounts and support functions on-line. Such a move reduces the need for customer service representatives, bank tellers, stockbrokers, insurance agents, and so on. For example, while the average cost of executing a transaction at a bank, such as shifting money from one account to another, is about $1.07, executing the same transaction over the Internet costs $0.01.[28] Similarly, the whole theory behind Internet-based retailers such as Amazon.com is that significant costs can be taken out of the retailing system by replacing physical stores and their supporting personnel with an on-line virtual store and automated ordering and checkout processes. Cost savings can also be realized by using Web-based information systems to automate many internal company activities, from managing expense reimbursements to benefits planning and hiring processes, thereby reducing the need for internal support personnel.

For many years, skeptics questioned the impact that computer-based information systems were having on productivity, but recent productivity data from America suggest that the productivity gains are starting to appear. For the 1996–1998 period, U.S. nonfarm productivity growth accelerated from a historic average of 1 percent per year to 2.2 percent a year. In late 1998 and early 1999, it accelerated again to over 3 percent per annum. The productivity growth was greatest in the computer industry itself, which is not surprising, given the efforts by companies like Cisco and Dell to implement Web-based sales and service functions.[29]

Infrastructure and Efficiency

The infrastructure sets the context within which all other value creation activities take place. It follows that the infrastructure can help in achieving efficiency goals. Above all, the infrastructure can foster a companywide commitment to efficiency and promote cooperation among different functions in pursuit of efficiency goals.

A companywide commitment to efficiency can be built through the leadership of top management. The leadership task is to articulate a vision that recognizes the need for all functions of the company to focus on improving their efficiency. It is not enough just to improve the efficiency of production, or marketing, or R&D. Achieving superior efficiency requires a companywide commitment to this goal, and this commitment can be articulated only by top management.

A further leadership task is to facilitate cross-functional cooperation needed to achieve superior efficiency. For example, designing products that are easy to manufacture requires that production and R&D personnel communicate; integrating JIT systems with production scheduling requires close communication between material management and production; designing self-managing teams to perform production tasks requires close cooperation between human resources and production; and so on.

TABLE 5.1

The Primary Roles of Different Value Creation Functions in Achieving Superior Efficiency

Value Creation Function	Primary Roles
Infrastructure (Leadership)	1. Provide companywide commitment to efficiency. 2. Facilitate cooperation among functions.
Production	1. Where appropriate, pursue economies of scale and learning economics. 2. Implement flexible manufacturing systems.
Marketing	1. Where appropriate, adopt aggressive marketing to ride down the experience curve. 2. Limit customer defection rates by building brand loyalty.
Materials Management	1. Implement JIT systems.
R&D	1. Design products for ease of manufacture. 2. Seek process innovations.
Information Systems	1. Use information systems to automate processes. 2. Use information systems to reduce costs of coordination.
Human Resources	1. Institute training programs to build skills. 2. Implement self-managing teams. 3. Implement pay for performance.

■ Summary: Achieving Superior Efficiency

Table 5.1 summarizes the primary roles that various functions must take in order to achieve superior efficiency. Bear in mind that achieving superior efficiency is not something that can be tackled on a function by function basis. It requires an organizationwide commitment and an ability to ensure close cooperation among functions. Top management, by exercising leadership and influencing the infrastructure, plays a major role in this process.

ACHIEVING SUPERIOR QUALITY

We note in Chapter 4 that superior quality gives a company two advantages. The enhanced reputation for quality lets the company charge a premium price for its product, and the elimination of defects from the production process increases efficiency and hence lowers costs. In this section, we examine the means a company can use to achieve superior quality. The main one is **total quality management** (TQM), a management philosophy that focuses on improving the quality of a company's products and services and stresses that all company operations should be oriented toward this goal.[30] A companywide philosophy, it requires the cooperation of all the different functions if it is to be successfully implemented. We first consider the total quality management concept and then discuss the various steps needed to implement TQM programs. Throughout, we highlight the roles that different functions must play in this process.

The TQM Concept

The total quality management concept was first developed by a number of U.S. consultants, including H. W. Edwards Deming, Joseph Juran, and A. V. Feigenbaum.[31] Originally, these consultants won few converts in the United States. In contrast, the Japanese embraced them enthusiastically and even named their premier annual prize for manufacturing excellence after Deming. The philosophy underlying TQM, as articulated by Deming, is based on the following five-step chain reaction:

1. Improved quality means that costs decrease because of less rework, fewer mistakes, fewer delays, and better use of time and materials.

2. As a result, productivity improves.

3. Better quality leads to higher market share and allows the company to raise prices.

4. This increases the company's profitability and allows it to stay in business.

5. Thus, the company creates more jobs.[32]

Deming identified fourteen steps that should be part of any TQM program; they are summarized in Table 5.2. (Deming continually changed these points in line with his belief in the importance of continuous quality improvement; those given here are the latest—1990—version.) In essence, Deming urged a company to have a definite strategic plan for where it is going and how it is going to get there. He argued that management should embrace the philosophy that mistakes, defects, and poor-quality materials are not acceptable and should be eliminated. Quality of supervision should be improved by allowing more time for supervisors to work with employees and giving them appropriate skills for the job. Furthermore, management should create an environment in which employees will not fear reporting problems or recommending improvements. Deming also believed that work standards should not only be defined as numbers or quotas, but should also include some notion of quality to promote the production of defect-free output. He argued that management has the responsibility to train employees in new skills to keep pace with changes in the workplace and that achieving better quality requires the commitment of everyone in the company.

It took the rise of Japan to the top rank of economic powers to alert western business to the importance of the TQM concept. Since the early 1980s, TQM practices have spread rapidly throughout western industry. Strategy in Action 5.4 describes one of the most successful implementations of a quality improvement process, General Electric's six sigma program. Despite such instances of spectacular success, TQM practices are still not universally accepted. A study by the American Quality Foundation found that only 20 percent of U.S. companies regularly review the consequences of quality performance, compared with 70 percent of Japanese companies.[33] Another study by Arthur D. Little of 500 American companies using TQM found that only 36 percent believed that TQM was increasing their competitiveness.[34] A prime reason for this, according to the study, was that many companies had not fully understood or embraced the TQM concept.

TABLE 5.2

Deming's Fourteen Points to Quality

1. Create constancy of purpose toward improvement of product and service, with the aim to become competitive and to stay in business, and to provide jobs.

2. Adopt the new philosophy. We are in a new economic age. Western management must awaken to the challenge, must learn their responsibilities, and take on leadership for change.

3. Cease dependence on inspection to achieve quality. Eliminate the need for inspection on a mass basis by building quality into the product in the first place.

4. End the practice of awarding business on the basis of price tag. Instead, minimize total cost.

5. Improve constantly and forever the system of production and service, to improve quality and productivity, and thus constantly decrease costs.

6. Institute training on the job.

7. Institute leadership. The aim of leadership should be to help people and machines and gadgets do a better job. Leadership of management is in need of an overhaul, as well as leadership of production workers.

8. Drive out fear, so that everyone may work effectively for the company.

9. Break down barriers between departments. People in research, design, sales, and production must work as a team, to foresee problems of production and in use that may be encountered with the product or service.

10. Eliminate slogans, exhortations, and targets for the work force asking for zero defects and new levels of productivity. Such exhortations only create adversarial relationships. The bulk of the causes of low quality and low productivity belong to the system and thus lie beyond the power of the work force.

11. (a) Eliminate work standards on the factory floor. Substitute leadership. (b) Eliminate management by objective. Eliminate management by numbers, numerical goals. Substitute leadership.

12. (a) Remove barriers that rob hourly workers of their right to pride of workmanship. The responsibility of supervisors must be changed from sheer numbers to quality. (b) Remove barriers that rob people in management and in engineering of their right to pride of workmanship.

13. Institute a vigorous program of education and self-improvement.

14. Put everybody in the company to work to accomplish the transformation. The transformation is everybody's job.

"Demming's 14 Points to Quality," from Gabor, Andrea, *The Man Who Discovered Quality: Howard W. Edwards Deming Brought the Quality Revolution to America—The Stories of Ford, Xerox, & GM* (New York: Random House, 1990).

▨ Implementing TQM

Among companies that have successfully adopted TQM, certain imperatives stand out. We discuss them in the order in which they are usually tackled in companies implementing TQM programs, and we highlight the role that the various functions play in regard to each precept. What cannot be stressed enough, however, is that implementing TQM requires close cooperation among all functions in the pursuit of

5.4 STRATEGY *in* ACTION

General Electric's Six Sigma Quality Improvement Process

Six sigma is a quality and efficiency program that has been adopted by several major corporations, such as Motorola, General Electric, and Allied Signal. It is a philosophy that aims to reduce defects, boost productivity, eliminate waste and cut costs throughout a company. The term *sigma* comes from the Greek letter that statisticians use to represent a standard deviation from a mean. The higher the number of sigmas, the smaller the number of errors. At sigma, a production process would be 99.99966 percent accurate, creating just 3.4 defects per million units. While it is almost impossible for a company to achieve such perfection, six sigma quality is a goal that several strive toward.

General Electric is perhaps the most fervent adopter of six sigma programs. Under the direction of long-serving CEO, Jack Welch, GE spent nearly $1 billion between 1995 and 1998 to convert all its divisions to the six sigma faith. Welch credits the six sigma program with raising GE's operating profit margins to 16.6 percent in 1998, up from 14.4 percent three years earlier.

One of the first products designed from start to finish using six sigma processes was a $1.25 million diagnostic computer tomography, or CT, scanner called the Lightspeed, which produces three-dimensional images of the human body. Introducing it in 1998, GE spent $50 million to run 250 separate six sigma analyses designed to improve the reliability and lower the manufacturing cost of the Lightspeed scanner. The new scanner captures multiple images simultaneously, requiring only twenty seconds to do full body scans that once took three minutes—important because patients must remain perfectly still during the scan. Not only is the Lightspeed fast, but the first customers also noticed that it ran without downtime from the start, a testament to the reliability of the product.

Achieving that reliability took a lot of work. GE's engineers deconstructed the scanner into its basic components and tried to improve the reliability of each through a detailed step-by-step analysis. For example, the most important part of CT scanners is the vacuum tubes, which focus x-ray waves. The tubes that GE used in previous scanners, which cost $60,000 each, had low reliability. Hospitals and clinics wanted the tubes to operate twelve hours a day for at least six months, but typically they lasted only half that long. Moreover, GE was scrapping some $20 million in tubes each year because they failed preshipping performance tests, while a disturbing number of faulty tubes were slipping past inspection only to be pronounced dead on arrival.

To try and solve the reliability problem, the six sigma team took the tubes apart. They knew that one problem involves a petroleum-based oil used in the tube to prevent short circuits by isolating the anode, which has a positive charge, from the negatively charged cathode. The oil often deteriorated after a few months, leading to short circuits, but the team did not know why. By using statistical "what if" scenarios on all parts of the tube, however, the researchers learned that the lead-based paint on the inside of the tube was adulterating the oil. Acting on this information, the team developed a paint that would preserve the tube and protect the oil.

By pursuing this and other improvements, the six sigma team was able to extend the average life of a vacuum tube in the CT scanner from three months to over a year. Although the improvements increased the cost of the tube from $60,000 to $85,000, the increased cost was outweighed by the reduction in replacement costs, making it an attractive proposition for customers.[35]

the common goal of improving quality; it is a process that cuts across functions. The role played by the different functions in implementing TQM is summarized in Table 5.3. Strategy in Action 5.5 at the end of this section describes the efforts of a service company to put TQM into practice and the benefits it has gained.

Build Organizational Commitment to Quality There is evidence that TQM will do little to improve the performance of a company unless it is embraced by

TABLE 5.3

The Role Played by Different Functions in Implementing TQM

Value Creation Function	Primary Roles
Infrastructure (Leadership)	1. Provide leadership and commitment to quality. 2. Find ways to measure quality. 3. Set goals and create incentives. 4. Solicit input from employees. 5. Encourage cooperation among functions.
Production	1. Shorten production runs. 2. Trace defects back to source.
Marketing	1. Focus on the customer. 2. Provide customer feedback on quality.
Materials Management	1. Rationalize suppliers. 2. Help suppliers implement TQM. 3. Trace defects back to suppliers.
R&D	1. Design products that are easy to manufacture.
Information Systems	1. Use information systems to monitor defect rates.
Human Resources	1. Institute TQM training programs. 2. Organize employees into quality teams.

everyone in the organization.[36] For example, when Xerox launched its quality program in 1983, its first step was to educate its entire work force, from top management down, in the importance and operation of the TQM concept. It did so by forming groups, beginning with a group at the top of the organization that included the CEO. The top group was the first to receive basic TQM training. Each member of this group was then given the task of training a group at the next level in the hierarchy, and so on down throughout the organization until all 100,000 employees had received basic TQM training. Both top management and the human resource function of the company can play a major role in this process. Top management has the responsibility of exercising the leadership required to make a commitment to quality an organizationwide goal. The human resource function must take on responsibility for companywide training in TQM techniques.

Focus on the Customer TQM practitioners see a focus on the customer as the starting point, and indeed, the raison d'être, of the whole quality philosophy.[37] The marketing function, because it provides the primary point of contact with the customer, should play a major role here. It needs to identify what the customers want from the good or service that the company provides; what the company actually provides to customers; and the gap between what customers want and what they actually get, which could be called the quality gap. Then, together with the other functions of the company, it needs to formulate a plan for closing the quality gap.

5.5   **STRATEGY** *in* **ACTION**

Total Quality Management at Intermountain Health Care

Intermountain Health Care is a nonprofit chain of twenty-four hospitals operating in Idaho, Utah, and Wyoming. Intermountain first adopted TQM for certain sections of its system in the mid 1980s, and in 1990 it adopted TQM systemwide. The goal of TQM was to find and eliminate inappropriate variations in medical care—to provide the patient with better health care and, in the process, to reduce costs. The starting point was to identify variations in practice across physicians, particularly with regard to the cost and success rate of treatments. These data were then shared among physicians within the Intermountain system. The next step was for the physicians to take the data and use them to eliminate poor practices and to generally upgrade the quality of medical care.

The results have been quite striking. One early improvement was an attempt by Intermountain's hospital in Salt Lake City to lower the rate of postoperative wound infections. Before the effort began in 1985, the hospital's postoperative infection rate was 1.8 percent; this was 0.2 points below the national average, but still unacceptably high from a TQM perspective. By using a bedside computer system to make sure that antibiotics were given to patients two hours before surgery, the hospital dropped the infection rate in half, to 0.9 percent, within a year. Since then, the postoperative infection rate has dropped further still, to 0.4 percent compared with the national average of 2 percent. Given that the average postoperative infection adds $14,000 to a hospital bill, this constitutes a big cost saving.

Intermountain is now focusing on dozens of problems, including situations in which the wrong type or dose of medication is given, the top cause of poor medical care. Intermountain expects its efforts in this area to quickly eliminate at least 60 percent of such mistakes and to reduce medical related costs by up to $2 million a year per hospital.[40]

Find Ways to Measure Quality   Another imperative of any TQM program is to create some metric that can be used to measure quality. This is relatively easy in manufacturing companies, where quality can be measured by criteria such as defects per million parts. It tends to be more difficult in service companies, but with a little creativity suitable metrics can be devised. For example, one of the metrics Florida Power & Light uses to measure quality is meter reading errors per month. Another is the frequency and duration of power outages. L.L. Bean, the Freeport, Maine, mail-order retailer of outdoor gear, uses the percentage of orders that are correctly filled as one of its quality measures. For some banks, the key measures are the number of customer defections per year and the number of statement errors per thousand customers. The common theme that runs through all these examples is identifying what quality means from a customer's perspective and devising a method to gauge this. Top management should take primary responsibility for formulating different metrics to measure quality, but to succeed in this effort, it must receive input from the various functions of the company.

Set Goals and Create Incentives   Once a metric has been devised, the next step is to set a challenging quality goal and to create incentives for reaching that goal. Xerox again provides us with an example. When it introduced its TQM program, Xerox's initial goal was to reduce defective parts from 25,000 per million to 1,000 per million. One way of creating incentives to attain such a goal is to link rewards, such as bonus pay and opportunities for promotion, to the goal. Thus, within many companies that have adopted self-managing teams, the bonus pay of team members is determined in part by their ability to attain quality goals. The task of setting goals and creating incentives is one of the key tasks of top management.

Solicit Input from Employees

Employees can be a vital source of information regarding the sources of poor quality. Therefore, some framework must be established for soliciting employee suggestions as to the improvements that can be made. Quality circles—which are meetings of groups of employees—have often been used to achieve this goal. Other companies have utilized self-managing teams as forums for discussing quality improvement ideas. Whatever the forum, soliciting input from lower-level employees requires that management be open to receiving, and acting on, bad news and criticism from employees. According to Deming, one problem with U.S. management is that it has grown used to "killing the bearer of bad tidings." But, he argues, managers who are committed to the quality concept must recognize that bad news is a gold mine of information.[38]

Identify Defects and Trace Them to the Source

Product defects most often occur in the production process. TQM preaches the need to identify defects during the work process, trace them to their source, find out what caused them, and make corrections so that they do not recur. Production and materials management typically has primary responsibility for this task.

To uncover defects, Deming advocates the use of statistical procedures to pinpoint variations in the quality of goods or services. Deming views variation as the enemy of quality.[39] Once variations have been identified, they must be traced to their source and eliminated. One technique that helps greatly in tracing defects to their source is reducing lot sizes for manufactured products. With short production runs, defects show up immediately. Consequently, they can be quickly traced to the source and the problem can be fixed. Reducing lot sizes also means that when defective products are produced, their number will not be large, thus decreasing waste. Flexible manufacturing techniques, discussed earlier, can be used to reduce lot sizes without raising costs. Consequently, adopting flexible manufacturing techniques is an important aspect of a TQM program.

Just-in-time (JIT) inventory systems also play a part. Under a JIT system, defective parts enter the manufacturing process immediately; they are not warehoused for several months before use. Hence defective inputs can be quickly spotted. The problem can then be traced to the supply source and corrected before more defective parts are produced. Under a more traditional system, the practice of warehousing parts for months before they are used may mean that large numbers of defects are produced by a supplier before they enter the production process.

Build Relationship with Suppliers

A major source of poor-quality finished goods is poor-quality component parts. To decrease product defects, a company has to work with its suppliers to improve the quality of the parts they supply. The primary responsibility in this area falls on the materials management function, since it is the function that interacts with suppliers.

To implement JIT systems with suppliers and to get suppliers to adopt their own TQM programs, two steps are necessary. First, the number of suppliers has to be reduced to manageable proportions. Second, the company must commit to building a cooperative long-term relationship with the suppliers that remain. Asking suppliers to invest in JIT and TQM systems is asking them to make major investments that tie them to the company. For example, in order to fully implement a JIT system, the company may ask a supplier to relocate its manufacturing plant so that it is next door to the company's assembly plant. Suppliers are likely to be hesitant about making such investments unless they feel that the company is committed to an enduring, long-term relationship with them.

Design for Ease of Manufacture   The more assembly steps a product requires, the more opportunities there are for making mistakes. Designing products with fewer parts should make assembly easier and result in fewer defects. Both R&D and manufacturing need to be involved in designing products that are easy to manufacture.

Break Down Barriers Between Functions   Implementing TQM requires organizationwide commitment and substantial cooperation among functions. R&D has to cooperate with production to design products that are easy to manufacture, marketing has to cooperate with production and R&D so that customer problems identified by marketing can be acted on, human resource management has to cooperate with all the other functions of the company in order to devise suitable quality-training programs, and so on. The issue of achieving cooperation among subunits within a company is explored in Chapter 11. What needs stressing at this point is that ultimately it is the responsibility of top management to ensure that such cooperation occurs.

ACHIEVING SUPERIOR INNOVATION

In many ways innovation is the single most important building block of competitive advantage. Successful innovation of products or processes gives a company something unique that its competitors lack. This uniqueness may allow a company to charge a premium price or lower its cost structure below that of its rivals. Competitors, however, will try to imitate successful innovations. Often they will succeed, although high barriers to imitation can slow down the speed of imitation. Therefore, maintaining a competitive advantage requires a continuing commitment to innovation.

Many companies have established a track record for successful innovation. Among them are Du Pont, which has produced a steady stream of successful innovations such as cellophane, nylon, Freon (used in all air conditioners), and Teflon (nonstick pans); Sony, whose successes include the Walkman and the compact disk; Merck, the drug company that during the 1980s produced seven major new drugs; 3M, which has applied its core competency in tapes and adhesives to developing a wide range of new products; and Intel, which has consistently managed to lead in the development of innovative new microprocessors to run personal computers.

■ The High Failure Rate of Innovation

Although innovation can be a source of competitive advantage, the failure rate of innovative new products is high. One study of product development in sixteen companies in the chemical, drug, petroleum, and electronics industries suggested that only about twenty percent of R&D projects ultimately result in a commercially successful product or process.[41] Another in-depth case study of product development in three companies (one in chemicals and two in drugs) reported that about 60 percent of R&D projects reached technical completion, 30 percent were commercialized, and only 12 percent earned an economic profit that exceeded the company's cost of capital.[42] Similarly, a famous study by the consulting division of Booz, Allen, & Hamilton found that over one-third of 13,000 new consumer and industrial products failed to meet company-specific financial and strategic performance criteria.[43] Another study found that 45 percent of new products introduced into the marketplace did not meet their profitability goals.[44] In sum, this evidence suggests that many R&D projects do not result in a commercial product and that between 33 percent and 60 percent of all new products that do reach the marketplace fail to generate an adequate economic return. Two well-publicized product failures have been Apple Computer's Newton, a personal digital assistant, and Sony's Betamax format in the video player and recorder market. Although many reasons have been advanced to explain why so many new products fail to generate an economic return, five explanations for failure appear on most lists: uncertainty, poor commercialization, poor positioning strategy, technological myopia, and a lack of speed in the development process.[45]

Uncertainty   New product development is an inherently risky process. It requires testing a hypothesis whose answer is impossible to know prior to market introduction: namely, is there sufficient market demand for this new technology? Although good market research can minimize the uncertainty about likely future demand for a new technology, the uncertainty cannot be eradicated altogether. Therefore, a certain failure rate is to be expected.

We would expect that failure rate to be higher for quantum product innovations than for incremental innovations. A **quantum innovation** represents a radical departure from existing technology—the introduction of something that is new to the world. The development of the World Wide Web can be considered a quantum innovation in communications technology. Other quantum innovations include the development of the first photocopier by Xerox, the first videocassette recorder by AMPEX, and the first contact lenses by Bausch & Lomb. **Incremental innovation** refers to an extension of existing technology. For example, Intel's Pentium Pro microprocessor is an incremental product innovation because it builds on the existing microprocessor architecture of Intel's X86 series.

The uncertainty of future demand for a new product is much greater if that product represents a quantum innovation that is new to the world than if it is an incremental innovation designed to replace an established product whose demand profile is already well known. Consequently, the failure rate tends to be higher for quantum innovations.

Poor Commercialization   A second reason frequently cited to explain the high failure rate of new product introductions is **poor commercialization**—a condition that occurs when there is an intrinsic demand for a new technology, but the technology is not well adapted to consumer needs because of factors such as poor design and poor quality. For instance, many of the early personal computers failed to sell because one needed to be a computer programmer to use them. It took Steve Jobs at Apple Computer to understand that if the technology could be made user-friendly (if it could be commercialized), there would be an enormous market for it.

Hence the original personal computers marketed by Apple incorporated little in the way of radically new technology, but they made existing technology accessible to the average person. The failure of Apple Computer to establish a market for the Newton—the personal digital assistant or hand-held computer that Apple introduced in the summer of 1993—can be traced to poor commercialization of a potentially attractive technology. Apple predicted a $1 billion market for the Newton, but sales failed to materialize when it became clear that the Newton's software could not adequately recognize messages written on the Newton's message pad. Despite this failure, many companies believe that there is an intrinsic demand for this kind of technology, but only if the product can be better commercialized.

Poor Positioning Strategy   Poor positioning strategy arises when a company introduces an intrinsically attractive new product, but sales fail to materialize because it is poorly positioned in the market place. **Positioning strategy** is the position a company adopts for a product on four main dimensions of marketing: price, distribution, promotion and advertising, and product features. Apart from poor product quality, another reason for the failure of the Apple Newton was poor positioning strategy. The Newton was introduced at such a high initial price (close to $1,000) that probably there would have been few takers even if the technology had been adequately commercialized. Poor positioning strategy may have also affected the recent introduction of the digital compact cassette (DCC), discussed in Strategy in Action 5.6. The DCC suffered from high prices, poor promotion, and a failure by the innovating companies to produce products for the portable and car market.

Technological Myopia   Another reason why many new product introductions fail is that companies often make the mistake of marketing a technology for which there is not enough consumer demand. **Technological myopia** occurs when a company gets blinded by the wizardry of a new technology and fails to consider whether there is consumer demand for the product. This problem may have been a factor in the failure of the desktop computer introduced by NeXT in the late 1980s. (NeXT was founded by Steve Jobs, the founder of Apple Computer.) Technologically, the NeXT machines were clearly ahead of their time, with advanced software and hardware features that would not be incorporated into most personal computers for another decade. However, consumer acceptance was very slow, primarily because of the complete lack of applications software such as spreadsheet and word-processing programs to run on the machines. Management at NeXT was so enthusiastic about the technology of their new computer that they ignored this basic market reality. After several years of slow sales, NeXT eventually withdrew the machines from the marketplace.

Slowness in Marketing   Finally, companies fail when they are slow to get their products to market. The longer the time between initial development and final marketing—that is, the slower the "cycle time"—the more likely it is that someone else will beat the firm to market and gain a first-mover advantage.[47] By and large, slow innovators update their products less frequently than fast innovators. Consequently, they can be perceived as technical laggards relative to the fast innovators. In the automobile industry, General Motors has suffered from being a slow innovator. Its product development cycle has been about five years, compared with two to three years at Honda, Toyota, and Mazda, and three to four years at Ford. Because they are

5.6 STRATEGY *in* ACTION

Whatever Happened to the Digital Compact Cassette?

The Digital Compact Cassette (DCC) was developed by Philips, the Dutch consumer electronics company. The DCC is a recordable audio digital technology that offers sound qualities superior to those of analog cassette technology. The DCC was designed to replace analog cassette tapes in much the same way that digital compact disks have replaced analog long-playing records. An attractive feature of the technology was a design that allowed users to play their analog cassette tapes on the DCC, in addition to DCC digital tapes. The thinking at Philips was that this feature would make the product very attractive to users, who would not have to replace their existing collection of analog cassette tapes when they purchased a DCC player. To try and ensure initial acceptance of the technology, Philips lined up a number of recording companies—including MCA, Polygram, EMI, and Warner—all of whom agreed to issue prerecorded DCC tapes in conjunction with the launch by Philips of the tapes players.

Brought out in 1993, the DCC was hailed in the press as the biggest new product introduction in the consumer electronics industry since the introduction of the compact disk a decade earlier. However, as initial demand failed to materialize, retailers with unsold DCC tapes and decks on their hands refused to keep devoting valuable shelf space to DCC products, and recording companies soon stopped issuing prerecorded DCC tapes. It was obvious within a year that the product was stillborn in the marketplace.

Why did the DCC fail to gain market acceptance despite its apparently attractive features? Poor positioning strategy is probably part of the explanation. Philips introduced the technology at a very high price—around $1,000 for a basic home deck—out of the reach of most consumers. Moreover, Philips failed to introduce a portable model (to compete with Sony's Walkman) or a model for cars (most consumers still have analog tape players in their cars). To make matters worse, the original promotional advertising failed to mention one of the most attractive features of the technology—that DCC tape drives could play existing analog tapes. Finally, Philips implemented a very abstract advertising campaign, which left most consumers confused about the nature of the new technology.

Another reason for the poor market acceptance was the limited value placed on the technology by many consumers. Most consumers did not see the DCC as a big advance over CD players. True, CD technology did not have recording capability, but CD players were increasingly turning up in cars and Sony had marketed a very successful portable version of the CD (the Discman)—both market niches that were natural targets for the DCC. Consequently, few consumers valued the technology enough to pay $1,000 or so for a player. Whether Philips would have been able to build sales for the DCC had it entered the market at a lower price point, with better advertising and a broader range of models, remains an open question, but success would probably have been more likely.[46]

---

based on five-year-old technology and design concepts, GM cars are already out-of-date when they reach the market. Another example of the consequences of slow innovation, the demise of Apollo Computer at the hands of Sun Microsystems, is presented in Strategy in Action 5.7.

▓ Building Competencies in Innovation

Companies can take a number of steps in order to build a competency in innovation and avoid failure. Three of the most important seem to be (1) building skills in basic and applied scientific research; (2) developing a good process for project selection and project management, and (3) integrating the different functions of the

Slow Cycle Time at Apollo Computer

In 1980, Apollo Computer created the market for engineering computer workstations. (Workstations are high-powered freestanding minicomputers.) Apollo was rewarded with rapid growth and a virtual monopoly position. Its first real competitor, Sun Microsystems, did not introduce a competing product until 1982. However, by 1988 Apollo had lost its lead in the workstation market to Sun. While Apollo was generating revenues of $600 million in 1988, Sun's revenues were more than $1 billion. Between 1984 and 1988, Sun's revenues from workstations grew at an annual rate of 100 percent, compared with Apollo's annual growth rate of 35 percent.

The cause of Apollo's slower growth was a slow cycle time. In the computer industry, innovations in microprocessor technology are proceeding at a furious pace. In order to stay abreast of new microprocessor technology, any manufacturer of computers must be continually updating their product. However, while Sun had succeeded in introducing a new product every twelve months and in doubling the power of its workstations every eighteen months on the average, Apollo's product development cycle had stretched out to more than two years. As a result, Apollo's products were regularly superseded by the more technologically advanced products introduced by Sun, and Apollo was falling further and further behind. Consequently, while Sun had increased its market share from 21 percent to 33 percent between 1985 and 1988, Apollo's fell from 41 percent to under 20 percent. In 1989, facing mounting problems, Apollo was acquired by Hewlett-Packard.[48]

company through cross-functional product development teams and partly parallel development processes.[49]

Building Skills in Basic and Applied Research Building skills in basic and applied research requires the employment of research scientists and engineers and the establishment of a work environment that fosters creativity. A number of top companies try to achieve this by setting up university-style research facilities, where scientists and engineers are given time to work on their own research projects, in addition to projects that are linked directly to ongoing company research. At Hewlett-Packard, for example, the company labs are open to engineers around the clock. Hewlett-Packard even encourages its corporate researchers to devote 10 percent of company time to exploring their own ideas—and does not penalize them if they fail. Similarly, at 3M there is a "15 percent rule," which allows researchers to spend 15 percent of the workweek researching any topic they want to investigate, as long as there is the potential of a payoff for the company. The most famous outcome of this policy is the ubiquitous yellow Post-it Notes. The idea for them evolved from a researcher's desire to find a way to keep the bookmark from falling out of his hymn book. Post-it Notes are now a major 3M consumer business, with revenues of around $300 million.

Project Selection and Management Project management is the overall management of the innovation process, from generation of the original concept, through development, and into final production and shipping. Project management requires three important skills: the ability to encourage as much generation of ideas as possible; the ability to select among competing projects at an early stage of development

FIGURE 5.8

The Development
Funnel

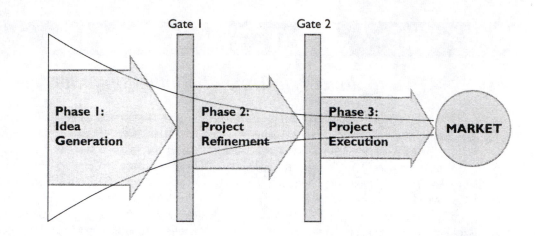

so that the most promising receive funding and potential costly failures are killed off; and the ability to minimize time to market. The concept of the development funnel, illustrated in Figure 5.8, summarizes what is required to build these skills.[50]

As Figure 5.8 shows, the development funnel is divided into three phases. The objective in phase 1 is to widen the mouth of the tunnel to encourage as much idea generation as possible. To this end, a company should solicit input from all its functions, as well as from customers, competitors, and suppliers.

At gate 1 the funnel narrows. Here ideas are reviewed by a cross-functional team of managers who were not involved in the original concept development. Those concepts that are ready to proceed then move on to phase 2 of the funnel, which is where the details of the project proposal are worked out. Note that gate 1 is not a go/no-go evaluation point. At this screen, ideas may be sent back for further concept development to be resubmitted for evaluation.

During phase 2, which typically lasts only one or two months, the data and information developed during phase 1 are put into a form that will enable senior management to evaluate proposed projects against competing projects. Normally, this requires the development of a careful project plan, complete with details of the proposed target market, attainable market share, likely revenues, development costs, production costs, key milestones, and the like. The next big selection point, gate 2, is a go/no-go evaluation point. Senior managers are brought in to review the various projects under consideration. Their task is to select those projects that seem likely winners and that make most sense from a strategic perspective, given the long-term goals of the enterprise. The overriding objective at this gate is to select projects whose successful completion will help maintain or build a competitive advantage for the company. A related objective is to ensure that the company does not spread its scarce capital and human resources too thinly over too many projects and that instead it concentrates resources on those projects where the probability of success and potential returns are most attractive. Any project selected to go forward at this stage will be funded and staffed, the expectation being that it will be carried through to market introduction. In phase 3, the project development proposal is executed by a cross-functional product development team.

Cross-Functional Integration   Tight cross-functional integration between R&D, production, and marketing can help a company to ensure that

1. product development projects are driven by customer needs.

2. new products are designed for ease of manufacture.

3. development costs are kept in check.

4. time to market is minimized.

Close integration between R&D and marketing is required to ensure that product development projects are driven by the needs of customers. A company's customers can be one of its primary sources of new product ideas. Identification of customer needs, and particularly unmet needs, can set the context within which successful product innovation takes place. As the point of contact with customers, the marketing function of a company can provide valuable information in this regard. Moreover, integration of R&D and marketing is crucial if a new product is to be properly commercialized. Without integration of R&D and marketing, a company runs the risk of developing products for which there is little or no demand.

The case of Techsonic Industries illustrates the benefits of integrating R&D and marketing. This Alabama company manufactures depth finders—electronic devices used in fishing to measure the depth of water beneath a boat and to track the prey. Techsonic had weathered nine new-product failures in a row when the company decided to conduct interviews across the country with those engaged in the sport of fishing to identify what they needed. It discovered an unmet need for a depth finder with a gauge that could be read in bright sunlight, so that is what Techsonic developed. In the year after the $250 depth finder hit the market, Techsonic's sales tripled to $80 million and its market share surged to 40 percent.[51]

Integrating of R&D and production can help a company ensure that products are designed with manufacturing requirements in mind, which lowers manufacturing costs and leaves less room for mistakes, thus increasing product quality. Such integration can also reduce development costs and speed products to market. If a new product is not designed with manufacturing capabilities in mind, it may prove too difficult to build, given existing manufacturing technology. In that case, it will have to be redesigned, and both overall development costs and the time it takes to bring the product to market may increase significantly. For example, making design changes during product planning could raise overall development costs by 50 percent and add 25 percent to the time it takes to bring the product to market.[52] Moreover, many quantum product innovations require new processes to manufacture them. That makes it all the more important to integrate R&D and production, since minimizing time to market and development costs may require the simultaneous development of new products and new processes.[53]

Product Development Teams   One of the best way to achieve cross-functional integration is to establish cross-functional product development teams. These are teams composed of representatives from R&D, marketing, and production. The objective of a team should be to take a product development project through from the initial concept development to market introduction. Certain attributes seem particularly important for a product development team to have if it is to function effectively and meet all its development milestones.[54]

First, the team should be led by a "heavyweight" project manager, who has both high status within the organization and the power and authority to obtain the financial and human resources that the team needs to succeed. This "heavyweight" leader should be dedicated primarily, if not entirely, to the project. The leader should be someone who believes in the project—that is, a champion of the project—and should also be skilled at integrating the perspectives of different functions and at helping personnel from different functions work together for a common goal. Moreover, the leader must also be able to act as the team's advocate to senior management.

Second, the team should include at least one member from each key function. The team members should have an ability to contribute functional expertise, high standing within their function, a willingness to share responsibility for team results, and an ability to put functional advocacy aside. Generally, it is preferable for core team members to be 100 percent dedicated to the project for its duration so that their focus is on the project, not on the ongoing work of their function.

Third, the team members should be physically colocated to create a sense of camaraderie and to facilitate communication.

Fourth, the team should have a clear plan and clear goals, particularly with regard to critical development milestones and development budgets. The team should have incentives to attain those goals—such as pay bonuses when major development milestones are hit.

Fifth, each team needs to develop its own processes for communication and conflict resolution. For example, one product development team at Quantum Corporation, a California-based manufacturer of disk drives for personal computers, instituted a rule that all major decisions would be made and conflicts resolved at meetings that were held every Monday afternoon. This simple rule helped the team to meet its development goals.[55]

Partly Parallel Development Processes One way in which a product development team can compress the time it takes to develop a product and bring it to market is to utilize a partly parallel development process. Traditionally, product development processes have been organized on a sequential basis, as illustrated in Figure 5.9a. A problem with this kind of process is that product development proceeds without consideration of manufacturing issues. Most significantly, since the basic design of a product is completed before the design of a manufacturing process and full-scale commercial production, there is no early warning system to indicate manufacturability. Consequently, the company may find that it cannot manufacture the product in a cost-efficient way and must send it back to the design stage for redesign. The result is that cycle time lengthens as the product iterates back and forth between stages.

To solve this problem, companies typically use a process similar to that illustrated in Figure 5.9b. In the partly parallel development process, development stages overlap so that, for example, work starts on the development of the production process before the product design is finalized. By reducing the need for expensive and time-consuming product redesigns, such a process can significantly reduce the time it takes to develop a new product and bring it to market.

What occurred after Intel introduced its 386 microprocessor in 1986 illustrates this point. A number of companies, including IBM and Compaq, were racing to be the first to introduce a 386-based personal computer. Compaq beat IBM by six months and gained a major share of the high-powered market, mainly because it used a cross-functional team and a partly parallel process to develop the product. The team included engineers (R&D) and marketing, production, and finance peo-

FIGURE 5.9

Sequential and Partly
Parallel Development
Processes

a: A Sequential Process

Opportunity
identification

Concept
development

R&D

Manufacturing

Product
design

R&D and Marketing

Process
design

Commercial
production

b: A Partly Parallel Process

Opportunity
identification

Concept
development

R&D and Manufacturing

Product
design

Process
design

Commercial
production

ple. Each function worked in parallel rather than sequentially. While the engineers were designing the product, the production people were setting up the manufacturing facilities, the marketing people were working on distribution and planning marketing campaigns, and the finance people were working on project funding.

■ Summary: Achieving Superior Innovation

The primary role that the various functions play in achieving superior innovation is summarized in Table 5.4. Two matters, especially, need noting. First, top management must bear primary responsibility for overseeing the whole development

TABLE 5.4

The Role Played by Various Functions in Achieving Superior Innovation

Value Creation Function	Primary Roles
Infrastructure (Leadership)	1. Manage overall project (i.e., manage the development function). 2. Facilitate cross-functional cooperation.
Production	1. Cooperate with R&D on designing products that are easy to manufacture. 2. Work with R&D to develop process innovations.
Marketing	1. Provide market information to R&D. Work with R&D to develop new products.
Materials Management	No primary responsibility.
R&D	1. Develop new products and processes. 2. Cooperate with other functions, particularly marketing and manufacturing, in the development process.
Information Systems	1. Use information systems to coordinate cross-functional and cross-company product development work.
Human Resources	1. Hire talented scientists and engineers.

process. This entails both managing the development funnel and facilitating cooperation between functions. Second, while R&D plays a central role in the innovation process, the effectiveness of R&D in developing new products and processes depends on its ability to cooperate with marketing and production.

ACHIEVING SUPERIOR CUSTOMER RESPONSIVENESS

To achieve superior customer responsiveness, a company must give customers what they want when they want it—so long as the company's long-term profitability is not compromised in the process. The more responsive a company is to the needs of its customers, the greater the brand loyalty it can command. In turn, strong brand loyalty may allow a company to charge a premium price for its products or to sell more goods and services to customers. Either way, the company that is responsive to its customers' needs will have a competitive advantage.

Achieving superior customer responsiveness means giving customers value for money, and steps taken to improve the efficiency of a company's production process and the quality of its output should be consistent with this aim. In addition, giving customers what they want may require the development of new products with new features. In other words, achieving superior efficiency, quality, and innovation are all part of achieving superior customer responsiveness. There are two other prerequisites for attaining this goal. The first is to focus on the company's customers and their needs, and the second, to find ways to better satisfy those needs.

■ Customer Focus

A company cannot be responsive to its customers' needs unless it knows what those needs are. Thus, the first step in building superior customer responsiveness is to motivate the whole company to focus on the customer. The means to this end are demonstrating leadership, shaping employee attitudes, and using mechanisms for bringing customers into the company.

Leadership Customer focus must start at the top of the organization. A commitment to superior customer responsiveness brings attitudinal changes throughout a company that can ultimately be built only through strong leadership. A mission statement (see Chapter 2) that puts customers first is one way to send a clear message to employees about the desired focus. Another avenue is top management's own actions. For example, Tom Monaghan, the founder of Domino's Pizza, stays close to the customer by visiting as many stores as possible every week, running some deliveries himself, insisting that other top managers do the same, and eating Domino's pizza regularly.

Employee Attitudes Achieving a superior customer focus requires that all employees see the customer as the focus of their activity. Leadership alone is not enough to attain this goal. All employees must be trained to focus on the customer, whether their function is marketing, manufacturing, R&D, or accounting. The objective should be to make employees think of themselves as customers—to put themselves in the customers' shoes. At that point, employees will be better able to identify ways to improve the quality of a customer's experience with the company.

To reinforce this mindset, incentive systems within the company should reward employees for satisfying customers. For example, senior managers at the Four Seasons hotel chain, who pride themselves on their customer focus, like to tell the story of Roy Dyment, a doorman in Toronto who neglected to load a departing guest's briefcase into his taxi. The doorman called the guest, a lawyer, in Washington D.C., and found that he desperately needed the briefcase for a morning meeting. Dyment hopped on a plane to Washington and returned it—without first securing approval from his boss. Far from punishing Dyment for making a mistake and for not checking with management before going to Washington, the Four Seasons responded by naming him Employee of the Year.[57] This action sent a powerful message to Four Seasons employees about the importance of satisfying customer needs.

Bringing Customers into the Company "Know thy customer" is one of the keys to achieving superior customer responsiveness. Knowing the customer not only requires that employees think like customers themselves; it also demands that they listen to what their customers have to say, and, as much as possible, bring them into the company. While this may not involve physically bringing customers into the company, it does mean bringing in customers' opinions by soliciting feedback from customers on the company's goods and services and by building information systems that communicate the feedback to the relevant people.

For an example, consider mail-order clothing retailer Lands' End. Through its catalog and customer service telephone operators, Lands' End actively solicits comments from its customers about the quality of its clothing and the kind of merchandise they want Lands' End to supply. Indeed, it was customers' insistence that prompted the company to move into the clothing segment. Lands' End used to supply equipment for sailboats through mail-order catalogs. However, it received so many requests from customers to include outdoor clothing in its offering that it responded by expanding the catalog to fill this need. Soon clothing became the main business and Lands' End dropped the sailboat equipment. Today, the company still pays close attention to customer requests. Every month a computer printout of customer requests and comments is given to managers. This feedback helps the company to fine-tune the merchandise it sells. Indeed, frequently new lines of merchandise are introduced in response to customer requests.[58]

■ Satisfying Customer Needs

Once a focus on the customer has been achieved, the next task is to satisfy the customer needs that have been identified. As already noted, efficiency, quality, and innovation are all crucial to satisfying those needs. Beyond that, companies can provide a higher level of satisfaction if they customize the product, as much as possible, to the requirements of individual customers and if they minimize the time it takes to respond to customer demands.

Customization   Varying the features of a good or service to tailor it to the unique needs of groups of customers or, in the extreme case, individual customers is known as **customization**. It used to be thought that customization raised costs. However, as noted earlier in this chapter, the development of flexible manufacturing technologies has made it feasible to produce a far greater variety of products than could previously be done without suffering a substantial cost penalty. Companies can now customize their products to a much greater extent than they could ten to fifteen years ago, particularly when flexible manufacturing technologies are linked with Web-based information systems. The Opening Case illustrates how Levi Strauss is using Web-based systems in conjunction with flexible manufacturing technology to customize its blue jeans for individual consumers. The same is true of service companies. For example, on-line retailers such as Amazon.com have used Web-based technologies to develop a home page for their stores that is customized for each individual user. When customers access Amazon.com, they are confronted with a list of recommendations for books or music to purchase that is based on an analysis of their prior buying history.

The trend toward customization has fragmented many markets, particularly consumer markets, into ever smaller niches. An example of this fragmentation occurred in Japan in the early 1980s, when Honda dominated the motorcycle market there. Second-place Yamaha decided to go after Honda's lead. In 1981, it announced the opening of a new factory, which, when operating at full capacity, would make Yamaha the world's largest manufacturer of motorcycles. Honda responded by proliferating its product line and stepping up its rate of new-product introduction. At the start of what became known as the "motorcycle wars," Honda had 60 motorcycles in its product line. Over the next eighteen months, Honda rapidly increased its range to 113 models, customizing them to ever smaller niches. Honda was able to accomplish this without bearing a significant cost penalty because it was a flexible manufacturer. The flood of Honda's customized models pushed Yamaha out of much of the market, effectively stalling its bid to overtake Honda.[59]

Response Time   Giving customers what they want when they want it requires speed of response to customer demands. To gain a competitive advantage, a company must often respond to consumer demands very quickly, whether the transaction is a furniture manufacturer's delivery of a product once it has been ordered, a bank's processing of a loan application, an automobile manufacturer's delivery of a spare part for a car that broke down, or the wait in a supermarket checkout line. We live in a fast-paced society, where time is a valuable commodity. Companies that can satisfy customer demands for rapid response can build brand loyalty and set a higher price for the product or service.

Increased speed lets a company charge a significant premium, as the mail delivery industry illustrates. The air express niche of the mail delivery industry is based on the notion that customers are often willing to pay considerably more for overnight Express Mail, as opposed to regular mail. Another example of the value of rapid response is Caterpillar, the manufacturer of heavy earthmoving equipment, which can get a spare part to any point in the world within twenty-four hours. Since downtime for heavy construction equipment is very costly, Caterpillar's ability to respond quickly in the event of equipment malfunction is of prime importance to its customers. As a result, many of them have remained loyal to Caterpillar despite the aggressive low-price competition from Komatsu of Japan.

In general, reducing response time requires (1) a marketing function that can quickly communicate customer requests to production, (2) production and materials management functions that can quickly adjust production schedules in response to unanticipated customer demands, and (3) information systems that can help production and marketing in this process.

■ Summary: Achieving Superior Customer Responsiveness

Table 5.5 summarizes the steps different functions must take if a company is to achieve superior customer responsiveness. Although marketing plays the critical role in helping a company attain this goal, primarily because it represents the point

TABLE 5.5

The Primary Role of Different Functions in Achieving Superior Customer Responsiveness

Value Creation Function	Primary Roles
Infrastructure (Leadership)	1. Through leadership by example, build a companywide commitment to customer responsiveness.
Production	1. Achieve customization by implementing flexible manufacturing. 2. Achieve rapid response through flexible manufacturing.
Marketing	1. Know the customer. 2. Communicate customer feedback to appropriate functions.
Materials Management	1. Develop logistics systems capable of responding quickly to unanticipated customer demands (JIT).
R&D	1. Bring customers into the product development process.
Information Systems	1. Use Web-based information systems to increase customer responsiveness.
Human Resources	1. Develop training programs that get employees to think like customers.

of contact with the customer, Table 5.5 shows that the other functions also have major roles to perform. Moreover, like achieving superior efficiency, quality, and innovation, achieving superior customer responsiveness requires top management to lead in building a customer orientation within the company.

SUMMARY OF CHAPTER

This chapter discusses the role that functional-level strategies play in achieving efficiency, quality, innovation, and customer responsiveness. It examines in detail the different steps that lead to this end and makes the following main points:

✓ A company can increase efficiency through a number of steps. These include exploiting economies of scale and learning effects, adopting flexible manufacturing technologies, reducing customer defection rates, implementing just-in-time systems, getting the R&D function to design products that are easy to manufacture, upgrading the skills of employees through training, introducing self-managing teams, linking pay to performance, building a companywide commitment to efficiency through strong leadership, and designing structures that facilitate cooperation among different functions in pursuit of efficiency goals.

✓ Superior quality can help a company both to lower its costs and to differentiate its product and charge a premium price.

✓ Achieving superior quality demands an organizationwide commitment to quality and a clear focus on the customer. It also requires metrics to measure quality goals and incentives that emphasize quality; input from employees regarding ways in which quality can be improved; a methodology for tracing defects to their source and correcting the problems that produce them; rationalization of the company's supply base; cooperation with the suppliers that remain to implement TQM programs; products that are designed for ease of manufacturing; and substantial cooperation among functions.

✓ The failure rate of new-product introductions is high due to factors such as uncertainty, poor commercialization, poor positioning strategy, technological myopia, and slow cycle time.

✓ To achieve superior innovation, a company must build skills in basic and applied research; design good processes for managing development projects; and achieve close integration between the different functions of the enterprise, primarily through the adoption of cross-functional product development teams and partly parallel development processes.

✓ Achieving superior customer responsiveness often requires that the company achieve superior efficiency, quality, and innovation.

✓ To achieve superior customer responsiveness, a company needs to give customers what they want when they want it. It must ensure a strong customer focus, which can be attained through leadership; training employees to think like customers; bring customers into the company by means of superior market research; customizing the product to the unique needs of individual customers or customer groups; and responding quickly to customer demands.

DISCUSSION QUESTIONS

1. How are the four generic building blocks of competitive advantage related to each other?

2. What role can top management play in helping a company achieve superior efficiency, quality, innovation, and customer responsiveness?

3. In the long run, will adoption of TQM practices give a company a competitive advantage, or will it be required just to achieve parity with competitors?

4. In what sense might innovation be called the single most important building block of competitive advantage?

Practicing Strategic Management

SMALL-GROUP EXERCISE
Identifying Excellence

Break up into groups of three to five people, and discuss the following scenario:

You are the management team of a start-up company, which will produce disk drives for the personal computer industry. You will sell your product to manufacturers of personal computers (original equipment manufacturers). The disk drive market is characterized by rapid technological change, product life cycles of only six to nine months, intense price competition, high fixed costs for manufacturing equipment, and substantial manufacturing economies of scale. Your customers—the original equipment manufacturers—issue very demanding technological specifications that your product has to comply with. The original equipment manufacturers also pressure you to deliver your product on time so that it fits in with their own product introduction schedule. In this industry, what functional competencies are the most important for you to build? How will you design your internal processes to ensure that those competencies are built within the company?

STRATEGIC MANAGEMENT PROJECT
Module 5

This module deals with the ability of your company to achieve superior efficiency, quality, innovation, and customer responsiveness. With the information you have at your disposal, answer the questions and perform the tasks listed:

1. Is your company pursuing any of the efficiency-enhancing practices discussed in this chapter?

2. Is your company pursuing any of the quality-enhancing practices discussed in this chapter?

3. Is your company pursuing any of the practices designed to enhance innovation discussed in this chapter?

4. Is your company pursuing any of the practices designed to increase customer responsiveness discussed in this chapter?

5. Evaluate the competitive position of your company in the light of your answers to questions 1–4. Explain what, if anything, the company needs to do to improve its competitive position.

ARTICLE FILE 5

Find an example of a company that is widely regarded as excellent. Identify the source of its excellence and relate it to the material discussed in this chapter. Pay particular attention to the role played by the various functions in building excellence.

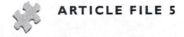

EXPLORING THE WEB
Visiting Applied Materials

Visit the Web site of Applied Materials, the world's largest manufacturer of semiconductor fabrication equipment at ⟨http://www.appliedmaterials.com⟩. Find and read the company's mission statement. What does this mission statement tell you about the kind of competitive advantage that Applied Materials is trying to build? How important are efficiency, quality, innovation, and customer responsiveness to this company?

Now go to the sections of Applied's Web site that detail the company's financial results, products, and press releases. Read through these sections and try to establish how successful Applied has been at meeting the objectives set down in its mission statement. What do you think the company has done at the functional level to increase its efficiency, customer responsiveness, innovative ability, and product quality?

Search the Web for a company whose home page describes in some detail its approach to achieving one of the following: superior productivity, product quality, customer service, or innovation. Using this information, document the company's functional-level strategy and assess whether the strategy makes sense, given what you have learned so far in this book.

Reengineering Lloyds Bank

LLOYDS BANK is one of the largest banks in Britain, with 29,000 employees and 1,800 branches nationwide. It is also one of Britain's most profitable banks, with one of the lowest ratios of operating costs to income in the British banking industry. Lloyds' senior management gives much of the credit for the bank's recent performance to its Service Quality Improvement Program (SQIP), an exercise in business process reengineering. Business process reengineering is an attempt to reorganize companies around their core processes as opposed to their traditional functions, such as the production department, marketing department, or human resource department. The term *core processes* has been defined as "a collection of activities that takes one or more kinds of input and creates an output that is of value to the customer." Processes often include activities such as customer service, order fulfillment, and product development.

Lloyds Bank turned to process reengineering in September 1992 in an attempt to increase the quality of its service and drive down the cost structure of its retail branch banking network. The catalyst was the growing competition from Britain's building societies (which are similar to U.S. savings and loans). The building societies had aggressively pursued Lloyds' retail customers following the deregulation of the British financial services industry, which had allowed banks and building societies to enter each other's markets for the first time. The bank was also worried about the impact of service expansion on its cost structure. During the 1980s, each time the bank entered a new service market (for example, home mortgage financing), it simply added more staff to a retail branch. As a result, by the early 1990s, branch costs were beginning to spiral out of control.

Under the traditional system at Lloyds, staff were given narrowly defined functional responsibilities within the context of a rigid hierarchical structure. One set of people would be responsible for managing checking accounts, another for reviewing a customer's credit, and still another for issuing credit cards, and so on. One consequence was that countless people and bits of paper were involved in what, from the customers' point of view, was a single process. For example, under the old system for opening an account at a Lloyds branch, an application form could spend a month wandering from desk to desk as different staff ordered bank cards, reviewed credit details, ordered checkbooks, opened savings accounts, and so on. Under Lloyds' new system, a single person is now responsible for a largely paperless "quality welcome" process, which entails reviewing the customer's credit history, setting up an account, and issuing credit cards, ATM cards, and checkbooks. With this new process, it usually takes less than a week for a new account to be fully functional.

Besides the "quality welcome" process, Lloyds identified five other core processes within its branches, including "lending control," "periodic payments," and "customer retention."

Each process was assigned a process owner, whose job it was to make sure that the process was reengineered to achieve Lloyds' goals of driving down costs and increasing the quality of customer service. The processes were tested in a make-believe branch before being introduced across the bank's network of retail branches in a series of waves starting in July 1993. The indications are that SQIP is having the desired effect. Lloyds' managers claim that the reengineering project has comfortably cleared the 12 percent return on capital hurdle required of business ideas. For example, the number of faulty checkbook orders fell by 30 percent in the first two months of the program—producing savings large enough to pay for the computers that monitor this activity under the new process. There is also evidence that the bank is meeting its central aim of improving customer service. Lloyds' own measure of customer satisfaction rose from 73 percent in mid 1993, when the project began, to 80 percent by mid 1995, putting the bank comfortably ahead of its two largest British rivals. Having said that, however, a 7 percent improvement in customer satisfaction is less than stunning.

Also on the down side, Lloyds has had to deal with morale problems in many of its branches, where the reengineering process is often perceived to be a subtle way of cutting jobs and, in some cases, closing down branches altogether. The bank closed 300 branches between 1990 and 1995, although management claims that this effort was independent of the reengineering process, which focuses on what is happening within branches.

Management does not question the fact that 200 jobs have been lost as a result of the reengineering process but points out that all these losses were voluntary. Those hit hardest by the reengineering effort seem to be middle-level managers, as opposed to branch employees. Between mid 1993 and mid 1995, the bank reduced the number of area directors from 80 to 41, largely because the reengineering effort enabled the bank to do more with less. Whatever the true cause of the job losses, there are concerns that employee morale problems are inhibiting Lloyd's ability to realize the full benefits of its reengineering efforts.[60]

Case Discussion Questions

1. What are the goals of the reengineering project at Lloyds Bank? If successful, how will this project affect the efficiency, quality, and customer responsiveness of Lloyds Bank?

2. Is the kind of process reengineering described here consistent with Deming's approach to total quality management, as described in this chapter?

3. Can you see a down side to Lloyds' reengineering effort? What is it? How might the impact of this down side be limited?

End Notes

1. E. Schonfeld, "The Customized, Digitized, Have It Your Way Economy," *Fortune*, September 28, 1998, p. 117; M. Knight, "Levi's to Close 11 Plants in Shift to Offshore Manufacturing," *Business and Industry*, February 24, 1999, p. 6; "The View from the Outside, Levi's Needs More Than a Patch," *New York Times*, February 28, 1999, p. 4.

2. *Chase press release*, "Chase and Chemical Merger Creating Largest Banking Company in the United States," March 21, 1996, (http://www.chase.com); S. Lipin, "Joining Fortunes," *Wall Street Journal*, August 28, 1995, p. 1; G. B. Knecht, "Chemical Merger with Chase Echoes Earlier Alliance," *Wall Street Journal*, September 1, 1995, p. 4.

3. For example, see F. M. Scherer, A. Beckenstein, E. Kaufer, and R. D. Murphy, *The Economies of Multiplant Operations* (Cambridge, Mass.: Harvard University Press, 1975).

4. H. Luft, J. Bunker, and A. Enthoven, "Should Operations Be Regionalized?" *New England Journal of Medicine*, 301 (1979) 1364–1369.

5. G. Hall and S. Howell, "The Experience Curve from an Economist's Perspective," *Strategic Management Journal*, 6 (1985), 197–212; M. Lieberman, "The Learning Curve and Pricing in the Chemical Processing Industries," *RAND Journal of Economics*, 15 (1984), 213–228.

6. Boston Consulting Group, *Perspectives on Experience* (Boston: Boston Consulting Group, 1972); Hall and Howell, "The Experience Curve,"; W. B. Hirschmann, "Profit from the Learning Curve," *Harvard Business Review* (January–February 1964), 125–139.

7. A. A. Alchian, "Reliability of Progress Curves in Airframe Production," *Econometrica*, 31 (1963), 679–693.

8. M. Borrus, L. A. Tyson, and J. Zysman, "Creating Advantage: How Government Policies Create Trade in the Semi-Conductor Industry," *Strategic Trade Policy and the New International Economics*, ed. P. R. Krugman (Cambridge, Mass.: MIT Press, 1986); S. Ghoshal and C. A. Bartlett, "Matsushita Electrical Industrial (MEI) in 1987," *Harvard Business School Case* No. 388-144, 1988.

9. G. Stalk and T. M. Hout, *Competing Against Time* (New York: Free Press, 1990); D. Miller, *The Icarus Paradox* (New York: Harper Business, 1990).

10. Abernathy and Wayne, "Limits of the Learning Curve," *Harvard Business Review*, pp. 109–119, 1980.

11. D. F. Barnett and R. W. Crandall, *Up from the Ashes: The Rise of the Steel Minimill in the United States* (Washington, D.C.: Brookings Institution, 1986).

12. See P. Nemetz and L. Fry, "Flexible Manufacturing Organizations: Implications for Strategy Formulation," *Academy of Management Review*, 13 (1988), 627–638; N. Greenwood, *Implementing Flexible Manufacturing Systems* (New York: Halstead Press, 1986); J. P. Womack, D. T. Jones, and D. Roos, *The Machine That Changed the World* (New York: Rawson Associates, 1990); and R. Parthasarthy and S. P. Seith, "The Impact of Flexible Automation on Business Strategy and Organizational Structure," *Academy of Management Review*, 17 (1992), 86–111.

13. B. J. Pine, *Mass Customization: The New Frontier in Business Competition* (Boston: Harvard Business School Press, 1993); S. Kotha, "Mass Customization: Implementing the Emerging Paradigm for Competitive Advantage," *Strategic Management Journal*, 16 (1995), 21–42; J. H. Gilmore and B. J. Pine II, "The Four Faces of Mass Customization," *Harvard Business Review* (January–February, 1997), 91–101.

14. "The Celling Out of America," *Economist*, December 17, 1994, pp. 63–64.

15. M. A. Cusumano, *The Japanese Automobile Industry* (Cambridge, Mass.: Harvard University Press, 1989); Ohno Taiichi, *Toyota Production System* (Cambridge, Mass.: Productivity Press, 1990); Womack, Jones, and Roos, *The Machine That Changed the World*.

16. F. F. Reichheld and W. E. Sasser, "Zero Defections: Quality Comes to Service," *Harvard Business Review* (September–October 1990), 105–111.

17. The example comes from Reichheld and Sasser, "Zero Defections," 105–111.

18. Ibid.

19. R. Narasimhan and J. R. Carter, "Organization, Communication and Coordination of International Sourcing," *International Marketing Review*, 7 (1990) 6–20.

20. H. F. Busch, "Integrated Materials Management," *IJDP & MM*, 18 (1990) 28–39.

21. Stalk and Hout, *Competing Against Time*.

22. A. Sorge and M. Warner, "Manpower Training, Manufacturing Organization, and Work Place Relations in Great Britain and West Germany," *British Journal of Industrial Relations*, 18 (1980), 318–333; R. Jaikumar, "Postindustrial Manufacturing," *Harvard Business Review* (November-December 1986), 72–83.

23. J. Hoerr, "The Payoff from Teamwork," *Business Week*, July 10, 1989, pp. 56–62.

24. "The Trouble with Teams," *Economist*, January 14, 1995, p. 61.

25. T. C. Powell and A. Dent-Micallef, "Information Technology as Competitive Advantage: The Role of Human, Business, and Technology Resource," *Strategic Management Journal*, 18 (1997), 375–405; B. Gates, *Business @ the Speed of Thought* (New York: Warner Books, 1999).

26. "Cisco@Speed," *Economist*, Special Report: Business and the Internet, June 26, 1999, p. 12; S. Tully, "How Cisco Mastered the Net," *Fortune*, August 17, 1997, p. 207–210; C. Kano. "The Real King of the Internet," *Fortune*, September 7, 1998, pp. 82–93.

27. Gates, *Business@the Speed of Thought*.

28. Ibid.

29. "Work in Progress," *Economist*, July 24, 1999.

30. See the articles published in the special issue on total quality management, *Academy of Management Review*, 19 (1994). The following paper provides a good overview of many of the issues involved from an academic perspective: J. W. Dean and D. E. Bowen, "Management Theory and Total Quality," *Academy of Management Review*, 19 (1994),

392–418. Also see T.C. Powell, "Total Quality Management as Competitive Advantage," *Strategic Management Journal*, 16 (1995), 15–37.

31. For general background information, see "How to Build Quality," *Economist*, September 23, 1989, pp. 91–92; A. Gabor, *The Man Who Discovered Quality* (New York: Penguin, 1990); and P. B. Crosby, *Quality Is Free* (New York: Mentor, 1980).

32. W. E. Deming, "Improvement of Quality and Productivity Through Action by Management," *National Productivity Review*, 1 (Winter 1981–1982), 12–22.

33. J. Bowles, "Is American Management Really Committed to Quality?" *Management Review* (April 1992), 42–46.

34. O. Port and G. Smith, "Quality," *Business Week*, November 30, 1992, pp. 66–75. See also "The Straining of Quality," *Economist*, January 14, 1995, pp. 55–56.

35. C. H. Deutsch, "Six Sigma Enlightenment," *New York Times*, December 7, 1998, p. 1; J. J. Barshay, "The Six Sigma Story," *Star Tribune*, June 14, 1999, p. 1; D. D. Bak, "Rethinking Industrial Drives," *Electrical/Electronics Technology*, November 30, 1998, p. 58.

36. Bowles, "Is American Management Really Committed to Quality?"; "The Straining of Quality."

37. Gabor, *The Man Who Discovered Quality*.

38. Deming, "Improvement of Quality and Productivity."

39. W. E. Deming, *Out of the Crisis* (Cambridge, Mass.: MIT Center for Advanced Engineering Study, 1986).

40. J. F. Siler and S. Atchison, "The Rx at Work in Utah," *Business Week*, October 25, 1991, p. 113.

41. E. Mansfield, "How Economists See R&D," *Harvard Business Review* (November–December, 1981), 98–106.

42. Ibid.

43. Booz, Allen, & Hamilton, "New Products Management for the 1980's," privately published research report, 1982.

44. A. L. Page, "PDMA's New Product Development Practices Survey: Performance and Best Practices." PDMA 15th Annual International Conference, Boston, October 16, 1991.

45. See S. L. Brown and K. M. Eisenhardt, "Product Development: Past Research, Present Findings, and Future Directions," *Academy of Management Review*, 20 (1995), 343–378; M. B. Lieberman and D. B. Montgomery, "First Mover Advantages," *Strategic Management Journal* (Special Issue 9, Summer 1988), 41–58; D. J. Teece, "Profiting from Technological Innovation: Implications for Integration, Collaboration, Licensing and Public Policy," *Research Policy*, 15 (1987), 285–305; G. J. Tellis and P. N. Golder, "First to Market,

First to Fail?" *Sloan Management Review* (Winter 1996), 65–75.

46. R. L. Hudson, "Philips Official Calls DCC Launch Flawed, Vows Division Comeback," *Wall Street Journal*, August 19, 1993, p. A7; (2) A. Kupfer, "The Next Wave in Cassette Tapes," *Fortune*, June 3, 1991, pp. 153–158; P. M. Reilly, "Sony's Digital Audio Format Pulls Ahead of Philips's, But Both Still Have Far to Go," *Wall Street Journal*, August 6, 1993, p. B1.

47. Stalk and Hout, *Competing Against Time*.

48. Ibid.; B. Buell and R. D. Hof, "Hewlett-Packard Rethinks Itself," *Business Week*, April 1, 1991, pp. 76–79.

49. Clark and Wheelwright, *Managing New Product and Process Development*.; M. A. Schilling and C. W. L. Hill, "Managing the New Product Development Process," *Academy of Management Executive*, 12, (August 1998), 67–81.

50. Clark and Wheelwright, *Managing New Product and Process Development*.

51. P. Sellers, "Getting Customers to Love You," *Fortune*, March 13, 1989, pp. 38–42.

52. O. Port, "Moving Past the Assembly Line," *Business Week*, Special Issue: Reinventing America, 1992, pp. 177–180.

53. G. P. Pisano and S. C. Wheelwright, "The New Logic of High Tech R&D," *Harvard Business Review*, September–October 1995, 93–105.

54. K. B. Clark and T. Fujimoto, "The Power of Product Integrity," *Harvard Business Review* (November–December 1990), 107–118; Clark and Wheelwright, *Managing New Product and Process*; Brown and Eisenhardt, "Product Development: Past Research, Present Findings, and Future Directions"; Stalk and Hout, *Competing Against Time*.

55. C. Christensen, "Quantum Corporation—Business and Product Teams," *Harvard Business School Case* No. 9-692-023.

56. S. Caminiti, "A Mail Order Romance: Lands' End Courts Unseen Customers," *Fortune*, March 13, 1989, pp. 43–44.

57. Sellers, "Getting Customers to Love You."

58. Caminiti, "A Mail Order Romance."

59. Stalk and Hout, *Competing Against Time*.

60. "The Black Horse Goes to the Vet," *Economist*, July 22, 1995, pp. 71–72; J. Kelley, "London Calling," *Journal of Business Strategy*, (March–April 1995), 22–26; K. Waterhouse and A. Morgan, "Using Research to Help Keep Good Customers," *Marketing and Research Today* (August 1994), 181–194; M. Hammer and J. Champy, *Reengineering the Corporation* (New York: Harper Business, 1993).

6 Business-Level Strategy

OPENING CASE

*How E*Trade Uses the Internet to Gain a Low-Cost Advantage*

AS WE SAW IN CHAPTER 3, in many industries new entrants have taken advantage of the opportunities opened up by the Internet to overcome barriers to entry and compete successfully against market leaders. Consider the situation of E*Trade, the on-line brokerage firm. As we discussed, for many years large established brokerages like Merrill Lynch had dominated the industry and used their protected positions to charge exorbitant brokerage fees. E*Trade's managers bought and developed software and hardware that allowed its customers to make their own trades, and to do so at a price as low as $19.95.[1]

However, the low-cost competition story in the brokerage industry did not end there. By 1999, E*Trade itself came under pressure from a new generation of on-line brokerage houses, such as Suretrade, Ameritrade and DLJ, which began offering customers trades for only $9.95 and even $7.95, undercutting E*Trade's prices by 100 percent. How could a company like E*Trade, which had made its reputation by being the low-cost leader in the industry, compete against companies that saw themselves as the new cost leaders?

The answer for E*Trade was to enhance its differentiated appeal to its customers by offering them a higher quality of service and a broader product line. E*Trade introduced a brand-new software package that made it even easier for customers to use the Internet to trade shares. What was very important, the new software was more reliable in that customers could make their trades when they wanted. Previously, E*Trade, like other brokerage firms, had experienced many problems when too many customers made trades at once; often the overloaded system simply crashed and customers were unable to buy or sell shares. E*Trade's new package also offered customers more financial research tools and gave them access to more information about specific companies to aid them in their investment decisions. In addition, E*Trade offered customers increased access to real-time stock quotes so that they could take advantage of second-to-second changes in stock prices to make money. Finally, it gave customers the opportunity to invest in Initial Public Offerings (IPOs) of shares from new companies where both potential risks and returns are high.

Furthermore, in 1999 E*Trade decided to merge with an on-line bank, Telebank, to provide its customers with a broad range of on-line banking services, such as paying bills on-line, and thus to become a one-stop on-line shopping site for all of a customer's financial needs.[2] It also took over a variety of other insurance and financial service companies to offer its customers a broad financial service product line.

The realization that it could not just be a low-cost company but also had to create a differentiation advantage in the quickly evolving on-line financial services industry has paid off for E*Trade. Its customers did not switch to the new low-cost leaders because customers perceived that for the $19.95 price they were receiving extra value for money in terms of service and reliability. E*Trade's customer accounts have increased steadily, and its stock price has soared as investors see that the company's competitive advantage is sustainable and that the company is likely to remain a dominant player in the changed industry environment. Indeed, E*Trade has shown the other firms in the industry that to remain viable they must all pursue a simultaneous low-cost and differentiation strategy—something that has become possible only because of the emergence of the Internet, which has created external economies that firms can exploit to increase their performance and competitive advantage.

OVERVIEW

As the E*Trade case suggests, this chapter examines how a company can compete effectively in a business or industry and scrutinizes the various strategies that it can adopt to maximize competitive advantage and profitability. Chapter 3, on the external industry environment, provides concepts for analyzing industry opportunities and threats. Chapters 4 and 5 discuss how a company develops functional-level strategies to build internal strengths and distinctive competencies to achieve a competitive advantage. The purpose of this chapter is to consider the business-level strategies that a company can use to exploit its competitive advantage and compete effectively in an industry. By the end of this chapter, you will be able to identify and distinguish between the principal kinds of business-level strategies that strategic managers can develop to give their companies a competitive advantage over their rivals.

WHAT IS BUSINESS-LEVEL STRATEGY?

Business-level strategy refers to the plan of action that strategic managers adopt for using a company's resources and distinctive competencies to gain a competitive advantage over its rivals in a market or industry. In Chapter 2, we discuss Derek F. Abell's view that the process of business definition entails decisions about (1) customers' needs, or *what* is to be satisfied; (2) customer groups, or *who* is to be satisfied; and (3) distinctive competencies, or *how* customer needs are to be satisfied.[3] These three decisions are the basis for choosing a business-level strategy because they determine how a company will compete in a business or industry. Consequently, we need to look at the ways in which a company makes these three decisions to gain a competitive advantage over its rivals.

■ Customers' Needs and Product Differentiation

Customers' needs are desires, wants, or cravings that can be satisfied by means of the characteristics of a product or service. For example, a person's craving for something sweet can be satisfied by a carton of Ben & Jerry's ice cream, a Snickers bar, or a spoonful of sugar. **Product differentiation** is the process of creating a competitive advantage by designing products—goods or services—to satisfy customers' needs. All companies must differentiate their products to a certain degree in order to attract customers and satisfy some minimal level of need. However, some companies differentiate their products to a much greater degree than others, and this difference can give them a competitive edge.

Some companies offer the customer a low-priced product without engaging in much product differentiation. Others seek to create something unique about their product so that they satisfy customers' needs in ways that other products cannot. The uniqueness may relate to the physical characteristics of the product, such as quality or reliability, or it may lie in the product's appeal to customers' psychological needs, such as the need for prestige or status.[4] Thus, a Japanese car may be differentiated by its reputation for reliability, and a Corvette or a Porsche may be differentiated by its ability to satisfy customers' needs for status.

■ Customer Groups and Market Segmentation

Market segmentation is the way a company decides to group customers, based on important differences in their needs or preferences, in order to gain a competitive advantage.[5] For example, General Motors groups its customers according to the amount of money they want and can afford to spend to buy a car, and for each group it builds different cars, which range from the low-priced GEO Metro to the high-priced Cadillac Seville.

In general, a company can adopt three alternative strategies toward market segmentation.[6] First, it can choose not to recognize that different groups of customers have different needs and instead adopt the approach of serving the average customer. Second, a company can choose to segment its market into different constituencies and develop a product to suit the needs of each. For example, in a recent catalog, Sony offered twenty-four different 19-inch color television sets, each targeted at a different market segment. Third, a company can choose to recognize that the market is segmented but concentrate on servicing only one market segment, or niche, such as the luxury-car niche pursued by Mercedes-Benz.

Why would a company want to make complex product/market choices and create a different product tailored to each market segment rather than create a single product for the whole market? The answer is that the decision to provide many products for many market niches allows a company to satisfy customers' needs better. As a result, customers' demand for the company's products rises and generates more revenue than would be the case if the company offered just one product for the whole market.[7] Sometimes, however, the nature of the product or the nature of the industry does not allow much differentiation, as is true, for instance, of bulk chemicals or cement.[8] These industries afford little opportunity for obtaining a competitive advantage through product differentiation and market segmentation because there is little opportunity for serving customers' needs and customer groups in different ways. Instead, price is the main criterion by which customers evaluate the product, and the competitive advantage lies with the company that has superior efficiency and can provide the lowest-priced product.

■ Distinctive Competencies

The third issue in business-level strategy is deciding which distinctive competencies to pursue to satisfy customers' needs and customer groups.[9] As we discuss in Chapter 4, there are four ways companies can obtain a competitive advantage: superior efficiency, quality, innovation, and responsiveness to customers. The Four Seasons hotel chain, for example, attempts to do all it can to provide its customers with the highest-quality accommodations and the best customer service possible. In making business strategy choices, a company must decide how to organize and combine its distinctive competencies to gain a competitive advantage. The source of these distinctive competencies is examined at length in Chapter 5.

CHOOSING A GENERIC BUSINESS-LEVEL STRATEGY

Companies pursue a business-level strategy to gain a competitive advantage that allows them to outperform rivals and achieve above-average returns. They can choose from three basic generic competitive approaches: cost leadership, differentiation, and focus, although, as we will see, these can be combined in different ways.[10] These strategies are called *generic* because all businesses or industries can pursue them regardless of whether they are manufacturing, service, or not-for-profit enterprises. Each of the generic strategies results from a company's making consistent choices on product, market, and distinctive competencies—choices that reinforce each other. Table 6.1 summarizes the choices appropriate for each of the three generic strategies.

■ Cost-Leadership Strategy

A company's goal in pursuing a **cost-leadership strategy** is to outperform competitors by doing everything it can to produce goods or services at a cost lower than theirs. Two advantages accrue from a cost-leadership strategy. First, because of its lower costs, the cost leader is able to charge a lower price than its competitors yet make the same level of profit. If companies in the industry charge similar prices for their products, the cost leader still makes a higher profit than its competitors because of its lower costs. Second, if rivalry within the industry increases and companies start to compete on price, the cost leader will be able to withstand competition

TABLE 6.1

Product/Market/Distinctive-Competency Choices and Generic Competitive Strategies

	Cost Leadership	*Differentiation*	*Focus*
Product Differentiation	Low (principally by price)	High (principally by uniqueness)	Low to high (price or uniqueness)
Market Segmentation	Low (mass market)	High (many market segments)	Low (one or a few segments)
Distinctive Competency	Manufacturing and materials management	Research and development, sales and marketing	Any kind of distinctive competency

better than the other companies because of its lower costs. For both these reasons, cost leaders are likely to earn above-average profits. How does a company become the cost leader? It achieves this position by means of the product/market/distinctive-competency choices that it makes to gain a low-cost competitive advantage (see Table 6.1).

Strategic Choices   The cost leader chooses a low level of product differentiation. Differentiation is expensive; if the company expends resources to make its products unique, then its costs rise.[11] The cost leader aims for a level of differentiation not markedly inferior to that of the differentiator (a company that competes by spending resources on product development), but a level obtainable at low cost.[12] The cost leader does not try to be the industry leader in differentiation; it waits until customers want a feature or service before providing it. For example, a cost leader does not introduce stereo sound in television sets. It adds stereo sound only when it is obvious that consumers want it.

The cost leader also normally ignores the different market segments and positions its product to appeal to the average customer. The reason the cost leader makes this choice is, again, that developing a line of products tailored to the needs of different market segments is an expensive proposition. A cost leader normally engages in only a limited amount of market segmentation. Even though no customer may be totally happy with the product, the fact that the company normally charges a lower price than its competitors attracts customers to its products.

In developing distinctive competencies, the overriding goal of the cost leader must be to increase its efficiency and lower its costs compared with its rivals. The development of distinctive competencies in manufacturing and materials management is central to achieving this goal. Companies pursuing a low-cost strategy may attempt to ride down the experience curve so that they can lower their manufacturing costs.

Achieving a low-cost position may also require that the company develop skills in flexible manufacturing and adopt efficient materials-management techniques. (As you may recall, Table 5.1 outlines the ways in which a company's functions can be used to increase efficiency.) Consequently, the manufacturing and materials-management functions are the center of attention for a company pursuing a cost-leadership strategy; the other functions shape their distinctive competencies to meet the needs of manufacturing and materials management.[13] For example, the sales function may develop the competency of capturing large, stable sets of customers' orders. In turn, this allows manufacturing to make longer production runs and so achieve economies of scale and reduce costs. The human resource function may focus on instituting training programs and compensation systems that lower costs by enhancing employees' productivity, and the research and development function may specialize in process improvements to lower the manufacturing costs. We saw in the Opening Case, for example, how E*Trade took advantage of advances in information technology to lower the costs associated with exchanging goods between buyers and sellers. Similarly, Dell Computer uses the Internet to lower the cost of selling its computers—Internet sales now account for more than 30 percent of its sales.

Many cost leaders gear all their strategic product/market/distinctive-competency choices to the single goal of squeezing out every cent of costs to sustain their competitive advantage. A company such as H. J. Heinz is another excellent example of a cost leader. Because beans and canned vegetables do not permit much of a markup, the profit comes from the large volume of cans sold. Therefore, Heinz goes to extraordinary lengths to try to reduce costs—by even one-twentieth of a cent per can—because this will lead to large cost savings and thus bigger profits over the long run. As you will see in the chapters in Part Four on strategy implementation, another source of cost savings in pursuing cost leadership is the design of the organizational structure to match this strategy, since structure is a major source of a company's costs. As we discuss in Chapter 12, a low-cost strategy usually implies tight production controls and rigorous use of budgets to control the production process.

Advantages and Disadvantages   The advantages of each generic strategy are best discussed in terms of Porter's five forces model, which is introduced in Chapter 3.[14] The five forces are threats from competitors, powerful suppliers, powerful buyers, substitute products, and new entrants. The cost leader is protected from *industry competitors* by its cost advantage. Its lower costs also mean that it will be less affected than its competitors by increases in the price of inputs if there are *powerful suppliers* and less affected by a fall in the price it can charge for its products if there are *powerful buyers*. Moreover, since cost leadership usually requires a big market share, the cost leader purchases in relatively large quantities, increasing its bargaining power over suppliers. If *substitute products* start to come into the market, the cost leader can reduce its price to compete with them and retain its market share. Finally, the leader's cost advantage constitutes a *barrier to entry*, since other companies are unable to enter the industry and match the leader's costs or prices. The cost leader is, therefore, relatively safe as long as it can maintain its cost advantage and price is the key for a significant number of buyers.

The principal dangers of the cost-leadership approach lurk in competitors' ability to find ways to produce at lower cost and beat the cost leader at its own game. For instance, if technological change makes experience-curve economies obsolete, new companies may apply lower-cost technologies that give them a cost advantage over the cost leader. The steel minimills discussed in Chapter 5 gained this advantage. Competitors may also draw a cost advantage from labor-cost savings. Foreign competitors in the Third World have very low labor costs; for example, wage costs in the United States are roughly 600 percent more than they are in Malaysia, China, or Mexico. Many U.S. companies now assemble their products abroad as part of their low-cost strategy; many are forced to do so simply to compete.

Competitors' ability to imitate easily the cost leader's methods is another threat to the cost-leadership strategy. For example, the ability of IBM-clone manufacturers to produce IBM-compatible products at costs similar to IBM's (but, of course, to sell them at a much lower price) was a major factor contributing to IBM's troubles.

Finally, the cost-leadership strategy carries a risk that the cost leader, in its single-minded desire to reduce costs, may lose sight of changes in customers' tastes. Thus, a company might make decisions that decrease costs but drastically affect demand for the product. For example, Joseph Schlitz Brewing lowered the quality of its beer's ingredients, substituting inferior grains to reduce costs. Consumers immediately caught on, with the result that demand for the product dropped dramatically. As mentioned earlier, the cost leader cannot abandon product differentiation, and even low-priced products, such as Timex watches, cannot be too inferior to the more expensive watches made by Seiko if the low-cost, low-price policy is to succeed.

■ Differentiation Strategy

The objective of the generic **differentiation strategy** is to achieve a competitive advantage by creating a product (good or service) that is perceived by customers to be *unique* in some important way. The differentiated company's ability to satisfy a customer's need in a way that its competitors cannot means that it can charge a *premium price* (a price considerably above the industry's average). The ability to increase revenues by charging premium prices (rather than by reducing costs as the cost leader does) allows the differentiator to outperform its competitors and gain above-average profits. The premium price is usually substantially above the price charged by the cost leader, and customers pay it because they believe the product's differentiated qualities are worth the difference. Consequently, the product is priced on the basis of what the market will bear.[15]

Thus, Mercedes-Benz cars are much more expensive in the United States than in Europe because they confer more status here. Similarly, a BMW is not a lot more expensive to produce than a Honda, but its price is determined by customers who perceive that the prestige of owning a BMW is something worth paying for. Similarly, Rolex watches do not cost much to produce; their design has not changed very much for years, and their gold content represents only a fraction of the price. Customers, however, buy a Rolex because of the unique quality they perceive in it: its ability to confer status on its wearer. In stereos, the name Bang & Olufsen of Denmark stands out; in jewelry, Tiffany; in airplanes, Learjets. All these products command premium prices because of their differentiated qualities.

Strategic Choices   As Table 6.1 shows, a differentiator chooses a high level of product differentiation to gain a competitive advantage. Product differentiation can be achieved in three principal ways, which are discussed in detail in Chapter 4: quality, innovation, and responsiveness to customers. For example, Procter & Gamble claims that its product quality is high and that Ivory soap is 99.44 percent pure. Maytag stresses reliability and the best repair record of any washer on the market. IBM promotes the quality service provided by its well-trained sales force.

Innovation is very important for technologically complex products, for which new features are the source of differentiation, and many people pay a premium price for new and innovative products, such as a state-of-the-art computer, stereo, or car.

When differentiation is based on responsiveness to customers, a company offers comprehensive after-sales service and product repair. This is an especially important consideration for complex products such as cars and domestic appliances, which are likely to break down periodically. Companies such as Maytag, Dell Computer, and BMW all excel in responsiveness to customers. In service organizations, quality-of-service attributes are also very important. Why can Neiman Marcus, Nordstrom, and Federal Express charge premium prices? They offer an exceptionally high level of service. Similarly, firms of lawyers or accountants stress the service aspects of their operations to clients: their knowledge, professionalism, and reputation.

Finally, a product's appeal to customers' psychological desires can become a source of differentiation. The appeal can be to prestige or status, as it is with BMWs and Rolex watches; to patriotism, as with Chevrolet; to safety of home and family, as with Prudential Insurance; or to value for money, as with Sears and JC Penney. Differentiation can also be tailored to age groups and to socioeconomic groups. Indeed, the bases of differentiation are endless.

A company that pursues a differentiation strategy strives to differentiate it self along as many dimensions as possible. The less it resembles its rivals, the more it is protected from competition and the wider is its market appeal. Thus, BMWs do not offer only prestige. They also offer technological sophistication, luxury, and reliability, as well as good, although very expensive, repair service. All these bases of differentiation help increase sales.

Generally, a differentiator chooses to segment its market into many niches. Now and then a company offers a product designed for each market niche and decides to be a **broad differentiator**, but a company might choose to serve just those niches in which it has a specific differentiation advantage. For example, Sony produces twenty-four models of television, filling all the niches from mid-priced to high-priced sets. However, its lowest-priced model is always priced about $100 above that of its competitors, bringing into play the premium-price factor. You have to pay extra for a Sony. Similarly, although Mercedes-Benz has filled niches below its old high-priced models with its S and C series, until recently it made no attempt to produce a car for every market segment. In 1996, however, it announced that it was planning to introduce a new line of less expensive cars to appeal to a wider market, and analysts were at once concerned that this would affect its differentiated appeal.

Finally, in choosing which distinctive competency to pursue, a differentiated company concentrates on the organizational function that provides the sources of its differentiation advantage. Differentiation on the basis of innovation and technological competency depends on the R&D function, as discussed in Chapter 5. Efforts to improve service to customers depend on the quality of the sales function. A focus on a specific function does not mean, however, that the control of costs is not important for a differentiator. A differentiator does not want to increase costs unnecessarily and tries to keep them somewhere near those of the cost leader. However, since developing the distinctive competency needed to provide a differentiation advantage is often expensive, a differentiator usually has higher costs than the cost leader.

Still, it must control all costs that do not contribute to its differentiation advantage so that the price of the product does not exceed what customers are willing to pay. Since bigger profits are earned by controlling costs and by maximizing revenues, it pays to control costs, though not to minimize them to the point of losing the source of differentiation.[16] The owners of the famous Savoy Hotel in London faced just this problem in the 1990s. The Savoy's reputation has always been based on the incredibly high level of service it offers its customers. Three hotel employees attend to the needs of each guest, and in every room a guest can summon a waiter, maid, or valet by pressing a button at the bedside. The cost of offering this level of service has been so high that the hotel makes less than 1 percent net profit every year.[17] Its owners are trying to find ways to reduce costs to increase profits. However, their problem is that if they reduce the number of hotel staff (the main source of the Savoy's high costs), they may destroy the main source of its differentiated appeal.

Advantages and Disadvantages   The advantages of the differentiation strategy can now be discussed in the context of the five forces model. Differentiation safeguards a company against competitors to the degree that customers develop *brand loyalty* for its products. Brand loyalty is a very valuable asset because it protects the company on all fronts. For example, powerful suppliers are rarely a problem because the differentiated company's strategy is geared more toward the price it can charge than toward the costs of production. Thus, a differentiator can tolerate moderate increases in the prices of its inputs better than the cost leader can. Differentiators are unlikely to experience problems with powerful buyers because the differentiator offers the buyer a unique product. Only it can supply the product, and it commands brand loyalty. Differentiators can pass on price increases to customers because customers are willing to pay the premium price. Differentiation and brand loyalty also create a barrier to entry for other companies seeking to enter the industry. New companies are forced to develop their own distinctive competency to be able to compete, and doing so is very expensive.

Finally, the threat of substitute products depends on the ability of competitors' products to meet the same customers' needs as the differentiator's products and to break customers' brand loyalty. This can happen, as when IBM-clone manufacturers captured a large share of the home computer market, but many people still want an IBM, even though there are many IBM clones available. The issue is, how much of a premium price a company can charge for uniqueness before customers switch products?

The main problems with a differentiation strategy center on the company's long-term ability to maintain its perceived uniqueness in customers' eyes. We have seen in the last ten years how quickly competitors move to imitate and copy successful differentiators. This has happened in many industries, such as computers, autos, and home electronics. Patents and first-mover advantages (the advantages of being the first to market a product or service) last only so long, and as the overall quality of products produced by all companies goes up, brand loyalty declines. The story of the way American Express lost its competitive advantage, told in Strategy in Action 6.1, highlights many of the threats that face a differentiator.

A strategy of differentiation, then, requires the firm to develop a competitive advantage by making choices about its product, market, and distinctive competency that reinforce each other and together increase the value of a good or service in the eyes of consumers. When a product has uniqueness in customers' eyes, differentiators can charge a premium price. However, the disadvantages of a differentiation strategy are the ease with which competitors can imitate a differentiator's product and the difficulty of maintaining a premium price. When differentiation stems from the design or physical features of the product, differentiators are at great risk because imitation is easy. The risk is that over time products such as VCRs or stereos become *commoditylike* products, for which the importance of differentiation diminishes as customers become more price sensitive. When differentiation stems from quality of service or reliability or from any *intangible source*, such as Federal Express's guarantee of fast delivery or the prestige of a Rolex, a company is much more secure. It is difficult to imitate intangibles, and the differentiator can reap the benefits of this strategy for a long time. Nevertheless, all differentiators must watch out for imitators and be careful that they do not charge a price higher than the market will bear.

Cost Leadership *and* Differentiation

Recently, changes in production techniques—in particular, the development of flexible manufacturing technologies (discussed in Chapter 5)—have made the choice between cost-leadership and differentiation strategies less clear-cut. With techno-

Who Wants an American Express Card?

American Express Company's green, gold, and platinum credit cards used to be closely linked with high status and prestige. Obtaining an American Express (AmEx) card required a high income, and obtaining a gold or platinum card required an even higher one. AmEx carefully differentiated its product by using famous people to advertise the virtues—exclusivity and uniqueness—of possessing its card. Consumers were willing to pay the high yearly fee to possess the card, even though every month they were required to pay off the debit balance they had accumulated. AmEx's cards were a premium product that allowed the company to charge both customers and merchants more because it offered quality service and conferred status on the user. For many years, its credit card operation was the money spinner of AmEx's Travel Related Services (TRS) Division, and the company's stock price soared as its profits surpassed $200 million by 1990.[18]

AmEx's differentiated strategy began to suffer in the 1990s, however. Rival companies such as MasterCard and Visa advertised that their cards can be used at locations where AmEx's are not accepted. Moreover, as these companies make clear, anybody can own a MasterCard or a Visa gold card; it is not just for the fortunate elite. In addition, various companies and banks have banded together to offer the consumer many other benefits of using their particular credit cards. For example, banks and airlines formed alliances that allow consumers to use a bank's credit card to accumulate miles toward the purchase of an airline's tickets. By 1995, thousands of other companies—among them, AT&T, General Motors, Yahoo!, Kroger's, and Dell—began issuing their own credit cards, which offer customers savings on their products, often without a yearly fee. The emergence of all these new credit cards broke the loyalty of AmEx customers and shattered the card's unique image. It lost its differentiated appeal and become one more credit card in an overcrowded market. More than 2 million of its users deserted Amex, and the firm lost hundreds of millions of dollars in the early 1990s.

However, Amex strove to fight back and restore profitability to its division. To reduce costs, it laid off more than 5,000 employees in the TRS division, started its own airline mileage program to entice its previous cardholders back, and made its card more available to potential users, such as college students. By lowering the fees it charges merchants, it also increased the number of outlets that accept the card. For example, the card can now be used at Kmart. Furthermore, in 1998, it spent $1.13 billion on marketing and promotion to rebuild its brand name.[19] Finally, in 1999, it announced that it was developing the "ultimate travel card," a new electronic smart card that it intended to make the global standard for travel and entertainment transactions. Among other things, this card permits electronic ticketing and boarding passes, automated car rental check-in, Internet identification and access, and payment functions, which include an electronic purse.[20] In this way, AMEX hopes to promote its differentiated image and once again become the credit card that everyone wants to use.

logical developments, companies have found it easier to obtain the benefits of both strategies. The reason is that the new flexible technologies allow firms to pursue a differentiation strategy at a low cost: that is, companies can combine these two generic strategies.

Traditionally, differentiation was obtainable only at high cost because the necessity of producing different models for different market segments meant that firms had to have short production runs, which raised manufacturing costs. In addition, the differentiated firm had to bear higher marketing costs than the cost leader because it was serving many market segments. As a result, differentiators had higher costs than cost leaders, which produced large batches of standardized products. However, flexible manufacturing may enable a firm pursuing differentiation to manufacture a range of products at a cost comparable to that of the cost leader. The use of robots and flexible manufacturing cells reduces the costs of retooling the production line and the costs associated with small production runs. Indeed, a factor promoting the current trend toward market fragmentation and niche marketing in many consumer goods industries, such as mobile phones, computers, and appliances, is the substantial reduction of the costs of differentiation by flexible manufacturing.

Another way that a differentiated producer may be able to realize significant economies of scale is by standardizing many of the component parts used in its end products. For example, in the 1990s Chrysler began to offer more than twenty different models of cars and minivans to different segments of the auto market. However, despite their different appearances, all twenty models were based on only three different platforms. Moreover, most of the cars used many of the same components, including axles, drive units, suspensions, and gear boxes. As a result, Chrysler was able to realize significant economies of scale in the manufacture and bulk purchase of standardized component parts.

A company can also reduce both production and marketing costs if it limits the number of models in the product line by offering packages of options rather than letting consumers decide exactly what options they require. It is increasingly common for auto manufacturers, for example, to offer an economy auto package, a luxury package, and a sports package to appeal to the principal market segments. Package offerings substantially lower manufacturing costs because long production runs of the various packages are possible. At the same time, the firm is able to focus its advertising and marketing efforts on particular market segments so that these costs are also decreased. Once again, the firm is getting gains from differentiation and from low cost at the same time.

Just-in-time inventory systems, too, can help reduce costs, as well as improve the quality and reliability of a company's products. This benefit is important to differentiated firms, for whom quality and reliability are essential ingredients of the product's appeal. Rolls-Royces, for instance, are never supposed to break down. Improved quality control enhances a company's reputation and thus allows it to charge a premium price, which is one object of TQM programs.

Taking advantage of the new production and marketing developments, some firms are managing to reap the gains from cost-leadership and differentiation strategies simultaneously. Since they can charge a premium price for their products compared with the price charged by the pure cost leader and since they have lower costs than the pure differentiator, they are obtaining at least an equal, and probably a higher, level of profit than firms pursuing only one of the generic strategies. Hence the combined strategy is the most profitable to pursue, and companies are quickly moving to take advantage of the new production, materials-management, and marketing techniques. Indeed, U.S. companies must take advantage of them if they are to regain a competitive advantage, for the Japanese pioneered many of these new developments. This explains why firms such as Toyota and Sony are currently much more profitable than their U.S. counterparts, General Motors and Zenith, respectively. However, American firms such as McDonald's, Motorola, and Ford, which is profiled in Strategy in Action 6.2, are pursuing both strategies simultaneously with great success.

6.2 STRATEGY *in* ACTION

Ford's Difficult Balancing Act

In the 1990s, Alex Trotman, Ford Motor's CEO at the time, faced the problem of how best to compete in an increasingly competitive car industry. On the one hand, Ford, like other large U.S. carmakers, had been forced to find ways to reduce costs to compete effectively against low-priced competitors from Japan and Europe. On the other, Ford had to differentiate its cars and make them stand out so that customers would be attracted to them and would buy them rather than the cars of its rivals.

To reduce costs, Ford forged ahead with a global cost-cutting plan called Ford 2000. The plan included producing very similar models of cars and trucks that could be sold globally to customers in all the countries of the world in which Ford does business. It also meant centralizing all car design activities at five global design centers to reduce costs. Finally, the plan reduced the number of different car platforms (the frames on which the car models are based) and the number of component parts, again to decrease costs. For example, instead of the more than thirty different kinds of car horns, Ford decided to use only three, which it bought in bigger volume from a few manufacturers. Ford projected a $1 billion saving in engineering costs and $11 billion in reduced plant investment costs from this plan.[21]

To make Ford's products unique, Trotman also authorized a radically new program of car styling. Throughout the 1970s and 1980s, Ford had been known for the big, boxy, plain look of its cars, a look that had changed little in decades. From the mid 1980s on, Ford began to restyle all its cars. Trotman's multibillion-dollar program culminated in the radical redesign of the best-selling car in the United States, the Ford Taurus, which Ford launched in the fall of 1995. The accentuated curves and oval shape of the Taurus reflected the redesign of Ford's other cars, such as the Lincoln Continental, the Mustang, and the Mondeo, Ford's first world car.

By 1996, however, it became clear to Trotman and other top Ford executives that the dual push to reduce costs on a global level while launching a whole new series of redesigned global cars was not working. The enormous development costs of the new cars had raised costs dramatically and forced up car prices. The typical well-equipped Taurus, for example, was retailing for more than $20,000, more than $3,000 above the old model, and customers were experiencing sticker shock. In essence, all the cost savings brought about by the Ford 2000 plan were being eaten up by the high costs associated with its push to produce a radically new, differentiated line of cars. By mid 1996 the Honda Accord had once again become the best-selling car in the United States, Ford's profits had plunged 58 percent, its stock price was flat, and many analysts were worried that Ford's new strategy was not working.[22]

In May 1996, Trotman announced a new plan to bring together the cost and differentiation sides of Ford's business-level strategy. He argued that Ford's basic strategy was correct and that all the benefits of the launch of new cars and the saving in costs would be reaped well into the next century. In the short term, however, to boost sales, Ford announced that it would bring out stripped-down models of the Taurus and other cars to reduce the price and attract more customers. In addition, recognizing that its new cars were costing too much to develop, Ford announced that it would close two of its global design centers and further consolidate its design program to reduce development costs. Trotman and his top management team continued to search for ways to align both the cost and differentiation sides of the business-strategy equation to provide Ford's customers with a well-designed car at a price they are willing to pay.

In 1999, a new CEO, Jacques Nasser, took control of the company and announced new moves to further the company's competitive advantage. First, he orchestrated Ford's purchase of Volvo to increase its product range. He also announced a new global push to reduce costs, including a new move to decentralize control to each of Ford's business units so that they might search out innovative ways to streamline their operations and increase efficiency.[23] By the end of the 1990s, Ford's strategy paid off as its sales and profits rose to record levels.

■ Focus Strategy

The third generic competitive strategy, the **focus strategy**, differs from the other two chiefly because it is directed toward serving the needs of a *limited customer group* or *segment*. A focus strategy concentrates on serving a particular market niche, which can be defined geographically, by type of customer, or by segment of the product line.[24] For example, a geographic niche can be defined by region or even by locality. Selecting a niche by type of customer might mean serving only the very rich, the very young, or the very adventurous. Concentrating only on a segment of the product line means focusing only on vegetarian foods, on very fast automobiles, on designer clothes, or on sunglasses. In following a focus strategy, a company is *specializing* in some way.

Once it has chosen its market segment, a company pursues a focus strategy through either a differentiation or a low-cost approach. Figure 6.1 shows these two different kinds of focused strategies and compares them with a pure cost-leadership or differentiation strategy.

In essence, a focused company is a specialized differentiator *or* a cost leader. If a company uses a focused low-cost approach, it competes against the cost leader in the market segments in which it has no cost disadvantage. For example, in local lumber or cement markets, the focuser has lower transportation costs than the low-cost national company. The focuser may also have a cost advantage because it is producing complex or custom-built products that do not lend themselves easily to economies of scale in production and, therefore, offer few experience-curve advantages. With a focus strategy, a company concentrates on small-volume custom products, for which it has a cost advantage, and leaves the large-volume standardized market to the cost leader.

If a company uses a focused differentiation approach, then all the means of differentiation that are open to the differentiator are available to the focused company. The point is that the focused company competes with the differentiator in only one or in just a few segments. For example, Porsche, a focused company, competes against General Motors in the sports car segment of the car market, not in other market segments. Focused companies are likely to develop differentiated product qualities successfully because of their knowledge of a small customer set (such as sports car buyers) or knowledge of a region.

FIGURE 6.1

Types of Business-Level Strategies

	Offers products to only one group of customers	Offers products to many kinds of customers
Offers low-priced products to customers	Focused Cost-Leadership Strategy	Cost-Leadership Strategy
Offers unique or distinctive products to customers	Focused Differentiation Strategy	Differentiation Strategy

6.3   STRATEGY *in* ACTION

Finding a Niche in the Outsourcing Market

Outsourcing occurs when one company contracts with another to have it perform one of the value creation functions for it. Increasingly, many companies are finding it very difficult to keep up with the pace of technological change in the computer software industry and are outsourcing their data-processing needs to specialized software companies. For example, Electronic Data Systems (EDS), founded by Ross Perot, has grown into a $15 billion computer services giant that manages other companies' data-processing operations using its own proprietary software. IBM is another large company that has moved to exploit this developing market; in 1999, it signed many billion-dollar contracts with large computer makers such as Dell and Motorola to be their primary computer parts supplier.

As you can imagine, however, different kinds of organizations, such as universities, banks, insurance agencies, local governments, and utilities, have different kinds of data-processing needs and problems. Consequently, each kind of company requires a specialized kind of software system that can be customized to its specific needs. As a result, it is difficult for any one software company to serve the needs of a wide range of different companies, and the outsourcing market in data processing is very fragmented. Large companies such as EDS have only a small market share; for example, EDS had just 18 percent market share in 1996. Consequently, opportunities abound.

Increasingly, small, specialized software companies have been springing up to manage the needs of particular kinds of clients. An example is Systems & Computer Technology, based in Malvern, Pennsylvania, which went head-to-head with EDS to secure a seven-year $35 million outsourcing contract to serve the data-processing needs of Dallas County. The company has yearly revenues of only $200 million, compared with EDS's $15 billion, but it won the contract because it specializes in servicing the needs of local government and institutions of higher education.[25] It could show Dallas County its twelve ongoing contracts with municipal clients, whereas EDS could offer its experience with only one, a hospital. The focused company won out over the differentiator.

Other focused companies are also springing up—for instance, the Bisys Group and Systematics Company, which serves the needs of banks and universities. It appears that in the data-processing industry, small, focused companies are strong competitors because of their ability to provide specialized, personal service to specific clients in a way that large differentiators cannot.[26] Indeed, EDS has run into problems in the late 1990s because of the emergence of agile, Internet-based competitors that can provide e-commerce solutions at a price much lower than EDS's.[27] In 1999, EDS replaced its CEO and announced the appointment of a new e-business chief to catch up and get back in the game.[28] Only time will tell if it can regain its dominant position in the fast-changing Internet services industry environment.

Furthermore, concentration on a small range of products sometimes allows a focuser to develop innovations faster than a large differentiator can. However, the focuser does not attempt to serve all market segments, for doing so would bring it into direct competition with the differentiator. Instead, a focused company concentrates on building market share in one market segment and, if successful, may begin to serve more and more market segments, chipping away the differentiator's competitive advantage. The emergence of small software companies to take advantage of specialized niches in the outsourcing market, discussed in Strategy in Action 6.3, illustrates how focused companies can obtain a competitive advantage.

Strategic Choices Table 6.1 illustrates the specific product/market/distinctive-competency choices made by a focused company. Differentiation can be high or low because the company can pursue a low-cost or a differentiation approach. As for customer groups, a focused company chooses specific niches in which to compete rather than going for a whole market, as a cost leader does, or filling a large number of niches, as a broad differentiator does. The focused firm can pursue any distinctive competency because it can seek any kind of differentiation or low-cost advantage. Thus, it might find a cost advantage and develop a superior efficiency in low-cost manufacturing within a region. Alternatively, it might develop superior skills in responsiveness to customers, based on its ability to serve the needs of regional customers in ways that a national differentiator would find very expensive.

The many avenues a focused company can take to develop a competitive advantage explain why there are so many small companies in relation to large ones. A focused company has enormous opportunity to develop its own niche and compete against low-cost and differentiated enterprises, which tend to be larger. A focus strategy provides an opportunity for an entrepreneur to find and then exploit a gap in the market by developing an innovative product that customers cannot do without.[29] The steel minimills discussed in Chapter 5 are a good example of how focused companies specializing in one market can grow so efficient that they become the cost leaders. Many large companies started with a focus strategy, and, of course, one means by which companies can expand is to take over other focused companies. For example, Saatchi & Saatchi DFS Compton, a specialist marketing company, grew by taking over several companies that were also specialists in their own markets, such as Hay Associates, the management consultants.

Advantages and Disadvantages   A focused company's competitive advantages stem from the source of its distinctive competency—efficiency, quality, innovation, or responsiveness to customers. The firm is protected from *rivals* to the extent that it can provide a product or service they cannot. This ability also gives the focuser power over its *buyers* because they cannot get the same thing from anyone else. With regard to *powerful suppliers*, however, a focused company is at a disadvantage, because it buys in small volume and thus is in the suppliers' power. However, as long as it can pass on price increases to loyal customers, this disadvantage may not be a significant problem. *Potential entrants* have to overcome the loyalty from customers the focuser has generated, and the development of customers' loyalty also lessens the threat from *substitute products*. This protection from the five forces allows the focuser to earn above-average returns on its investment. Another advantage of the focus strategy is that it permits a company to stay close to its customers and to respond to their changing needs. The difficulty a large differentiator sometimes experiences in managing a large number of market segments is not an issue for a focuser.

Since a focuser produces a small volume, its production costs often exceed those of a low-cost company. Higher costs can also reduce profitability if a focuser is forced to invest heavily in developing a distinctive competency—such as expensive product innovation—in order to compete with a differentiated firm. However, once again, flexible manufacturing systems are opening up new opportunities for focused firms because small production runs become possible at a lower cost. Increasingly, small specialized firms are competing with large companies in specific market segments in which their cost disadvantage is much reduced.

A second problem is that the focuser's niche can suddenly disappear because of technological change or changes in consumers' tastes. Unlike the more generalist differentiator, a focuser cannot move easily to new niches, given its concentration of resources and competency in one or a few niches. For example, a clothing manufacturer that focuses on heavy metal enthusiasts would find it difficult to shift to other segments if heavy metal loses its appeal, and a Mexican restaurant would find it difficult to move to Chinese food if customers' tastes change. The disappearance of niches is one reason that so many small companies fail.

Finally, there is the prospect that differentiators will compete for a focuser's niche by offering a product that can satisfy the demands of the focuser's customers; for example, GM's and Ford's new luxury cars are aimed at Lexus, BMW, and Mercedes-Benz buyers. A focuser is vulnerable to attack and, therefore, has to defend its niche constantly.

Stuck in the Middle

Each generic strategy requires a company to make consistent product/market/distinctive-competency choices to establish a competitive advantage. In other words, a company must achieve a fit among the three components of business-level strategy. Thus, for example, a low-cost company cannot strive for a high level of market segmentation, as a differentiator does, and provide a wide range of products because doing so would raise production costs too much and the company would lose its low-cost advantage. Similarly, a differentiator with a competency in innovation that tries to reduce its expenditures on research and development or one with a competency in responsiveness to customers through after-sales service that seeks to economize on its sales force to decrease costs is asking for trouble because it will lose its competitive advantage as its distinctive competency disappears.

Choosing a business-level strategy successfully means giving serious attention to all elements of the competitive plan. Many companies, through ignorance or through mistakes, do not do the planning necessary for success in their chosen strategy. Such companies are said to be **stuck in the middle** because they have made product/market choices in such a way that they have been unable to obtain or sustain a competitive advantage.[30] As a result, they have no consistent business-level strategy, experience below-average performance, and suffer when industry competition intensifies.

Some stuck-in-the-middle companies may have started out by pursuing one of the three generic strategies but then made wrong resource allocation decisions or experienced a hostile, changing environment. It is very easy to lose control of a generic strategy unless strategic managers keep close track of the business and its environment, constantly adjusting product/market choices to suit changing conditions within the industry. The experience of Holiday Inns in the 1980s, described in Strategy in Action 6.4, shows how a company can become stuck in the middle because of environmental changes.

As the experience of Holiday Inns suggests, there are many paths to being stuck in the middle. Quite commonly, a focuser can get stuck in the middle when it becomes overconfident and starts to act like a broad differentiator. People Express, the defunct airline, exemplified a company in this situation. It started out as a specialized air carrier serving a narrow market niche: low-priced travel on the eastern seaboard. In pursuing this focus strategy based on cost leadership, it was very successful, but when it tried to expand to other geographic regions and began taking over other airlines to gain a larger number of planes, it lost its niche. People Express became one more carrier in an increasingly competitive market, in which it had no special competitive advantage against the other national carriers. The result was financial troubles. People Express was swallowed up by Texas Air and incorporated into Continental Airlines. By contrast, Southwest Airlines, the focused low-cost company, has continued to focus on this strategy and has grown successfully.

Holiday Inns' Rough Ride

The history of the Holiday Inns motel chain is one of the great success stories in U.S. business. Its founder, Kemmons Wilson, vacationing in the early 1950s, found existing motels to be small, expensive, and of unpredictable quality. This discovery, along with the prospect of unprecedented highway travel that would come with the new interstate highway program, triggered a realization: There was an unmet customer need, a gap in the market for quality accommodations. Holiday Inns was founded to meet that need.

From the beginning, Holiday Inns set the standard for offering motel features such as air conditioning and icemakers while keeping room rates reasonable. These amenities enhanced the motels' popularity, and motel franchising, Wilson's invention, made rapid expansion possible. By 1960, Holiday Inns' motels dotted the U.S. landscape; they could be found in virtually every city and on every major highway. Before the 1960s ended, more than 1,000 of them were in full operation, and occupancy rates averaged 80 percent. The concept of mass accommodation had arrived.[31]

By the 1970s, however, the motel chain was in trouble. The service offered by Holiday Inns appealed to the average traveler, who wanted a standardized product (a room) at an average price. In essence, Holiday Inns had been targeting the middle of the hotel-room market. The problem was that travelers were beginning to make different demands on hotels and motels. Some wanted luxury and were willing to pay higher prices for better accommodations and service. Others sought low prices and accepted rock-bottom quality and service in exchange. Although the market had fragmented into different groups of customers with different needs, Holiday Inns was still offering an undifferentiated, average-cost, average-quality product.[32]

Holiday Inns missed the change in the market and thus failed to respond appropriately to it, but the competition did not. Companies such as Hyatt siphoned off the top end of the market, where quality and service sold rooms.

Chains such as Motel 6 and Days Inns captured the basic-quality, low-price end of the market. In between were many specialty chains that appealed to business travelers, families, or self-caterers (people who want to be able to cook in their hotel rooms). Holiday Inns' position was attacked from all sides. The company's earnings declined as occupancy rates dropped drastically, and marginal Holiday Inns motels began to close as competition increased.

Wounded but not dead, Holiday Inns began a counterattack. The original chain was upgraded to suit quality-oriented travelers. At the same time, to meet the needs of different kinds of travelers, Holiday Inns created new hotel and motel chains, including the luxury Crowne Plazas; the Hampton Inns, which serve the low-priced end of the market; and the all-suite Embassy Suites. Holiday Inns tried to meet the demands of the many niches, or segments, of the hotel market that have emerged as customers' needs have changed over time.[33]

These moves were successful in the early 1990s, and Holiday Inns grew to become one of the largest suppliers of hotel rooms in the industry. However, by 1996, it became clear that Holiday Inns was once again losing its differentiated appeal as its revenues and profits fell. A new CEO, Thomas R. Oliver, was brought in to remake Holiday Inns. His solution? To upgrade the Holiday Inns flagship chain with new furniture, food, and a large new advertising budget.

While this worked, other moves to restore profitability created new problems. Oliver also wanted to open other budget chains aimed at the business traveler. However, he wanted to use the Holiday Inns name on them to give them instant name recognition. Many of the regular Holiday Inns franchisees objected, since this would reduce the differentiated appeal of their chain. For example, Oliver plans to open a chain called the Staybridge Suites by Holiday Inns which are tailored to long-term business customers. Whatever the outcome of these efforts, one thing is clear: Holiday Inns needs to remake its image in the highly competitive hotel room industry.

Differentiators, too, can fail in the market and end up stuck in the mid
petitors attack their markets with more specialized or low-cost products that blunt
their competitive edge. This happened to IBM in the large-frame computer market
as personal computers became more powerful and able to do the job of the much
more expensive mainframes. The increasing movement toward flexible manufacturing systems aggravates the problems faced by cost leaders and differentiators. Many
large firms will become stuck in the middle unless they make the investment
needed to pursue both strategies simultaneously. No company is safe in the jungle
of competition, and each must be constantly on the lookout to exploit competitive
advantages as they arise and to defend the advantages it already has.

To sum up, successful management of a generic competitive strategy requires
strategic managers to attend to two main matters. First, they need to ensure that the
product/market/distinctive-competency decisions they make are oriented toward
one specific competitive strategy. Second, they need to monitor the environment so
that they can keep the firm's sources of competitive advantage in tune with changing opportunities and threats.

STRATEGIC GROUPS AND BUSINESS-LEVEL STRATEGY

As implied by the preceding discussion, companies in an industry can pursue many
different kinds of business-level strategies that differ from each other with respect
to factors such as the choice of market segments to serve, product quality, technological leadership, customer service, pricing policy, and advertising policy. As a result, within most industries, strategic groups emerge, each of which is composed of
companies pursuing the same generic strategy.[34] Thus, for example, all the companies inside an industry pursuing a low-cost strategy form one strategic group; all
those seeking to pursue a broad differentiation strategy constitute another strategic
group; and all those pursing a focus-differentiation strategy or a focused low-cost
strategy form yet other strategic groups.

For instance, in the pharmaceutical industry, which we discuss in Chapter 3,
there are two main strategic groups.[35] One group includes such companies as
Merck, Eli Lilly, and Pfizer (see Figure 3.5), which pursue a differentiation strategy
characterized by heavy R&D spending and a focus on developing new proprietary
blockbuster drugs. The other strategic group might be characterized as the *low-cost
strategic group* because it focuses on the manufacture of low-priced generic drugs.
Companies in this group are pursuing a low-cost strategy because they are not investing millions of dollars in R&D, and, as a result, they cannot expect to charge a
premium price.

The concept of strategic groups has a number of implications for business-level
strategy. First, a company's immediate competitors are those companies pursuing
the same strategy in its strategic group. Consumers tend to view the products of
such enterprises as being direct substitutes for each other. Thus, a major threat to a
company's profitability may arise primarily from within its own strategic group, not
necessarily from the other companies in the industry pursuing different generic
business-level strategies. For example, the main competition for Toyota comes from
Honda, Ford, and GM, not from Rolls-Royce.

Second, different strategic groups can have a different standing with respect to each of Porter's five competitive forces because, as already discussed, the five forces affect companies in different ways. In other words, the risk of new entry by potential competitors, the degree of rivalry among companies within a group, the bargaining power of buyers, the bargaining power of suppliers, and the competitive force of substitute products can all vary in intensity among different strategic groups within the same industry.

In the pharmaceutical industry, for example, companies in the differentiation strategic group have historically been in a very powerful position vis-à-vis buyers because their products are patented. Besides, rivalry within this group has been limited to competition to be the first to patent a new drug and achieve a **first-mover advantage**, the advantage that a company that is first to market a new product is said to possess. In contrast, companies in the low-cost group have been in a much weaker position, since they lack patents for their products and buyers can choose among very similar competing generic drugs. Moreover, price competition among the companies in this group has been quite intense, reflecting the lack of product differentiation. Thus, companies within this group have earned somewhat lower returns than companies in the proprietary group.

As discussed in Chapter 3, mobility barriers are factors that inhibit the movement of companies between groups in an industry. The relative height of mobility barriers determines how successfully companies in one group can compete with companies in another. For example, can a differentiation strategic group also pursue a low-cost strategy and thus achieve the low-cost/differentiation strategy previously discussed? To the degree that companies in one group can develop or obtain the functional and financial resources they need to either lower their costs or embark on a major R&D expansion, they may be able to compete successfully with companies in another strategic group. In effect, they have created yet another strategic group—a combined low-cost and differentiation strategic group, which, as we have seen, has the strongest competitive advantage and the greatest ability to earn above-average profits. In fact, the need to pursue a simultaneous global low-cost/differentiation strategy has been the major driving force behind the wave of merger activities that swept through the large drug companies in the 1990s. For example, the U.S. company Upjohn merged with the Swedish company Pharmacia to pursue a global low-cost/differentiation strategy. Thus, the strategic group map in the pharmaceutical industry is changing dramatically as firms fight to survive in the rapidly consolidating global pharmaceutical industry. So far, Pfizer, Merck, and Eli Lilly are still pursuing a pure differentiated strategy, but the other merged companies are moving quickly to reposition themselves as low-cost differentiators.

CHOOSING AN INVESTMENT STRATEGY AT THE BUSINESS LEVEL

We have been discussing business-level strategy in terms of making product/market/distinctive-competency choices to gain a competitive advantage. There is a second major choice to be made at the business level, however—the choice of which type of investment strategy to pursue in support of the competitive strategy.[36]

An **investment strategy** sets the amount and type of resources—human, functional, and financial—that must be invested to gain a competitive advantage.

Generic competitive strategies provide competitive advantages, but they are expensive to develop and maintain. A simultaneous differentiation/cost-leadership strategy is the most expensive, because it requires that a company invest resources not only in functions such as R&D, sales, and marketing to develop distinctive competencies, but also in functions such as manufacturing and materials management to find ways to reduce costs. Differentiation is the next most expensive generic strategy and then cost leadership, which is less expensive to maintain once the initial investment in a manufacturing plant and equipment has been made. Cost leadership does not require such sophisticated research and development or marketing efforts as a differentiation strategy. The focus strategy is cheapest because fewer resources are needed to serve one market segment than to serve the whole market.

In deciding on an investment strategy, a company must evaluate the potential returns from investing in a generic competitive strategy against the cost. In this way, it can determine whether it is likely to be profitable to pursue a certain strategy and how profitability will change as competition within the industry changes. Two factors are crucial in choosing an investment strategy: the strength of a company's position in an industry relative to its competitors and the stage of the industry's life cycle in which the company is competing.[37]

■ Competitive Position

Two attributes can be used to determine the strength of a company's relative competitive position. First, the larger a company's *market share*, the stronger is its competitive position and the greater are the potential returns from future investment. A large market share provides experience-curve economies and suggests that the company has earned brand loyalty. One of the main reasons a wave of mergers has taken place in the pharmaceutical industry, for example, is that the merging of two or more different companies creates a much larger customer base that can be more efficiently served by one global sales force rather than the two global sales forces that previously existed. Thus, large market share may help an organization to lower its costs on a global, as well as a national, basis.

The uniqueness, strength, and number of a company's *distinctive competencies* are the second measure of competitive position. If it is difficult to imitate a company's research and development expertise, its manufacturing and marketing skills, its knowledge of particular customer segments, and its unique reputation or brand name capital, the company's relative competitive position is strong and its returns from the generic strategy increase. Once again, an attempt to build new and improved distinctive competencies has been a principal reason for the merger of pharmaceutical companies. For example, Ciba-Geigy and Sandoz, two giant Swiss pharmaceutical companies, recently merged because they were developing complementary kinds of drugs for treating the same broad range of diseases. By pooling their skills and abilities, they have created the second largest pharmaceutical company in the world, and they hope to use their combined distinctive competencies to compete head-to-head with U.S. companies such as Pfizer and Merck.

In general, companies with the largest market share and the strongest distinctive competencies are in the best position to build and sustain their competitive advantage. A unique distinctive competency leads to increased demand for the company's products, and, as a result of the revenues obtained from larger market share, the company has more resources to invest in developing its distinctive competency.

These two attributes reinforce one another and explain why some companies get stronger and stronger over time. Companies with a smaller market share and little potential for developing a distinctive competency are in a much weaker competitive position.[38]

Life Cycle Effects

The second main factor influencing the investment attractiveness of a generic strategy is the *stage of the industry life cycle*. Each life cycle stage is accompanied by a particular industry environment, presenting different opportunities and threats. Each stage, therefore, has different implications for the investment of resources needed to obtain a competitive advantage. Competition is strongest in the shakeout stage of the life cycle and least important in the embryonic stage, for example. The risks of pursuing a strategy change over time. The difference in risk explains why the potential returns from investing in a competitive strategy depend on the life cycle stage.

Choosing an Investment Strategy

Table 6.2 summarizes the relationship among the stage of the life cycle, the competitive position, and the investment strategy at the business level.

Embryonic Strategy   In the embryonic stage, all companies, weak and strong, emphasize the development of a distinctive competency and a product/market policy. During this stage, investment needs are great because a company has to establish a competitive advantage. Many fledgling companies in the industry are seeking resources to develop a distinctive competency. Thus, the appropriate business-level investment strategy is a **share-building strategy**. The aim is to build market share

TABLE 6.2

Choosing an Investment Strategy at the Business Level

	Strong Competitive Position	*Weak Competitive Position*
Stage of Industry Life Cycle		
Embryonic	Share building	Share building
Growth	Growth	Market concentration
Shakeout	Share increasing	Market concentration or harvest/liquidation
Maturity	Hold-and-maintain or profit	Harvest or liquidation/ divestiture
Decline	Market concentration or harvest (asset reduction)	Turnaround, liquidation, or divestiture

by developing a stable and unique competitive advantage to attract customers who have no knowledge of the company's products.

Companies require large amounts of capital to build research and development competencies or sales and service competencies. They cannot generate much of this capital internally. Thus, a company's success depends on its ability to demonstrate a unique competency to attract outside investors, or venture capitalists. If a company gains the resources to develop a distinctive competency, it will be in a relatively stronger competitive position. If it fails, its only option may be to exit the industry. In fact, companies in weak competitive positions at all stages in the life cycle may choose to exit the industry to cut their losses.

Growth Strategies At the growth stage, the task facing a company is to consolidate its position and provide the base it needs to survive the coming shakeout. Thus, the appropriate investment strategy is the **growth strategy**. The goal is to maintain a company's relative competitive position in a rapidly expanding market and, if possible, to increase it—in other words, to grow with the expanding market. However, other companies are entering the market and catching up with the industry's innovators. As a result, first movers require successive waves of capital infusion to sustain the momentum generated by their success in the embryonic stage. For example, differentiators need to engage in massive research and development to preserve their technological lead, and cost leaders need to invest in state-of-the-art machinery and computers to obtain new experience-curve economies. All this investment is very expensive.

The growth stage is also the time when companies try to consolidate existing market niches and enter new ones so that they can increase their market share. Increasing the level of market segmentation to become a broad differentiator is expensive as well. A company has to invest resources to develop a new sales and marketing competency. Consequently, at the growth stage, companies fine-tune their competitive strategy (which we discuss at length in the next chapter) and make business-level investment decisions about the relative advantages of a differentiation, low-cost, or focus strategy, given financial needs and relative competitive position. For instance, if one company has emerged as the cost leader, some companies may decide to compete head-to-head with it and enter this strategic group, whereas others will not. Instead, they will pursue a growth strategy using a differentiation or focus approach and invest resources in developing unique competencies. As a result, strategic groups start to develop in an industry as each company seeks the best way to invest its scarce resources to maximize its competitive advantage.

Companies must spend a lot of money just to keep up with growth in the market, and finding additional resources to develop new skills and competencies is a difficult task for strategic managers. Consequently, companies in a weak competitive position at this stage engage in a **market concentration strategy** to consolidate their position. They seek to specialize in some way and may adopt a focus strategy and move to a focused strategic group to reduce their investment needs. If very weak, they may choose to exit the industry and sell out to a stronger competitor.

Shakeout Strategies By the shakeout stage, demand increases slowly, and competition by price or product characteristics becomes intense. Companies in strong competitive positions need resources to invest in a **share-increasing strategy** to attract customers from weak companies that are exiting the market. In other words, companies attempt to maintain and increase market share despite fierce competition. The way companies invest their resources depends on their generic strategy.

For cost leaders, because of the price wars that can occur, investment in cost control is crucial if they are to survive the shakeout stage, and they must do all they can to reduce costs. Differentiators in a strong competitive position choose to forge ahead and become broad differentiators. Their investment is likely to be oriented toward marketing, and they are likely to develop a sophisticated after-sales service network. They also widen the product range to match the range of customers' needs. Differentiators in a weak position reduce their investment burden by withdrawing to a focused strategy—the **market concentration strategy**—to specialize in a particular niche or product. Weak companies exiting the industry engage in a **harvest** or **liquidation strategy**, both of which are discussed later in this chapter.

Maturity Strategies   By the maturity stage, a relatively stable strategic group structure has emerged in the industry, and companies have learned how their competitors will react to their competitive moves. At this point, companies want to reap the rewards of their previous investments in developing a generic strategy. Until now, profits have been reinvested in the business, and dividends have been small. Investors in strong companies have obtained their rewards through the appreciation of the value of their stock, because the company has reinvested most of its capital to maintain and increase market share. As market growth slows in the maturity stage, a company's investment strategy depends on the level of competition in the industry and the source of the company's competitive advantage.

In environments where competition is high because technological change is occurring or where barriers to entry are low, companies need to defend their competitive position. Strategic managers need to continue to invest heavily in maintaining the company's competitive advantage. Both low-cost companies and differentiators adopt a **hold-and-maintain strategy** to support their generic strategies. They expend resources to develop their distinctive competency so as to remain the market leaders. For example, differentiated companies may invest in improved after-sales service, and low-cost companies may invest in the latest production technologies, such as robotics.

It is at this point, however, that companies realize they must begin to pursue both a low-cost and a differentiation strategy if they are to protect themselves from aggressive competitors (both at home and abroad) that are watching for any opportunity or perceived weakness to take the lead in the industry. Differentiators take advantage of their strong position to develop flexible manufacturing systems to reduce their production costs. Cost leaders move to start differentiating their products to expand their market share by serving more market segments. For example, Gallo moved from the bulk-wine segment and began marketing premium wines and wine coolers to take advantage of its low production costs. In 1996, Gallo's new premium brand, Falling Leaf, became the best-selling chardonnay in the United States. Similarly, in the fast-food industry in the 1990s, McDonald's experienced intense pressure to lower its costs after Taco Bell began to offer its $.99 tacos. To counter this competitive attack, McDonald's sought new ways to lower its costs and widen its menu.

Historically, however, many companies have felt protected from competition within the industry in the maturity stage. Consequently, they decide to exploit their competitive advantage to the fullest by engaging in a **profit strategy**. A company pursuing this strategy attempts to maximize the present returns from its previous investments. Typically, it reinvests proportionally less in improvement of its functional resources and increases returns to shareholders. The profit strategy works well only as long as competitive forces remain relatively constant, so that the company can maintain the profit margins developed by its competitive strategy. However, it must be alert to threats from the environment and must take care not to become complacent and unresponsive to environmental changes.

All too often market leaders fail to exercise vigilance in managing the environment, imagining that they are impervious to competition. Thus, General Motors felt secure against foreign-car manufacturers until changes in oil prices precipitated a crisis. Kodak, which had profited for so long from its strengths in film processing, was slow to respond to the threat of electronic imaging techniques. Paradoxically, the most successful companies often fail to sense changes in the market. As Strategy in Action 6.5 shows, Gucci is another example of a company that over time failed to pursue a hold-and-maintain strategy to manage the competitive environment.

6.5 STRATEGY *in* ACTION

Gucci Loses Its Grip

Gucci has one of the most readily recognized brand name of all luxury goods companies. Its leather products, such as shoes and handbags, and its clothes are global status symbols worn by the world's wealthiest people. However, the power of its brand name was put at great risk in the middle 1990s because its CEO, Maurizio Gucci, and its designers had lost track of its customers' desires and its industry environment. Unlike competitors such as Versace, Ferragamo, and Giorgio Armani, the company failed to innovate and offer styles that appealed to a new, more casual global audience. To save money as its losses mounted, Gucci reduced its advertising budget. This was a disastrous move, for it sharpened the perception that Gucci was outmoded and out of touch with the luxury market. The company became caught in a vicious cycle downward.

It was saved by a tragedy. Maurizio Gucci's wife arranged to have him gunned down in a Milan doorway in 1995; as a result Domenico De Sole became CEO, and he had a clear vision of what to do. Lacking money because of mounting losses, De Sole named a Texan, Thomas Ford, as Gucci's chief designer and invested all the company's resources in producing a revolutionary, new, Ford-designed line of clothes for both men and women to attract back Gucci's customers. An instant success, the clothes generated much attention and free advertising for Gucci. All of a sudden, customers flocked back to Gucci stores, and, as they bought clothes, they also bought Gucci's signature leather products, such as $500 shoes and handbags. The company's sales and profits increased, and De Sole invested the proceeds in advertising, tripling the advertising budget. He thus changed the vicious cycle downward into a virtuous cycle upward.

Gucci has gone from strength to strength under De Sole and Ford; it regained its status as one of the foremost brand names in the world. In fact, it became so successful that it attracted the attention of LVMH, the French luxury goods company that owns such brand names as Moet et Chandon, and Louis Vuitton. LVMH first bought a significant number of Gucci shares, and it looked like it might try to take over the company; however, De Sole fought back. In October 1999, it appeared that Gucci might take over Fendi, another Italian fashion house, as De Sole strove to keep Gucci under his control. No matter what happens, Gucci's global future looks bright indeed.

Decline Strategies   The decline stage of an industry's life cycle begins when demand for the industry's product starts to fall. There are many possible reasons for decline, including foreign competition and the loss of a company's distinctive competency as its rivals enter with new or more efficient technologies. Thus, a company must decide what investment strategy to adopt in order to deal with new circumstances within its industry. Table 6.2 lists the strategies that companies can resort to when their competitive position is declining.[39]

The initial strategies that companies can adopt are market concentration and asset reduction.[40] With a **market concentration strategy**, a company attempts to consolidate its product and market choices. It narrows its product range and exits marginal niches in an attempt to redeploy its resources more effectively and improve its competitive position. Reducing customer groups served may also allow a company to pursue a focus strategy in order to survive the decline stage. (As noted earlier, weak companies in the growth stage tend to adopt this strategy.) That is what International Harvester did as the demand for farm machinery fell. It now produces only medium-sized trucks under the Navistar name.

An **asset reduction strategy** requires a company to limit or decrease its investment in a business and to extract, or milk, the investment as much as it can. This approach is sometimes called a **harvest strategy** because a company will exit the industry once it has harvested all the returns it can. It reduces to a minimum the assets it employs in the business and forgoes investment for the sake of immediate profits.[41] A market concentration strategy, on the other hand, generally indicates that a company is trying to turn around its business so that it can survive in the long run.

Low-cost companies are more likely to pursue a harvest strategy simply because a smaller market share means higher costs, and they are unable to move to a focus strategy. Differentiators, in contrast, have a competitive advantage in this stage if they can move to a focus strategy.

At any stage of the life cycle, companies that are in weak competitive positions may apply **turnaround strategies**.[42] The questions that a company has to answer are whether it has the resources available to develop a viable business-level strategy to compete in the industry and how much that will cost. If a company is stuck in the middle, for example, it must assess the investment costs of developing a low-cost or differentiation strategy. Perhaps a company pursuing a low-cost strategy has not made the right product or market choices, or perhaps a differentiator has been missing niche opportunities. In such cases, the company can redeploy resources and change its strategy.

Sometimes a company's loss of competitiveness may be due to poor strategy implementation. If so, the company must move to change its structure and control systems rather than its strategy. For example, Dan Schendel, a prominent management researcher, found that 74 percent of the turnaround situations he and his colleagues studied were due to inefficient strategy implementation. The strategy-structure fit at the business level is thus very important in determining competitive strength.[43] We discuss it in detail in Chapter 13.

If a company decides that turnaround is not possible, either for competitive or for life cycle reasons, then the two remaining investment alternatives are **liquidation** and **divestiture**. As the terms imply, the company moves to exit the industry either by liquidating its assets or by selling the whole business. Both can be regarded as radical forms of harvesting strategy, because the company is seeking to get back as much as it can from its investment in the business. Often, however, it can only exit at a loss and take a tax write-off. Timing is important, because the earlier a company senses that divestiture is necessary, the more it can get for its assets. There are many stories about companies that buy weak or declining companies, thinking they can turn them around, and then realize their mistake as the new acquisitions become a drain on their resources. Often the acquired companies have lost their competitive advantage, and the cost of regaining it is too great. However, there have also been spectacular successes, such as that achieved by Lee Iacocca, who engaged in a low-cost strategy at Chrysler that set the scene for its success in the 1990s.

SUMMARY OF CHAPTER

The purpose of this chapter is to discuss the factors that must be considered if a company is to develop a business-level strategy that allows it to compete effectively in the marketplace. The formulation of business-level strategy means matching the opportunities and threats in the environment to the company's strengths and weaknesses by making choices about products, markets, and distinctive competencies, as well as the investments necessary to pursue the choices. All companies, from one-person operations to the strategic business units of large corporations, must develop a business strategy if they are to compete effectively and maximize their long-term profitability. The chapter makes the following main points:

- Business-level strategy refers to the way strategic managers devise a plan of action for using a company's resources and distinctive competencies to gain a competitive advantage over rivals in a market or industry.

- At the heart of developing a generic business-level strategy are choices concerning product differentiation, market segmentation, and distinctive competency.

- The combination of those three choices results in the specific form of generic business-level strategy employed by a company.

- The three pure generic competitive strategies are cost leadership, differentiation, and focus. Each has advantages and disadvantages. A company must constantly manage its strategy; otherwise, it risks being stuck in the middle.

- Increasingly, developments in manufacturing technology are allowing firms to pursue both a cost-leadership and a differentiation strategy and thus obtain the economic benefits of both strategies simultaneously. Technical developments also allow small firms to compete with large firms on an equal footing in particular market segments and hence increase the number of firms pursuing a focus strategy.

- Companies can also adopt two forms of focus strategy: a focused low-cost strategy and a focused differentiation strategy.

- Most industries are composed of strategic groups. Strategic groups are groups of companies pursuing the same or a similar business-level strategy. The members of a strategic group constitute a company's immediate competitors.

- Since different strategic groups are characterized by different opportunities and threats, it may pay a company to switch strategic groups. The feasibility of doing so is a function of the height of mobility barriers.

- The second choice facing a company is an investment strategy for supporting the competitive strategy. The choice of investment strategy depends on two main factors: (1) the strength of a company's competitive position in the industry and (2) the stage of the industry's life cycle.

- The main types of investment strategy are share building, growth, share increasing, hold-and-maintain, profit, market concentration, asset reduction, harvest, turnaround, liquidation, and divestiture.

DISCUSSION QUESTIONS

1. Why does each generic competitive strategy require a different set of product/market/distinctive-competency choices? Give examples of pairs of companies in (a) the computer industry and (b) the auto industry that pursue different competitive strategies.

2. How can companies pursuing a cost-leadership, differentiation, or focus strategy become stuck in the

middle? In what ways can they regain their competitive advantage?

3. Over an industry's life cycle, what investment strategy choices should be made by (a) differentiators in a strong competitive position and (b) differentiators in a weak competitive position?

4. How do technical developments affect the generic strategies pursued by firms in an industry? How might they do so in the future?

5. Why is it difficult for a company in one strategic group to change to a different strategic group?

Practicing Strategic Management

 SMALL-GROUP EXERCISE
Finding a Strategy for a Restaurant

Break up into groups of three to five people, and discuss the following scenario:

You are a group of partners contemplating opening a new restaurant in your city. You are trying to decide what business-level strategy would provide your restaurant with the best competitive advantage to make it as profitable as possible.

1. Create a strategic group of the restaurants in your city and define their generic strategies.

2. Identify which restaurants you think are the most profitable and why.

3. On the basis of this analysis, decide what kind of restaurant you want to open and why.

STRATEGIC MANAGEMENT PROJECT
Module 6

This part of the project focuses on the nature of your company's business-level strategy. If your company operates in more than one business, concentrate either on its core, or most central, business, or on its most important businesses. Using all the information you have collected on your company, answer the following questions:

1. How differentiated are the products/services of your company? What is the basis of their differentiated appeal?

2. What is your company's strategy toward market segmentation? If it segments its market, on what basis does it do so?

3. What distinctive competencies does your company have? (To answer this question, use the information from the module on functional-level strategy in the last chapter.) Is efficiency, quality, innovation, responsiveness to customers, or a combination of these factors the main driving force in your company?

4. Based on these product/market/distinctive-competency choices, what generic business-level strategy is your company pursuing?

5. What are the advantages and disadvantages associated with your company's choice of business-level strategy?

6. How could you improve its business-level strategy to strengthen its competitive advantage?

7. Is your company a member of a strategic group in an industry? If so, which group?

8. What investment strategy is your company pursuing to support its generic strategy? How does this match the strength of its competitive position and the stage of its industry's life cycle?

 ARTICLE FILE 6

Find an example (or several examples) of a company pursuing one or more of the three generic business-level strategies. Which strategy is it? What product/market/distinctive-competency choices is it based on? What are its advantages and disadvantages?

 EXPLORING THE WEB
Visiting the Luxury-Car Market

Enter the Web sites of three luxury-car makers such as Lexus (www.lexususa.com), BMW (www.bmwusa.com), or Cadillac (www.cadillac.com), all of which compete in the same strategic group. Scan the sites to determine the key features of each company's business-level strategy. In what ways are their strategies similar and different? Which of these companies do you think has a competitive advantage over the others? Why?

Search the Web for a company pursuing a low-cost strategy, a differentiation strategy, or both. What product/market/distinctive-competency choices has the company made to pursue this strategy? How successful has the company been in its industry using this strategy?

Liz Claiborne, Inc.

DESIGNER LIZ CLAIBORNE founded her company in 1976 with the help of three partners. By 1990, the company had more than $2 billion in annual sales, and its stock had become a Wall Street favorite. The secret of the company's success was Liz Claiborne's decision to focus on the rapidly growing professional women's segment of the clothing market. By 1976, women were entering the work force in rapidly increasing numbers, but relatively few companies were producing clothes for this segment. Those that did cater to it were very high-priced firms such as Ellen Tracy, Donna Karan, and Anne Klein. Liz Claiborne decided to find out what kinds of clothing professional women wanted. Then she used her considerable talents to create a design team to focus on providing attractively designed clothing for professional women at reasonable prices. In doing so, she tapped an unmet customer need, and the result was dramatic as sales boomed.

To protect her firm's image, Liz Claiborne sold her clothing through established retailers, such as Macy's, Bloomingdale's, and Dillard's. Retailers were required to buy at least $50,000 worth of her collection, and the company controlled the way its suits and dresses were sold in each store—for example, the way clothes were hung and displayed. This attention to detail was part of her strategy of focusing on the upscale professional clothing niche. To promote its growth, the company then started to find new outlets for its clothes and opened a chain of Liz Claiborne boutiques and factory outlets. The Liz Claiborne team also used its design skills to produce a line of men's sportswear and to develop new products such as perfume, shoes, and accessories. By 1988, the Liz Claiborne name had become famous.

However, by 1990 the company's growth had slowed, and the company was in trouble. Competitors, recognizing the niche pioneered by Liz Claiborne, had begun to offer their own lines of professional women's clothing. Expensive designers such as Anne Klein and Donna Karan had new lines of cheaper clothing, priced to compete directly with Liz Claiborne. In addition, low-cost manufacturers had begun to produce clothing lines that undercut Liz Claiborne's prices, often using look-alike designs. This competition from both the top and the bottom end of the market took sales away from the company.

Another problem for Liz Claiborne came from the retail end. Many of the company's best customers, retailers such as Macy's, were in deep financial difficulty and were cutting back on purchases to reduce their debt. At the same time, cost-conscious consumers were buying more and more clothing from stores such as Casual Corner and JC Penney and even from discount stores such as Kmart and Wal-Mart, which do not sell the Liz Claiborne line but carry the low-priced lines of competitors. As customers switched to both cheaper stores and cheaper lines, Liz Claiborne's sales suffered.

Given this deteriorating situation, the company moved quickly to change its strategy. Jerry Chazen, who replaced Liz Claiborne as CEO of the company on her retirement, decided to broaden the company's product line and produce low-cost lines of clothing. To do so and at the same time protect the Liz Claiborne brand name, he bought Russ Togs, a clothing maker that produces three brands of women's clothing: Crazy Horse, The Villager, and Red Horse. As part of the company's new strategy, each of these clothing makers' lines was redesigned and targeted at a different price range in the women's clothing market. For example, Russ Togs, a sportswear line, was upgraded to sell a new line of clothing for 20 to 30 percent less than the Liz Claiborne line. Moreover, this clothing is sold through discount merchandisers such as Wal-Mart and in low-priced department stores such as Sears and JC Penney. In this way, the Liz Claiborne company began to serve the general women's clothing market, not just the professional women's clothing niche.[44]

Top management found that this new strategy bolstered the company's sagging sales and it led to a new period of growth and expansion in the late 1990s. In addition, they have taken the company's existing design skills and capabilities and applied them in other new market segments. Now, however, the company is going head-to-head with low-cost producers and has had to find new ways to reduce costs in order to compete. In 1999, the company reported record operating profits due to a growth in sales in its main product lines. Liz Claiborne has turned the corner and is once again a major player in the volatile women's clothing industry.[45]

Case Discussion Questions

1. What factors led to the success of Liz Claiborne, Inc.?

2. What changes has the company recently made in its strategy? Why?

End Notes

1. www.E*trade.com (1999).

2. Press releases, www.E*trade.com (1999).

3. D. F. Abell, *Defining the Business: The Starting Point of Strategic Planning* (Englewood Cliffs, N.J.: Prentice-Hall, 1980), p. 169.

4. R. Kotler, *Marketing Management*, 5th ed. (Englewood Cliffs, N.J.: Prentice-Hall, 1984); M. R. Darby and E. Karni, "Free Competition and the Optimal Amount of Fraud," *Journal of Law and Economics*, 16 (1973), 67–86.

5. Abell, *Defining the Business*, p. 8.

6. M. E. Porter, *Competitive Advantage: Creating and Sustaining Superior Performance* (New York: Free Press, 1985).

7. R. D. Buzzell and F. D. Wiersema, "Successful Share Building Strategies," *Harvard Business Review* (January–February 1981), 135–144; L. W. Phillips, D. R. Chang, and R. D. Buzzell, "Product Quality, Cost Position, and Business Performance: A Test of Some Key Hypotheses," *Journal of Marketing*, 47 (1983), 26–43.

8. M. E. Porter, *Competitive Strategy: Techniques for Analyzing Industries and Competitors* (New York: Free Press, 1980), p. 45.

9. Abell, *Defining the Business*, p. 15.

10. Although many other authors have discussed cost leadership and differentiation as basic competitive approaches— e.g., F. Scherer, *Industrial Market Structure and Economic Performance*, 2nd. ed. (Boston: Houghton Mifflin, 1980)— Porter's model (Porter, *Competitive Strategy*) has become the dominant approach. Consequently, this model is the one developed here and the discussion draws heavily on his definitions. The basic cost-leadership/differentiation dimension has received substantial empirical support; see, for instance, D. C. Hambrick, "High Profit Strategies in Mature Capital Goods Industries: A Contingency Approach," *Academy of Management Journal*, 26 (1983), 687–707.

11. Porter, *Competitive Advantage*, p. 37.

12. Ibid., pp. 13–14.

13. D. Miller, "Configurations of Strategy and Structure: Towards a Synthesis," *Strategic Management Journal*, 7 (1986), 217–231.

14. Porter, *Competitive Advantage*, pp. 44–46.

15. C. W. Hofer and D. Schendel, *Strategy Formulation: Analytical Concepts* (St. Paul, Minn.: West, 1978).

16. W. K. Hall, "Survival Strategies in a Hostile Environment," *Harvard Business Review*, 58 (1980), 75–85; Hambrick, "High Profit Strategies," pp. 687–707.

17. J. Guyon, "Can the Savoy Cut Costs and Be the Savoy?" *Wall Street Journal*, October 25, 1994, p. B1.

18. L. Nathans Spiro and M. Landler, "Less-Than-Fantastic Plastic," *Business Week*, November 9, 1992, pp. 100–101; Edward Baig, "Platinum Cards: Move over, Amex," *Business-Week*, August 19, 1996, p. 84; John N. Frank, "American Express's Attention Getter," *Credit Card Management* (August 1996), 36–37.

19. L. Beyer, "Breaking Tradition," *Credit Card Management*, 12, (1999) pp. 57–60.

20. R. Rolfe, "The Smart Centurion," *Credit Card Management*, 12 (1999), pp. 132–136.

21. D. McGinn, "For Ford, Making Wall Street Happy Is Job One," *Newsweek*, April 8, 1996, p. 48.

22. O. Suris, "Ford's Earnings Plunged 58% in 1st Quarter," *Wall Street Journal*, April 18, 1996, p. 7.

23. K. Kerwin and K. Naughton, "Remaking Ford," *Business Week*, 1999, October 11, pp. 68–75.

24. Porter, *Competitive Strategy*, p. 46.

25. J. W. Verity, "They Make a Killing Minding Other People's Business," *Business Week*, November 30, 1992, p. 96.

26. M. Willis, "Outsourcing Benefits Administration: A Disciplined Process for Conducting a Thorough Cost-Benefit Analysis," *Compensation & Benefits Management* (Winter 1996), 45–53; J. Gebhart, "Beyond the Information Systems Outsourcing Bandwagon: The Insourcing Response," *Sloan Business Review* (Winter 1996), 177.

27. B. Caldwell and J. Mateyaschuk, "Reviving EDS," *Informationweek*, 742 (1999), 18–19.

28. W. Zellner, "Can EDS Catch Up With the Net," *Business Week*, May 17, 1999, p.112.

29. P. F. Drucker, *The Practice of Management* (New York: Harper, 1954).

30. Porter, *Competitive Advantage*, pp. 44–46.

31. "The Holiday Inns Trip; A Breeze for Decades, Bumpy Ride in the 1980s," *Wall Street Journal*, February 11, 1987, p.1.

32. Holiday Inns, Annual Report, 1985.

33. Bureau of Labor Statistics, *U.S. Industrial Output* (Washington, D.C., 1986); M. Gleason and A. Salomon, "Fallon's Challenge: Make Holiday Inn More 'In'," *Advertising Age*, September 2, 1996, p. 14; J. Miller, "Amenities Range from Snacks to Technology," *Hotel and Motel Management*, July 3, 1996, pp. 38–40.

34. The development of strategic group theory has been a strong theme in the strategy literature. Important contributions include R. E. Caves and M. Porter, "From Entry Barriers to Mobility Barriers," *Quarterly Journal of Economics* (May 1977), 241–262; K. R. Harrigan, "An Application of Clustering for Strategic Group Analysis," *Strategic Management Journal*, 6 (1985), 55–73; K. J. Hatten and D. E. Schendel, "Heterogeneity Within an Industry: Firm Conduct in the U.S. Brewing Industry, 1952–1971," *Journal of Industrial Economics*, 26 (1976), 97–113; M. E. Porter, "The Structure Within Industries and Companies' Performance," *Review of Economics and Statistics*, 61 (1979), 214–227.

35. For details on strategic group structure in the pharmaceutical industry, see K. Cool and I. Dierickx, "Rivalry, Strategic Groups, and Firm Profitability," *Strategic Management Journal*, 14 (1993), 47–59.

36. Hofer and Schendel, *Strategy Formulation*, pp. 102–104.

37. Our discussion of the investment, or posturing, component of business-level strategy draws heavily on Hofer and Schendel's discussion in *Strategy Formulation*, especially Chapter 6.

38. Hofer and Schendel, *Strategy Formulation*, pp. 75–77.

39. K. R. Harrigan, "Strategy Formulation in Declining Industries," *Academy of Management Review*, 5 (1980), 599–604.

40. Hofer and Schendel, *Strategy Formulation*, pp. 169–172.

41. L. R. Feldman and A. L. Page, "Harvesting: The Misunderstood Market Exit Strategy," *Journal of Business Strategy*, 4 (1985), 79–85.

42. C. W. Hofer, "Turnaround Strategies," *Journal of Business Strategy*, 1 (1980), 19–31.

43. Hofer and Schendel, *Strategy Formulation*, p. 172.

44. N. Darnton, "The Joy of Polyester," *Newsweek*, August 3, 1992, p. 61.

45. C. Miller, "Liz Claiborne Throws a Curve with New Brand for Gen Xers," *Marketing News*, July 1, 1996, pp. 1, 10; E. Underwood, "Claiborne Back in Media," *Brandweek*, January 15, 1996, p. 2.

7 Competitive Strategy and the Industry Environment

OPENING CASE

How eBay Revolutionized the Auction Business

IN THE 1990S, many entrepreneurs have tried to use new information technologies, and particularly the Internet, to provide new or improved services to customers. Their goal in exploring the potential of the new technology was to find ways of gaining a competitive advantage over existing firms in a particular industry environment. Nowhere has this been more evident than in the auction industry.

Traditionally, auctions have been events bringing buyers and sellers face to face to determine the fair market value of a product. Auction houses range from the most prestigious ones, such as Sotheby's and Christie's, which sell fine art and antiques, to small local auction companies that sell the contents of someone's house.

In the early 1990s, Pierre Omidyar had an idea for a new kind of auction company, an on-line one, which he believed would revolutionize the selling of all kinds of products—not just fine arts and antiques, but any kind of collectible, from cars to Beanie Babies—by bringing buyers and sellers together through the Internet. He left his job at Microsoft and began to write the software that would provide the platform for an on-line auction service. The result was eBay, launched on Labor Day 1995.[1]

On the eBay Web site, sellers are able to electronically describe their product, post a photograph, and set an initial price, which buyers can then bid up. The highest bidder wins. The company charges a modest fee to list the product plus a low percentage of the final sales price. Sellers have the advantage that their product appears before buyers in every part of the United States, as well as abroad—wherever someone has a computer and can log on to eBay's on-line auction site. Buyers enjoy access to a huge array of merchandise, which can be quickly scanned by using the appropriate keywords on eBay's search engine.

Thus, eBay provides a low-cost forum where buyers and sellers can meet to buy and sell products. The company makes its money from the sheer volume of products that it sells. Every day, millions are listed, so that even with low fees eBay is able to generate high profits.

As you can imagine, eBay's low-cost approach has generated many imitators; after all, it is relatively easy to write a software program and develop an on-line auction site. However, eBay's early start has also given it another major competitive advantage. As the first in the on-line auction business, it has developed a loyal following of both buyers and sellers, who will not switch to other on-line auction companies even when they provide the service for free. By 1999, for instance, Yahoo! and MSN, and hundreds of small specialized companies, had developed their own on-line auction businesses and decided to charge users nothing for their services. Most of them, however, including Yahoo!'s auction site, have not attracted many buyers and sellers. The reason is simple. Sellers know that eBay's site attracts many more buyers than does Yahoo!'s and consequently that they are likely to obtain the highest price there; and eBay buyers know that they will find the greatest selection at that site and so focus their search

there. Thus, besides achieving a low-cost competency, eBay has developed a substantial reputation, which has given it a differentiation advantage as well.

Other on-line companies, however, are not willing to give away the lucrative on-line auction market to eBay; they are searching for new ways to fight back. In June 1999, for example, bookseller Amazon.com announced that it was forming an alliance with Sotheby's to create an upmarket on-line auction service. Other companies have also been seeking partners. In October 1999, Yahoo!, Amazon.com, and others announced that they were banding together to combine their auction businesses and offer a credible alternative to eBay.[2]

After this announcement, eBay's price on the stock market fell. It had soared several thousand percent because investors thought that eBay's strategy had given it a sustainable competitive advantage over its rivals. Through his innovative use of new information technology, Omidyar had brought increased value for millions of buyers and sellers and in the meantime had created more than $1 billion of value for himself in his eBay stock. Now the question arises whether eBay can maintain this value.

OVERVIEW

Chapter 6 examines the different kinds of generic business-level strategies that companies can adopt to obtain a competitive advantage and outperform their rivals. If strategic managers do succeed in developing a successful generic business-level strategy, they face still another crucial task: choosing an appropriate competitive strategy to position their company so that it can sustain its competitive advantage over time in different kinds of industry environments. That is the issue we explore in this chapter.

First, we focus on how companies in *fragmented industries* try to develop competitive strategies that support their generic strategies. Second, we consider the challenges of developing a competitive advantage in *embryonic* and *growth industries*. Third, we probe the nature of competitive relations in *mature industries*. We concentrate here on how a set of companies that have been pursuing successful generic competitive strategies (such as the major burger chains) can use a variety of competitive tactics and gambits to manage the high level of competitive interdependence found in such industries. Finally, we assess the problems of managing a company's generic competitive strategy in *declining industries*, in which rivalry between competitors is high because market demand is slowing or falling. By the end of this chapter, you will understand how the successful pursuit of a generic strategy depends on the selection of the right competitive strategy to manage the industry environment.

STRATEGIES IN FRAGMENTED INDUSTRIES

A **fragmented industry** is one consisting of a large number of small and medium-sized companies. The video-rental industry, for example, is still very fragmented, as is the restaurant industry, the health-club industry, and the legal-services industry. There are several reasons why an industry may consist of many small companies rather than a few large ones.[3] Some industries offer few economies of scale, and so large companies do not have an advantage over smaller enterprises. Indeed, in some industries there are diseconomies of scale. For instance, many home buyers prefer to deal with local real estate agencies, which they perceive as having better local knowledge than national chains. Similarly, in the restaurant business, many customers prefer the unique style of a local restaurant. Because they lack economies of scale, fragmented industries are often characterized by low barriers to entry (and new entries keep the industry fragmented). That is the situation in the restaurant industry, since the costs of opening a restaurant are very moderate and can be borne by a single entrepreneur. High transportation costs, too, can keep an industry fragmented, for regional production may be the only efficient way to satisfy customers' needs, as in the cement business. Finally, an industry may be fragmented because customers' needs are so specialized that only small job lots of products are required, and thus there is no room for a large mass-production operation to satisfy the market.

For some fragmented industries, these factors dictate the competitive strategy to pursue, and the *focus strategy* stands out as the principal choice. Companies may specialize by customer group, customer need, or geographic region; consequently, many small specialty companies operate in local or regional market segments. All kinds of custom-made products—furniture, clothing, hats, boots, and so on—fall into this category, as do all small service operations that cater to particular customers' needs, such as laundries, restaurants, health clubs, and furniture-rental stores. Indeed, service companies make up a large proportion of the enterprises in fragmented industries because they provide personalized service to clients and, therefore, need to be responsive to their needs.

Strategic managers, however, are eager to gain the cost advantages of pursuing a low-cost strategy or the sales/revenue-enhancing advantages of differentiation by circumventing the problems of a fragmented industry. Because returns from consolidating a fragmented industry are often huge, during the last thirty years many companies have developed competitive strategies to achieve such consolidation. Among these companies are the large retailers Wal-Mart, Sears, and JC Penney; fast-food chains such as McDonald's and Burger King; video-rental chains such as Blockbuster Entertainment with its Blockbuster Video stores; and chains of health clubs, repair shops, and even lawyers and consultants. To grow, consolidate their industries, and become the industry leaders, these companies utilize three main competitive strategies: (1) chaining, (2) franchising, (3) horizontal merger and (4) using the Internet.

Chaining

Companies such as Wal-Mart and Midas International pursue a **chaining** strategy to obtain the advantages of cost leadership. They establish networks of linked merchandising outlets so interconnected that they function as one large business entity. The amazing buying power that these companies possess through their nationwide store chains allows them to negotiate large price reductions with their suppliers, which in turn promotes their competitive advantage. They overcome the barrier of high transportation costs by establishing sophisticated regional distribution centers, which can economize on inventory costs and maximize responsiveness to the needs of stores and customers. (This is Wal-Mart's specialty.) Last but not least, they realize economies of scale from sharing managerial skills across the chain and from advertising nationally rather than locally.

Franchising

For differentiated companies in fragmented industries, such as McDonald's or Century 21 Real Estate, the competitive advantage comes from a business strategy that employs franchise agreements. In **franchising** the franchisor (parent) grants the franchisee the right to use the parent's name, reputation, and business skills at a particular location or area. If the franchisee also acts as the manager, he or she is strongly motivated to control the business closely and make sure that quality and standards are consistently high so that customers' needs are always satisfied. Such motivation is particularly critical in a strategy of differentiation, for which a company's ability to maintain its uniqueness is very important. Indeed, one reason industries fragment is the difficulty of controlling the many small outlets that must be operated while at the same time retaining their uniqueness. Franchising solves this problem.[4] In addition, franchising lessens the financial burden of swift expansion and so permits rapid growth of the company. Finally, a differentiated large company can reap the advantages of large-scale advertising, as well as economies in purchasing, management, and distribution, as McDonald's does very efficiently. Indeed, McDonald's is able to pursue cost leadership and differentiation simultaneously only because franchising allows costs to be controlled locally and differentiation to be achieved by marketing on a national level.

Horizontal Merger

Companies such as Anheuser-Busch, Dillard Department Stores, and Blockbuster Entertainment have been choosing a business-level strategy of **horizontal merger** to consolidate their respective industries. For example, Dillard arranged the merger of regional store chains in order to form a national company. By pursuing horizontal merger, companies are able to obtain economies of scale or secure a national market for their product. As a result, they are able to pursue a cost-leadership or a differentiation strategy, or both.

Using the Internet

The latest means by which companies have been able to consolidate a fragmented industry is the Internet, and eBay, profiled in the Opening Case, is a good example of this approach. Before eBay, the auction business was extremely fragmented, and local auctions in cities were the usual way in which people could dispose of their antiques and collectibles. With the advent of eBay, sellers using it know that they are getting wide visibility for their collectibles, and therefore are likely to receive a higher price for their product. Amazon.com's success in the book market has led to the closing of many small bookstores, which simply cannot compete either by price or selection. The trend toward using the Internet seems likely to further consolidate even relatively oligopolistic industries.

The challenge in a fragmented industry is to choose the most appropriate means—franchising, chaining, horizontal merger, or Internet—of overcoming a fragmented market so that the competitive advantages associated with the different business-level strategies can be realized. It is difficult to think of any major service activities—from consulting and accounting firms to businesses satisfying the smallest consumer need, such as beauty parlors and car-repair shops—that have not been merged or consolidated by chaining, franchising, and now by the Internet.

STRATEGIES IN EMBRYONIC AND GROWTH INDUSTRIES

Embryonic industries are typically created by the innovations of pioneering companies that become the first movers in a new market. For example, Apple singlehandedly created the market for personal computers, Xerox created the market for photocopiers, and McDonald's created the market for fast food. In most cases, the pioneering company can initially earn enormous profits from its innovation because it is the only company in the industry for a time. For example, before the entry of IBM into the personal computer market in 1981, Apple enjoyed a virtual monopoly. Similarly, during the seventeen years before its patents expired, Xerox enjoyed a monopoly in the market for photocopiers, earning enormous profits as a result.[5]

However, innovators' high profits also attract potential imitators and second movers, as the companies that enter the market later are known. Typically, second movers enter during the growth stage of an industry and may cause the pioneering, first-mover company to lose its commanding competitive position. Figure 7.1 shows how the profit rate enjoyed by the innovator in an embryonic industry can decline as imitators crowd into the market during its growth stage. Thus, Apple's onetime monopoly position was competed away as hordes of other personal computer makers entered the market in the early and mid 1980s, trying to share in Apple's success. Once its patents expired, Xerox, too, faced many imitators, and some of them, such as Canon and Ricoh, were ultimately very successful in the photocopier market. In the fast-food market, the early success of McDonald's drew imitators, including Burger King, Wendy's, and Foodmaker, with its Jack-in-the-Box restaurants.

Although their market share has declined since their early days, companies such as Apple, Xerox, and McDonald's are still major competitors. Other early innovators were not so lucky. For example, in the mid 1970s, EMI pioneered the development of the CAT scanner. Widely regarded as the most important advance in radiology since the x-ray, the CAT scanner takes three-dimensional x-ray pictures of the body. Despite being the pioneer, however, EMI soon saw imitators such as General Electric capture the market. EMI itself withdrew from the CAT market in the early 1980s. Similarly, Bowman invented the pocket calculator, only to see Texas Instruments reap the long-run rewards of the innovation, and Royal Crown Cola pioneered the introduction of diet colas, but it was Coca-Cola and PepsiCo that made

FIGURE 7.1

How an Innovator's
Profits Can Be
Competed Away

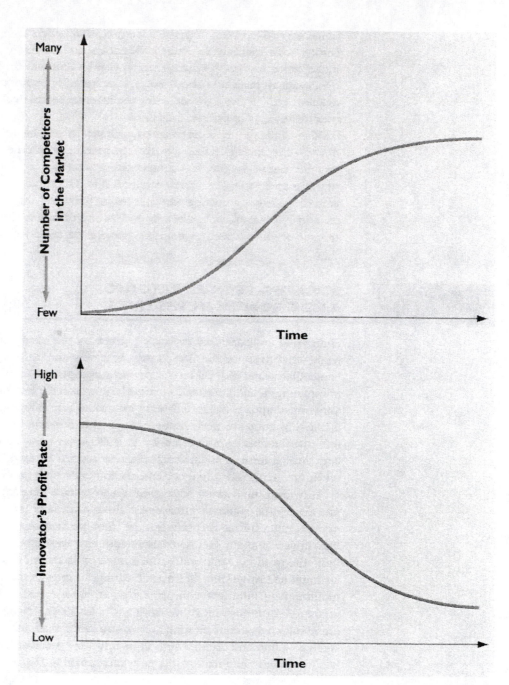

enormous profits from the concept. Thus, first movers often lose out to second
movers as competition in an industry becomes intense.

Given the inevitability of imitation, the key issue for an innovating company in
an embryonic industry is how to exploit its innovation and build an enduring long-
run competitive advantage based on low cost or differentiation. Three strategies are
available to the company: (1) to develop and market the innovation itself; (2) to develop and market the innovation jointly with other companies through a strategic

alliance or joint venture; and (3) to license the innovation to others and let them develop the market.

The optimal choice of strategy depends on the answers to three questions. First, does the innovating company have the *complementary assets* to exploit its innovation and obtain a competitive advantage? Second, how difficult is it for imitators to copy the company's innovation—in other words, what is the *height of barriers to imitation?* And third, are there *capable competitors* that could rapidly imitate the innovation? Before we discuss the optimal choice of innovation strategy, we need to examine the answers to these three questions.

▨ Complementary Assets

Complementary assets are those required to exploit a new innovation and gain a competitive advantage successfully.[6] Among the most important complementary assets are competitive manufacturing facilities capable of handling rapid growth in customers' demand while maintaining high product quality. State-of-the-art manufacturing facilities enable the innovator to move quickly down the experience curve without encountering production bottlenecks and/or problems with the quality of the product. The inability to satisfy demand because of these problems, however, creates the opportunity for imitators to enter the marketplace. For example, Compaq Computer was able to grow rapidly in the market for MS-DOS personal computers during the 1990s at the expense of the product's pioneer, IBM, largely because IBM lacked what Compaq possessed: the state-of-the-art manufacturing facilities to build low-cost computers.

Complementary assets also include marketing know-how, an adequate sales force, access to distribution systems, and an after-sales service and support network. Furthermore, the Internet is making it easier for small companies to develop a nationwide presence since it offers a low-cost way to advertise and sell products to customers. All these assets can help an innovator build brand loyalty. They also help the innovator achieve market penetration more rapidly.[7] In turn, the resulting increases in volume facilitate more rapid movement down the experience curve.

Developing such complementary assets can be very expensive, and embryonic companies often need large infusions of capital for this purpose. That is the reason first movers often lose out to late movers that are large, successful companies, often established in other industries, with the resources to develop a presence in the new industry quickly. Hewlett-Packard and 3M exemplify companies that can move quickly to capitalize on the opportunities arising when other companies open up new product markets, such as compact disks or floppy disks. For instance, Hewlett-Packard began producing personal computers that competed directly with those of Compaq, IBM, and Apple, the early movers.

▨ Height of Barriers to Imitation

Barriers to imitation are introduced in Chapter 4, in the discussion of the durability of competitive advantage. As you may recall, **barriers to imitation** are factors that prevent rivals from imitating a company's distinctive competencies. Barriers to imitation also prevent rivals, particularly second or late movers, from imitating a company's innovation. Although ultimately any innovation can be copied, the higher the barriers, the longer it takes for rivals to imitate.

Barriers to imitation give an innovator time to establish a competitive advantage and build more enduring barriers to entry in the newly created market. Patents, for example, are among the most widely used barriers to imitation. By protecting its photocopier technology with a thicket of patents, Xerox was able to delay any significant imitation of its product for seventeen years. However, patents are often easy to "invent around." For example, one study found that this happened to 60 percent of patented innovations within four years.[8] If patent protection is weak, a company might try to slow imitation by developing new products and processes in secret. The most famous example of this approach is Coca-Cola, which has kept the formula for Coke a secret for generations. But Coca-Cola's success in this regard is an exception. A study of 100 companies has estimated that proprietary information about a company's decision to develop a major new product or process is known to its rivals within about twelve to eighteen months of the original development decision.[9]

■ Capable Competitors

Capable competitors are companies that can move quickly to imitate the pioneering company. Competitors' capability to imitate a pioneer's innovation depends primarily on two factors: (1) R&D skills and (2) access to complementary assets. In general, the greater the number of capable competitors with access to the R&D skills and complementary assets needed to imitate an innovation, the more rapid is imitation likely to be.

In this context, R&D skills refer to the ability of rivals to reverse-engineer an innovation in order to find out how it works and quickly develop a comparable product. As an example, consider the CAT scanner. GE bought one of the first CAT scanners produced by EMI, and its technical experts reverse-engineered it. Despite the product's technological complexity, GE developed its own version of it, which allowed GE to imitate EMI quickly and ultimately to replace EMI as the major supplier of CAT scanners.

With regard to complementary assets, the access that rivals have to marketing, sales know-how, or manufacturing capabilities is one of the key determinants of the rate of imitation. If would-be imitators lack critical complementary assets, not only do they have to imitate the innovation, but they may also have to imitate the innovator's complementary assets. This is expensive, as AT&T discovered when it tried to enter the personal computer business in 1984. AT&T lacked the marketing assets (sales force and distribution systems) necessary to support personal computer products. The lack of these assets and the time it takes to build them partly explain why four years after it originally entered the market AT&T had lost $2.5 billion and still had not emerged as a viable contender.

■ Three Innovation Strategies

The way in which these three factors—complementary assets, height of barriers to imitation, and the capability of competitors—influence the choice of innovation strategy is summarized in Table 7.1. The competitive strategy of *developing and marketing the innovation alone* makes most sense when (1) the innovator has the complementary assets necessary to develop the innovation, (2) the barriers to imitating a new innovation are high, and (3) the number of capable competitors is limited. Complementary assets allow rapid development and promotion of the

TABLE 7.1

Strategies for Profiting from Innovation

Strategy	Does Innovator Have All Required Complementary Assets?	Likely Height of Barriers to Imitation	Number of Capable Competitors
Going it alone	Yes	High	Few
Entering into alliance	No	High	Limited
License innovation	No	Low	Many

innovation. High barriers to imitation buy the innovator time to establish a competitive advantage and build enduring barriers to entry through brand loyalty and/or experience-based cost advantages. The fewer the capable competitors, the less likely it is that any one of them will succeed in circumventing barriers to imitation and quickly imitating the innovation. The availability of the Internet makes this strategy more viable since a company can promote an innovation much more easily and inexpensively.

The competitive strategy of *developing and marketing the innovation jointly with other companies through a strategic alliance or joint venture* makes most sense when (1) the innovator lacks complementary assets, (2) barriers to imitation are high, and (3) there are several capable competitors. In such circumstances, it makes sense to enter into an alliance with a company that already has the complementary assets, in other words, with a capable competitor. Theoretically, such an alliance should prove to be mutually beneficial, and each partner can share in high profits that neither could earn on its own. The attempt by Body Shop International, described in Strategy in Action 7.1, to go it alone in the effort to enter the U.S. market rather than to form an alliance with U.S. partners illustrates the benefit of alliances in quickly exploiting an innovation.

The third strategy, *licensing,* makes most sense when (1) the innovating company lacks the complementary assets, (2) barriers to imitation are low, and (3) there are many capable competitors. The combination of low barriers to imitation and many capable competitors makes rapid imitation almost certain. The innovator's lack of complementary assets further suggests that an imitator will soon capture the innovator's competitive advantage. Given these factors, since rapid diffusion of the innovator's technology through imitation is inevitable, by licensing out its technology the innovator can at least share in some of the benefits of this diffusion.[11]

STRATEGY IN MATURE INDUSTRIES

As a result of fierce competition in the shakeout stage, an industry becomes consolidated, and so a mature industry is often dominated by a small number of large companies. Although a mature industry may also contain many medium-sized

STRATEGY *in* ACTION

The Body Shop Opens Too Late

In 1976, Anita Roddick, a former flower child and the owner of a small hotel in southern England, had an idea. Rising sentiment against the use of animals in testing cosmetics and a wave of environmentalism that focused on "natural" products gave her the idea for a range of skin creams, shampoos, and lotions made from fruit and vegetable oils rather than animal products. Her products, moreover, would not be tested on animals. Roddick began to sell her line of new products from a small shop in Brighton, a seaside town, and the results surpassed her wildest expectations. Her line of cosmetics was an instant success, and to capitalize on it, she began to franchise the right to open stores called The Body Shop to sell her products. By 1993, there were more than 700 of these stores around the world, with combined sales of more than $250 million.

In Britain and Europe, to speed the growth of the company, Roddick mainly franchised her stores through alliances with other individuals and companies. In her push to enter the U.S. market in 1988, however, she decided to own her stores and forgo the rapid expansion that franchising would have made possible. This was a costly mistake. Large U.S. cosmetic companies such as Estée Lauder and entrepreneurs such as Leslie Wexner of The Limited were quick to see the opportunities that Roddick had opened up in this rapidly growing market segment. They moved fast to imitate her product lines, which was not technically difficult to do, and began to market their own natural cosmetics. For example, Estée Lauder

brought out its Origins line of cosmetics, and Wexner opened the Bath and Body Works to sell his own line of natural cosmetics. Both these ventures have been very successful and have gained a large share of the market.

Realizing the competitive threat from imitators, in 1990 Roddick began to move quickly to franchise The Body Shop in the United States, and by 1993 more than 150 stores had opened. Although the stores have been successful, the delay in opening them gave Roddick's competitors the opportunity to establish their own brand names and robbed her enterprise of the uniqueness that its products enjoy throughout Europe. Given that the United States is by far the world's biggest cosmetics market and natural cosmetics are its fastest-growing segment, this mistake cost Body Shop billions of dollars in lost revenues.

Roddick acknowledged that her strategy was a mistake; however, during the 1990s, she failed to energize her company, and in 1998 a new CEO, Patrick Gourmay, took over. He moved quickly to revive flagging sales by opening new stores at a very fast rate, by increasing the level of product innovation, and by using the Internet to raise sales. In 1999, for example, he was aiming for product innovation growth of 60 percent as opposed to the 25 percent that the company had managed earlier.[10] Gourmay has obviously learnt the lesson well: when an innovation is easy to imitate and there are many capable competitors, a company must do all it can to speed the development and sale of a new product.

companies and a host of small specialized ones, the large companies determine the nature of the industry's competition because they can influence the five competitive forces. Indeed, these are the companies that developed the most successful generic business-level strategies in the industry.

By the end of the shakeout stage, strategic groups of companies pursuing similar generic competitive strategies have emerged in the industry. As we discuss in Chapter 6, all the companies pursuing a low-cost strategy can be viewed as composing one strategic group; all those pursuing differentiation constitute another; and the focusers form a third. Companies in an industry constantly analyze each other's business-level strategies, and they know that if they move to change their strategies, their actions are likely to stimulate a competitive response from rivals in their strategic group and from companies in other groups that may be threatened by the change in strategy.

For example, a differentiator that starts to lower its prices because it has adopted a more cost-efficient technology not only threatens other differentiators in its group, but also threatens low-cost companies, which see their competitive edge being eroded. These other companies may now change their strategies in response—most likely by reducing their prices, too, as is currently happening in the personal computer industry. Thus, the way one company changes or fine-tunes its business-level strategy over time affects the way the other companies in the industry pursue theirs. Hence, by the mature stage of the industry life cycle, companies have learned just how *interdependent* their strategies are.

In fact, the main challenge facing companies in a mature industry is to adopt a competitive strategy that *simultaneously* allows each individual company to protect its competitive advantage and preserves industry profitability. No generic strategy will generate above-average profits if competitive forces in an industry are so strong that companies are at the mercy of each other, potential entrants, powerful suppliers, powerful customers, and so on. As a result, in mature industries, competitive strategy revolves around understanding how large companies try *collectively* to reduce the strength of the five forces of industry competition to preserve both company and industry profitability.

Interdependent companies can help protect their competitive advantage and profitability by adopting competitive moves and tactics to reduce the threat of each competitive force. In the next sections, we examine the various price and nonprice competitive moves and tactics that companies use—first, to deter entry into an industry, and second, to reduce the level of rivalry within an industry. We then discuss methods that companies can employ to gain more control over suppliers and buyers.

STRATEGIES TO DETER ENTRY IN MATURE INDUSTRIES

Companies can utilize three main methods to deter entry by potential rivals and hence maintain and increase industry profitability. As Figure 7.2 shows, these methods are product proliferation, price cutting, and excess capacity.

FIGURE 7.2

Strategies for Deterring Entry of Rivals

Product Proliferation

Companies seldom produce just one product. Most commonly, they produce a range of products aimed at different market segments so that they have broad product lines. Sometimes, to diminish the threat of entry, companies expand the range of products they make to fill a wide variety of niches. Such expansion creates a barrier to entry because potential competitors now find it harder to break into an industry in which all the niches are filled.[12] This strategy of pursuing a broad product line to deter entry is known as **product proliferation.**

Because the large U.S. carmakers were so slow to fill the small-car niches (they did *not* pursue a product proliferation strategy), they were vulnerable to the entry of the Japanese into these market segments in the United States. American carmakers had no excuse for this situation, for in their European operations they had a long history of small-car manufacturing. They should have seen the opening and filled it ten years earlier, but their view was that small cars meant small profits. In the breakfast-cereal industry, on the other hand, competition is based on the production of new kinds of cereal to satisfy or create new desires by consumers. Thus, the number of breakfast cereals proliferates, making it very difficult for prospective entrants to attack a new market segment.

Figure 7.3 indicates how product proliferation can deter entry. It depicts product space in the restaurant industry along two dimensions: (1) atmosphere, which ranges from fast food to candlelight dining; and (2) quality of food, which ranges from average to gourmet. The circles represent product spaces filled by restaurants located along the two dimensions. Thus, McDonald's is situated in the average quality/fast-food area. A gap in the product space gives a potential entrant or an existing

FIGURE 7.3

Product Proliferation in the Restaurant Industry

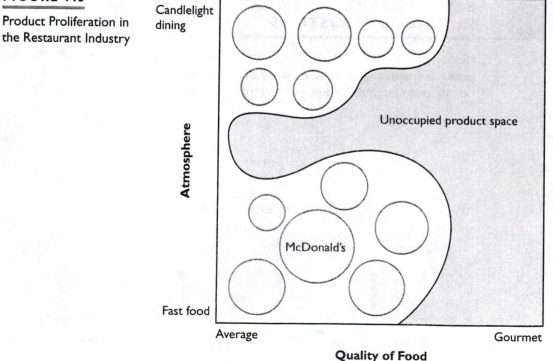

rival an opportunity to enter the market and make inroads. The shaded unoccupied product space represents areas where new restaurants can enter the market. Filling all the product spaces, however, creates a barrier to entry and makes it much more difficult for a new company to gain a foothold in the market and differentiate itself.

▩ Price Cutting

In some situations, pricing strategies involving **price cutting** can be used to deter entry by other companies, thus protecting the profit margins of companies already in an industry. One price-cutting strategy, for example, is to charge a high price initially for a product and seize short-term profits but then to cut prices aggressively in order to build market share *and* deter potential entrants simultaneously.[13] The incumbent companies thus signal to potential entrants that if they enter the industry, the incumbents will use their competitive advantage to drive down prices to a level at which new companies will be unable to cover their costs.[14] This pricing strategy also allows a company to ride down the experience curve and obtain substantial economies of scale. Since costs fall with prices, profit margins could still be maintained.

This strategy, though, is unlikely to deter a strong potential competitor—an established company that is trying to find profitable investment opportunities in other industries. It is difficult, for example, to imagine that 3M would be afraid to enter an industry because companies there threaten to drive down prices. A company such as 3M has the resources to withstand any short-term losses. Hewlett-Packard also had few worries about entering the highly competitive personal computer industry because of its powerful set of distinctive competencies. Hence, it may be in the interest of incumbent companies to accept new entry gracefully, giving up market share gradually to the new entrants to prevent price wars from developing, and thus save their profits, if this is feasible.

Most evidence suggests that companies first skim the market and charge high prices during the growth stage, maximizing short-run profits.[15] Then they move to increase their market share and charge a lower price to expand the market rapidly; develop a reputation; and obtain economies of scale, driving down costs and barring entry. As competitors do enter, the incumbent companies reduce prices to retard entry and give up market share to create a stable industry context—one in which they can use nonprice competitive tactics, such as product differentiation, to maximize long-run profits. At that point, nonprice competition becomes the main basis of industry competition, and prices are quite likely to rise as competition stabilizes. Thus, competitive tactics such as pricing and product differentiation are linked in mature industries; competitive decisions are taken to maximize the returns from a company's generic strategy. The airline industry, discussed in Strategy in Action 7.2, offers an illustration of how and when companies use both price and nonprice competitive tactics to build barriers to entry that deter new entrants and reduce rivalry.

▩ Maintaining Excess Capacity

The third competitive technique that allows companies to deter entry involves maintaining excess capacity, that is, producing more of a product than customers currently demand. Existing industry companies may deliberately develop some limited amount of excess capacity because it serves to warn potential entrants that if they enter the industry, existing firms can retaliate by increasing output and forcing

7.2   STRATEGY *in* ACTION

Ups and Downs in the Airline Industry

Before deregulation in 1978, competition over fares and ticket prices was not permitted in the airline industry, and the airlines had to find other ways to compete. Their response was to attract customers by offering more frequent flights and better service—a form of product differentiation. Since all airlines imitated one another, however, no airline was able to get a competitive advantage over its rivals, and each airline's costs rose dramatically because of the expense of extra flights, improved meals, and so on. To cover the higher costs, the airlines constantly applied for fare increases. As a result, customers paid higher and higher fares to compensate for the airlines' inefficiency. In an attempt to cure this problem, the U.S. Congress decided to deregulate the industry, permitting competition in ticket prices and allowing free entry into the industry. The airlines did not want deregulation. (Why should they? They were receiving a nice profit as a protected industry.) However, deregulation did take place in 1979, and the result was chaos.

Deregulation destroyed the old competitive tactics and maneuvers the airlines had long adopted. Before deregulation, the major airlines knew each other's competitive moves by heart. In the new world of price competition, entry into the industry was easy, and a host of small airlines entered to compete with the major companies. During regulation, no airline had had to develop a generic strategy. There had been no incentive to keep costs low because cost increases could be passed on to consumers. In addition, all firms had used the same means to differentiate themselves, so that no airline had a competitive advantage in being unique. With no rules to tell them how to compete and no experience of free competition, the airlines waged a price war as new, low-cost entrants such as People Express and Southwest Airlines sought to gain market share from the major players.

To survive in this environment, the major airlines have adopted new competitive tactics to protect their business-level strategies. One of these tactics is the development of hub-and-spoke networks, which have allowed them to build national route structures at low cost. These networks also make it difficult for new firms to enter the industry, because the major airlines hold most of the available gates at large airports. Through nonprice means, the major companies have tried to create new barriers to entry, thereby reducing the threat of new entrants. They have tried to develop new competitive rules of the game to stabilize competition within the industry and prevent price competition.

The use of all these price and nonprice techniques did reduce the number of new entrants, and by 1995 the industry had become profitable, after losing billions of dollars in the early 1990s. However, since 1995, there have been increasing customer complaints about lost bags, poor quality or nonexistent food, cramped seats, and higher fares as the major airlines have sought to reduce their costs and increase their profits. In addition, the wave of strategic alliances in the industry, for example, between American Airlines and British Airlines and between Continental Airlines and Northwest Airlines have led many analysts to conclude that customers may see even more price hikes and cuts in quality as the airlines enjoy their strong bargaining position.

down prices until entry would become unprofitable. However, the threat to increase output has to be *credible,* that is, companies in an industry must collectively be able to raise the level of production quickly if entry appears likely.

STRATEGIES TO MANAGE RIVALRY IN MATURE INDUSTRIES

Beyond seeking to deter entry, companies also wish to develop a competitive strategy to manage their competitive interdependence and decrease rivalry. As we noted earlier, unrestricted competition over prices or output reduces the level of company and industry profitability. Several competitive tactics and gambits are available to companies to manage industry relations. The most important are price signaling, price leadership, nonprice competition, and capacity control.

■ Price Signaling

Most industries start out fragmented, with small companies battling for market share. Then, over time, the leading players emerge, and companies start to interpret each other's competitive moves. Price signaling is the first means by which companies attempt to structure competition within an industry in order to control rivalry among competitors.[16] **Price signaling** is the process by which companies increase or decrease product prices to convey their intentions to other companies and so influence the way they price their products.[17] There are two ways in which companies use price signaling to help defend their generic competitive strategies.

First, companies may use price signaling to announce that they will respond vigorously to hostile competitive moves that threaten them. For example, companies may signal that if one company starts to cut prices aggressively, they will respond in kind—hence the term **tit-for-tat strategy** is often used to describe this kind of market signaling. The outcome of a tit-for-tat strategy is that nobody gains. Similarly, as we note in the last section, companies may signal to potential entrants that if the latter do enter the market, they will fight back by reducing prices and the new entrants may incur significant losses.

A second, and very important, use of price signaling is to allow companies indirectly to coordinate their actions and avoid costly competitive moves that lead to a breakdown in the pricing policy within an industry. One company may signal that it intends to lower prices because it wishes to attract customers who are switching to the products of another industry, not because it wishes to stimulate a price war. On the other hand, signaling can be used to improve profitability within an industry. The airline industry is a good example of the power of price signaling. In the 1980s, signals of lower prices set off price wars, but in the 1990s, the airlines have used price signaling to obtain uniform price increases. Nonrefundable tickets, too, originated as a market signal by one company that was quickly copied by all other companies in the industry. In sum, price signaling allows companies to give one another information that enables them to understand each other's competitive product/ market strategy and make coordinated competitive moves.

■ Price Leadership

Price leadership—the taking on by one company of the responsibility for setting industry prices—is a second tactic used to enhance the profitability of companies in a mature industry.[18] Formal price leadership, or price setting by companies jointly, is illegal under antitrust laws, so the process of price leadership is often very subtle. In the auto industry, for example, auto prices are set by imitation. The price set by the weakest company—that is, the one with the highest costs—is often used as the basis for competitors' pricing. Thus, U.S. carmakers set their prices, and Japanese carmakers then set theirs with reference to the U.S. prices. The Japanese are happy to do this because they have lower costs than U.S. companies and are making higher profits than U.S. carmakers without competing with them by price. Pricing is done by market segment. The prices of different auto models in the model range indicate the customer segments that the companies are aiming for and the price range they believe the market segment can tolerate. Each manufacturer prices a model in the segment with reference to the *prices* charged by its competitors, not by reference to competitors' costs. Price leadership allows differentiators to charge a premium price and also helps low-cost companies by increasing their margins.

Although price leadership can stabilize industry relationships by preventing head-to-head competition and thus raise the level of profitability within an industry, it has its dangers. Price leadership helps companies with high costs, allowing them to survive without becoming more productive or more efficient. Thus, it may foster complacency; companies may keep extracting profits without reinvesting any to improve their productivity. In the long term, such behavior will make them vulnerable to new entrants that have lower costs because they have developed new productive techniques. That is what happened in the U.S. auto industry after the Japanese entered the market. Following years of tacit price fixing, with General Motors as the leader, the carmakers were subjected to growing low-cost Japanese competition, to which they were unable to respond. Indeed, many U.S. auto companies have survived into the 1990s only because the Japanese carmakers were foreign firms. Had the foreign firms been new U.S. entrants, the government would probably not have taken steps to protect Chrysler, Ford, or General Motors, and they would be much smaller companies today.

◼ Nonprice Competition

A third very important aspect of product/market strategy in mature industries is the use of **nonprice competition** to manage rivalry within an industry. Using various tactics and maneuvers to try to prevent costly price cutting and price wars does not preclude competition by product differentiation. Indeed, in many industries, product differentiation is the principal competitive tactic used to prevent competitors from obtaining access to a company's customers and attacking its market share. In other words, companies rely on product differentiation to deter potential entrants and manage rivalry within their industry. Product differentiation allows industry rivals to compete for market share by offering products with different or superior features or by applying different marketing techniques. In Figure 7.4, product and market segment dimensions are used to identify four nonprice competitive strategies based on product differentiation. (Notice that this model applies to new market segments, not new markets.)[19]

FIGURE 7.4

Four Nonprice
Competitive Strategies

| 7.3 | STRATEGY *in* ACTION |

Warfare in Toyland

Toys 'R' Us, based in Paramus, New Jersey, grew at an astonishing 25 percent annual rate throughout the 1980s and today holds a 20 percent share of the $15 billion retail toy market, which makes it the industry leader. To reach its commanding position, the company used a strategy of market penetration based on developing a nationwide chain of retail outlets and a cost-leadership strategy. To lower costs, Toys 'R' Us developed efficient materials-management techniques for ordering and distributing toys to its stores. It also provided only a low level of customer service. Together, these moves allowed it to obtain a very low expense-to-sales ratio of 17 percent. Toys 'R' Us then used its low costs to promote a philosophy of everyday low pricing. The company deliberately set out to undercut the prices of its rivals, and it succeeded. In fact, its two largest competitors in the 1980s, Child World and Lionel, went bankrupt.[22] Pursuing a market-penetration strategy based on low cost thus brought spectacular results for Toys 'R' Us.

In the 1990s, however, the company's commanding position was threatened by a new set of rivals, which were also pursuing market-penetration strategies. Companies such as Wal-Mart, Kmart, and Target Stores rapidly expanded the number of their stores and beat Toys 'R' Us at its own game by selling toys at prices that were often below those of Toys 'R' Us. Indeed, Toys 'R' Us saw its sales fall from 25 percent in 1990 to 17 percent by 1999, and Wal-Mart is now the market leader with 18 percent.

The new competition squeezed profits for Toys 'R' Us and forced the company to turn to nonprice competition to attract customers. For example, Toys 'R' Us promoted its wide range of products as a competitive advantage; it made its stores more attractive; and it also increased the level of customer service by offering customers more personalized attention. In addition, it also went on-line and is in the process of developing a major Web presence. However, it was slow to do so and eToys, an Internet start-up, is the current leader in this market segment.[23] However, analysts feel that Toys 'R' Us, under newly appointed CEO Bob Moog, is rebuilding its brand name and that the company is poised to regain its leading position in the industry.

Market Penetration   When a company concentrates on expanding market share in its existing product markets, it is engaging in a strategy of **market penetration.**[20] Market penetration involves heavy advertising to promote and build product differentiation. In a mature industry, the thrust of advertising is to influence consumers' brand choice and create a brand-name reputation for the company and its products. In this way, a company can increase its market share by attracting the customers of its rivals. Because brand-name products often command premium prices, building market share in this situation is very profitable.

In some mature industries—for example, soap and detergent, disposable diapers, and brewing—a market-penetration strategy becomes a way of life.[21] In these industries, all companies engage in intensive advertising and battle for market share. Each company fears that by not advertising it will lose market share to rivals. Consequently, in the soap and detergent industry, for instance, Procter & Gamble spends more than 20 percent of sales revenues on advertising, with the aim of maintaining and perhaps building market share. These huge advertising outlays constitute a barrier to entry for prospective entrants. As Strategy in Action 7.3 details, Toys 'R' Us rose to prominence in the retail toy market by pursuing a market-penetration strategy.

Product Development **Product development** is the creation of new or improved products to replace existing ones.[24] The wet-shaving industry is another industry that depends on product replacement to create successive waves of consumer demand, which then create new sources of revenue for companies in the industry. Gillette, for example, periodically comes out with a new and improved razor—such as the Sensor shaving system—which often gives a massive boost to its market share. Similarly, in the car industry, each major car company replaces its models every three to five years to encourage customers to trade in their old models and buy the new one.

Product development is important for maintaining product differentiation and building market share.[25] For instance, the laundry detergent Tide has gone through more than fifty different changes in formulation during the past forty years to improve its performance. The product is always advertised as Tide, but it is a different product each year. The battle over diet colas is another interesting example of competitive product differentiation by product development. Royal Crown Cola developed Diet Rite, the first diet cola. However, Coca-Cola and PepsiCo responded quickly with their versions of the diet drink, and by massive advertising, they soon took over the market. Refining and improving products is an important competitive tactic in defending a company's generic competitive strategy in a mature industry, but this kind of competition can be as vicious as a price war because it is very expensive and raises costs dramatically.

Market signaling to competitors can also be an important part of a product development strategy. One company may let the others know that it is proceeding with product innovations that will provide a competitive advantage the others will be unable to imitate effectively because their entry into the market will be too late. For example, software companies such as Microsoft often announce new operating systems years in advance. The purpose of such an announcement is to deter prospective competitors from making the huge investments needed to compete with the industry leaders and to let its customers know that the company still has the competitive edge so important to retaining customers' loyalty. However, preemptive signaling can backfire, as IBM found out when it announced that its PS/2 operating system would not be compatible with the operating systems presently standard in the industry. Other companies in the industry collectively signaled to IBM and IBM's customers that they would band together to protect the existing operation systems, thus preserving industry standards and preventing IBM from obtaining a competitive advantage from its new technology. IBM subsequently backed down. If a preemptive move is to succeed, competitors must believe that a company will act according to its signals and stick to its position. If the threat is not credible, the signaling company weakens its position.

Market Development **Market development** finds new market segments for a company's products. A company pursuing this strategy wants to capitalize on the brand name it has developed in one market segment by locating new market segments in which to compete. In this way, it can exploit the product differentiation advantages of its brand name. The Japanese auto manufacturers provide an interesting example of the use of market development. When they first entered the market, each Japanese manufacturer offered a car, such as the Toyota Corolla and the Honda Accord, aimed at the economy segment of the auto market. However, the Japanese upgraded each car over time, and now each is directed at a more expensive market segment. The Accord is a leading contender in the mid-size-car segment, while the Corolla fills the small-car segment that used to be occupied by the Celica, which is now aimed at a sportier market segment. By redefining their product offerings, Japanese manufacturers have profitably developed their market segments and successfully attacked their industry rivals, wresting market share from these companies. Although the Japanese used to compete primarily as low-cost producers, market development has allowed them to become differentiators as well. Toyota is an example of a company that has used market development to pursue simultaneously a low-cost and a differentiation strategy.

Product Proliferation **Product proliferation** can be used to manage rivalry within an industry and to deter entry. The strategy of product proliferation generally means that large companies in an industry all have a product in each market segment or niche and compete head-to-head for customers. If a new niche develops, such as sports utility vehicles, designer sunglasses, or Internet Web sites, then the leader gets a first-mover advantage, but soon all the other companies catch up, and once again competition is stabilized and rivalry within the industry is reduced. Product proliferation thus allows the development of stable industry competition based on product differentiation, not price—that is, nonprice competition based on the development of new products. The battle is over a product's perceived quality and uniqueness, *not* over its price.

■ Capacity Control

Although nonprice competition helps mature industries avoid the cutthroat price reductions that shrink both company and industry levels of profitability, in some industries price competition does periodically break out. This occurs most commonly when there is industry overcapacity—that is, when companies collectively produce too much output so that lowering the price is the only way to dispose of it. If one company starts to cut prices, the others quickly follow because they fear that the price cutter will be able to sell all its inventory and they will be left holding unwanted goods. **Capacity control** strategies are the last set of competitive tactics and maneuvers for managing rivalry within an industry that we discuss in this chapter.

Excess capacity may be caused by a shortfall in demand, as when a recession lowers the demand for cars and causes car companies to give customers price incentives to purchase a new car. In this situation, companies can do nothing except wait for better times. By and large, however, excess capacity results from companies within an industry simultaneously responding to favorable conditions: they all invest in new plants to be able to take advantage of the predicted upsurge in demand. Paradoxically, each individual company's effort to outperform the others means that collectively the companies create industry overcapacity, which hurts them all. Figure 7.5 illustrates this situation. Although demand is rising, the consequence of each company's decision to increase capacity is a surge in industry capacity, which drives down prices.

To prevent the accumulation of costly excess capacity, companies must devise strategies that let them control—or at least benefit from—capacity expansion programs. Before we examine these strategies, however, we need to consider in greater detail the factors that cause excess capacity.[26]

FIGURE 7.5

Changes in Industry
Capacity and Demand

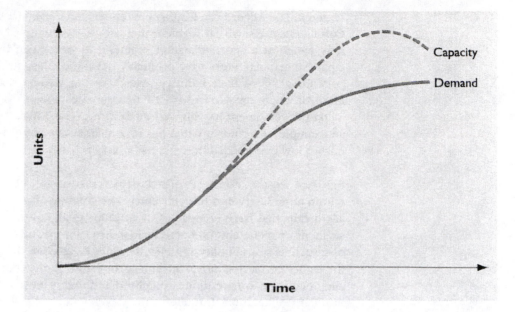

Factors Causing Excess Capacity The problem of excess capacity often derives from technological factors. Sometimes new, low-cost technology is the culprit because, to prevent being left behind, all companies introduce it simultaneously. Excess capacity occurs because the new technology can produce more than the old. In addition, new technology is often introduced in large increments, which generate overcapacity. For instance, an airline that needs more seats on a route must add another plane, thereby adding hundreds of seats even though only fifty are needed. To take another example, a new chemical process may operate efficiently only at the rate of 1,000 gallons a day, whereas the previous process was efficient at 500 gallons a day. If all companies within an industry change technologies, industry capacity may double and enormous problems can result.

Overcapacity may also be caused by competitive factors within an industry. Obviously, entry into an industry is one such factor. Japan's entry into the semiconductor industry caused massive overcapacity and price declines for the Organization of Petroleum Exporting Countries microchips. Sometimes the age of a company's plant is the source of the problem. For example, in the hotel industry, given the rapidity with which the quality of hotel furnishings declines, customers are always attracted to new hotels. The building of new hotel chains alongside the old chains, however, can cause excess capacity. Often companies are simply making simultaneous competitive moves based on industry trends, but those moves eventually lead to head-to-head competition. Most fast-food chains, for instance, establish new outlets whenever demographic data show population increases. However, the companies seem to forget that all chains use the same data. Thus, a locality that has no fast-food outlets may suddenly see several being built at the same time. Whether they can all survive depends on the growth rate of demand relative to the growth rate of the fast-food chains.

Choosing a Capacity-Control Strategy Given the various ways in which capacity can expand, companies clearly need to find some means of controlling it. If they are always plagued by price cutting and price wars, companies will be unable to recoup the investments in their generic strategies. Low profitability within an industry caused by overcapacity forces not just the weakest companies but sometimes the major players as well to exit the industry. In general, companies have two strategic choices. Either (1) each company individually must try to preempt its rivals and seize the initiative, or (2) the companies collectively must find indirect means of coordinating with each other so that they are all aware of the mutual effects of their actions.

To *preempt* rivals, a company must foresee a large increase in demand in the product market and then move rapidly to establish large-scale operations that will be able to satisfy the predicted demand. By achieving a first-mover advantage, the company may deter other firms from entering the market since the preemptor will usually be able to move down the experience curve, reduce its costs, and therefore its prices as well, and threaten a price war if necessary.

This strategy, however, is extremely risky, for it involves investing resources in a generic strategy before the extent and profitability of the future market are clear. Wal-Mart, with its strategy of locating in small rural towns to tap an underexploited market for discount goods, preempted Sears and Kmart. Wal-Mart has been able to engage in market penetration and market expansion because of the secure base it established in its rural strongholds.

A preemptive strategy is also risky if it does not deter competitors and they decide to enter the market. If the competitors have a stronger generic strategy or more resources, such as AT&T or IBM, they can make the preemptor suffer. Thus, for the strategy to succeed, the preemptor must generally be a credible company with enough resources to withstand a possible price war.

To *coordinate* with rivals as a capacity-control strategy, caution must be exercised since collusion on the timing of new investments is illegal under antitrust law. However, tacit coordination is practiced in many industries as companies attempt to understand and forecast the competitive moves of each other. Generally, companies use market signaling and engage in a kind of tit-for-tat strategy to secure coordination. They make announcements about their future investment decisions in trade journals and newspapers. In addition, they share information about their production levels and their forecasts of demand within an industry to bring supply and demand into equilibrium. Thus, a coordination strategy reduces the risks associated with investment in the industry.

SUPPLY AND DISTRIBUTION STRATEGY IN MATURE INDUSTRIES

As you saw in Chapter 3, when an industry becomes consolidated and comprises a few large companies, it gains strength over its suppliers and customers. Suppliers become dependent on the industry for buying their inputs and on customers for obtaining the industry's outputs. By the mature stage, to protect their market share and improve product quality, many companies want to take over more of the distribution of their products and control the source of inputs crucial to the production process. When they seek ownership of supply or distribution operations, they are pursuing a strategy of *vertical integration,* which is considered in detail in Chapter 9. In this chapter, we discuss how the way a company controls its supplier and distributor relationships protects its generic strategy and helps it develop a competitive advantage.

By controlling supplier and distributor relationships, a company can safeguard its ability to dispose of its outputs or to acquire inputs in a timely, reliable manner. This in turn, can reduce costs and improve product quality. One way to analyze the issues involved in choosing a distribution/supplier strategy is to contrast the situation that exists between a company and its suppliers and distributors in Japan with the situation that exists in the United States.

In the United States, it is common for a company and its suppliers and distributors to have an anonymous relationship in which each party tries to strike the best bargain to make the most profit. Often purchasing and distribution personnel are routinely rotated to prevent kickbacks. In contrast, the relationship between a company and its suppliers and distributors in Japan is based on long-term personal relationships and trust. Suppliers in Japan are sensitive to the needs of the company, respond quickly to changes in the specification of inputs, and adjust supply to meet the requirements of a company's just-in-time inventory system. The results of this close relationship are lower costs and the ability to respond to unexpected changes in customers' demand. Developing close supplier/distributor relationships is a tactic that supports Japanese companies' generic strategies. Clearly, it pays a company to develop a long-term relationship with its suppliers and distributors, and more and more U.S. companies such as Xerox, Motorola, Kodak, McDonald's, and Wal-Mart have formed close linkages with their suppliers.

A company has many options to choose from in deciding on the appropriate way to distribute its products to gain a competitive advantage. It may distribute its products to an independent distributor, which in turn distributes them to retailers. Alternatively, a company might distribute directly to retailers or even to the final customer. More and more companies are using this option as they turn to the Internet to market and sell their products. Strategy in Action 7.4 illustrates this shift.

In general, the *complexity of a product* and the *amount of information* needed about its operation and maintenance determine the distribution strategy chosen. Car companies, for example, use franchisees rather than "car supermarkets" to control the distribution of their autos. The reason is the high level of after-sales service and support needed to satisfy customers. Carmakers are able to penalize franchisees by withholding cars from a dealership if customers' complaints rise, giving them effective control over franchisees' behavior.

On the other hand, large electronics manufacturers and producers of consumer durables such as appliances generally prefer to use a network of distributors to control distribution. To enhance market share and control the way products are sold and serviced, manufacturers choose five or six large distributors per state to control distribution. The distributors are required to carry the full line of a company's products and invest in after-sales service facilities. The result is that the manufacturer receives good feedback on how its products are selling, and the distributor becomes knowledgeable about a company's products and thus helps the company maintain and increase its control over the market. The company is able to discipline its distributors if they start to discount prices or otherwise threaten the company's reputation or generic strategy.

Large manufacturers such as Johnson & Johnson, Procter & Gamble, and General Foods typically sell directly to a retailer and avoid giving profits to a distributor or wholesaler. They do so in part because they have lower profit margins than the

7.4   STRATEGY *in* ACTION

Compaq and Dell Go Head-to-Head in Distribution

As new developments in technology alter the nature of competition in the personal computer industry, the distribution strategies of its major players are also changing. These changes are evident in the struggle between Dell Computer and Compaq Computer for domination of the personal computer market. Founded by a team of engineers, Compaq has from the start emphasized the engineering and research side of the PC business. For example, it was the first company to bring out a computer using Intel's new 486 chip. Its differentiation strategy was to produce high-end PCs based on the newest technology, which would command a premium price. Compaq specialized in the business market, and it developed a sophisticated, 2,000-strong dealer network to distribute, sell, and service its expensive PCs.[27]

Dell, on the other hand, focused from the beginning on the marketing and distribution end of the PC business. Its low-cost strategy was to assemble a PC and then sell it directly to consumers through mail-order outlets, cutting out the dealer in order to offer a rock-bottom price. The company was viewed by its managers primarily as a distribution or mail-order company, not as an engineering one.

As computers increasingly became commodity products and prices fell drastically, Compaq realized that its strategy of selling only through high-priced dealers would mean disaster. It changed its strategy to produce a low-cost computer, and in the 1990s began its own mail-order distribution, offering its machines directly to consumers, and more recently to businesses.

However, Compaq has not been as successful as Dell in its on-line distribution strategy, both because Dell was first to engage in such distribution and established a first-mover advantage, and because Dell has established a more customer-friendly Web site and enjoys the record for fewest customer complaints. Moreover, while each company offers next-day delivery and installation of computers, as well as extended warranties, Dell has reached ahead in providing the best on-line customer service, and indeed is making quality customer service, as well as price, a main focus of its competitive advantage.[28]

In 1999, Compaq's new CEO, Michael Capellas, announced a bold new Internet distribution and sales strategy to make Compaq the leader in on-line selling to businesses and consumers.[29] Clearly, the battle between these companies is not over.

makers of electronic equipment and consumer durables. However, this strategy also allows them to influence a retailer's behavior directly. For example, they can refuse to supply a particular product that a retailer wants unless the retailer stocks the entire range of the company's products. In addition, the companies are assured of shelf space for new products. Coca-Cola and PepsiCo are two companies that are able to influence retailers to reduce the shelf space given to competing products or even to exclude them. They can do so because soft drinks have the highest profit margins of any product sold in supermarkets. Gallo is one of the few winemakers that control the distribution and retailing of their products. This is one reason that Gallo is so consistently profitable.

In sum, devising the appropriate strategy for acquiring inputs and disposing of outputs is a crucial part of competitive strategy in mature industry environments. Companies can gain a competitive advantage through the means they choose to control their relationships with distributors and suppliers. By selecting the right strategy, they are able to control their costs, their price and nonprice strategies, their reputation, and the quality of their products. These are crucial issues in mature industries.

STRATEGIES IN DECLINING INDUSTRIES

Sooner or later many industries enter into a decline stage, in which the size of the total market starts to shrink. The railroad, tobacco, and steel industries are at this stage. Industries start declining for a number of reasons, including technological change, social trends, and demographic shifts. The railroad and steel industries began to decline when technological changes brought viable substitutes for the products these industries manufactured. The advent of the internal combustion engine drove the railroad industry into decline, and the steel industry fell into decline with the rise of plastics and composite materials. As for the tobacco industry, changing social attitudes toward smoking, which are themselves a product of growing concerns about the health effects of smoking, have caused decline.

There are four main strategies that companies can adopt to deal with decline: (1) a **leadership strategy,** by which a company seeks to become the dominant player in a declining industry; (2) a **niche strategy,** which focuses on pockets of demand that are declining more slowly than the industry as a whole; (3) a **harvest strategy,** which optimizes cash flow; and (4) a **divestment strategy,** by which a company sells off the business to others. Before examining each of these strategies in detail, it is important to note that the choice of strategy depends in part on the *intensity* of the competition.

◼ The Severity of Decline

When the size of the total market is shrinking, competition tends to intensify in a declining industry and profit rates tend to fall. The intensity of competition in a declining industry depends on four critical factors, which are indicated in Figure 7.6. First, the intensity of competition is greater in industries in which decline is rapid as opposed to industries, such as tobacco, in which decline is slow and gradual.

Second, the intensity of competition is greater in declining industries in which exit barriers are high. As you recall from Chapter 3, high exit barriers keep compa-

FIGURE 7.6

Factors That Determine the Intensity of Competition in Declining Industries

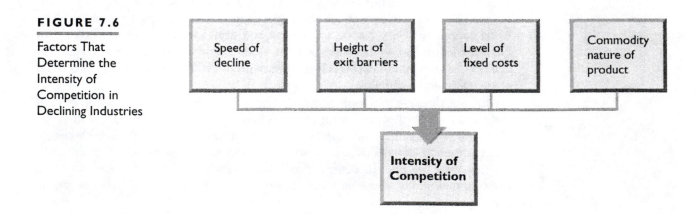

nies locked into an industry even when demand is falling. The result is the emergence of excess productive capacity, and hence an increased probability of fierce price competition.

Third, and related to the previous point, the intensity of competition is greater in declining industries in which fixed costs are high (as in the steel industry). The reason is that the need to cover fixed costs, such as the costs of maintaining productive capacity, can make companies try to utilize any excess capacity they have by slashing prices—an action that can trigger a price war.

Finally, the intensity of competition is greater in declining industries in which the product is perceived as a commodity (as it is in the steel industry) in contrast to industries in which differentiation gives rise to significant brand loyalty, as was true until very recently of the declining tobacco industry.

Not all segments of an industry typically decline at the same rate. In some segments, demand may remain reasonably strong, despite decline elsewhere. The steel industry illustrates this situation. Although bulk steel products, such as sheet steel, have suffered a general decline, demand has actually risen for specialty steels, such as those used in high-speed machine tools. Vacuum tubes provide another example. Although demand for them collapsed when transistors replaced them as a key component in many electronics products, for years afterward vacuum tubes still had some limited applications in radar equipment. Consequently, demand in this vacuum tube segment remained strong despite the general decline in the demand for vacuum tubes. The point, then, is that there may be *pockets of demand* in an industry in which demand is declining more slowly than in the industry as a whole or not declining at all. Price competition thus may be far less intense among the companies serving such pockets of demand than within the industry as a whole.

■ Choosing a Strategy

As already noted, four main strategies are available to companies in a declining industry: a leadership strategy, a niche strategy, a harvest strategy, and a divestment strategy. Figure 7.7 provides a simple framework for guiding strategic choice. Note that intensity of competition in the declining industry is measured on the vertical axis and that a company's strengths *relative* to remaining pockets of demand are measured on the horizontal axis.

Leadership Strategy A leadership strategy aims at growing in a declining industry by picking up the market share of companies that are leaving the industry. A leadership strategy makes most sense (1) when the company has distinctive strengths that allow it to capture market share in a declining industry and (2) when the speed of decline and the intensity of competition in the declining industry are moderate. Philip Morris has pursued such a strategy in the tobacco industry. By aggressive marketing, Philip Morris has increased its market share in a declining industry and earned enormous profits in the process.

The tactical steps companies might use to achieve a leadership position include aggressive pricing and marketing to build market share; acquiring established competitors to consolidate the industry; and raising the stakes for other competitors, for

FIGURE 7.7

Strategy Selection in a
Declining Industry

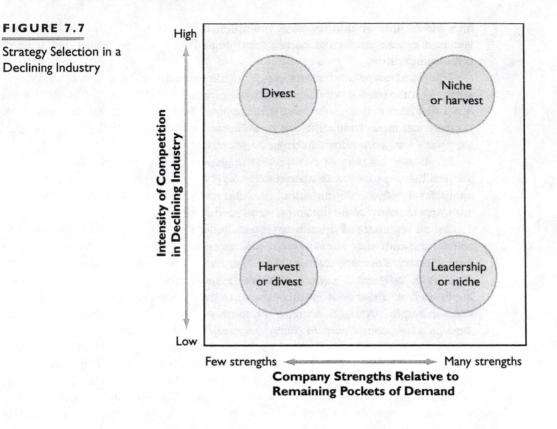

**Company Strengths Relative to
Remaining Pockets of Demand**

instance, by making new investments in productive capacity. Such competitive tactics signal to other competitors that the company is willing and able to stay and compete in the declining industry. These signals may persuade other companies to exit the industry, which would further enhance the competitive position of the industry leader. Strategy in Action 7.5 offers an example of a company, Richardson Electronics, that has prospered by taking a leadership position in a declining industry. It is one of the last companies in the vacuum tube business.

Niche Strategy   A niche strategy focuses on those pockets of demand in the industry in which demand is stable or declining less rapidly than the industry as a whole. The strategy makes sense when the company has some unique strengths related to those niches where demand remains relatively strong. As an example, consider Naval, a company that manufactures whaling harpoons, as well as small guns to fire them, and makes money doing so. This might be considered rather odd, since whaling has been outlawed by the world community. However, Naval survived the terminal decline of the harpoon industry by focusing on the one group of people who are still allowed to hunt whales, although only in very limited numbers—North American Eskimos. Eskimos are permitted to hunt bowhead whales, provided that they do so only for food and not for commercial purposes. Naval is the sole supplier of small harpoon whaling guns to Eskimo communities, and its monopoly position allows it to earn a healthy return in this small market.[31]

7.5 STRATEGY in ACTION

How to Make Money in the Vacuum Tube Business

At its peak in the early 1950s, the vacuum tube business was a major industry in which companies such as Westinghouse, General Electric, RCA, and Western Electric had a large stake. Then along came the transistor, making most vacuum tubes obsolete, and one by one all the big companies exited the industry. Richardson Electronics, however, not only stayed in the business but also demonstrated that high returns are possible in a declining industry. Primarily a distributor (although it does have some manufacturing capabilities), Richardson bought the remains of a dozen companies in the United States and Europe as they exited the vacuum tube industry. Richardson now has a warehouse that stocks more than 10,000 different types of vacuum tubes. The company is the world's only supplier of many of them, which helps explain why its gross margin is in the 35 percent to 40 percent range.

Richardson survives and prospers because vacuum tubes are vital parts of some older electronic equipment that would be costly to replace with solid-state equipment. In addition, vacuum tubes still outperform semiconductors in some limited applications, including radar and welding machines. The U.S. government and General Motors are big Richardson customers.

Speed is the essence of Richardson's business. The company's Illinois warehouse offers overnight delivery to some 40,000 customers, processing 650 orders a day, whose average price is $550. Customers such as GM don't really care whether a vacuum tube costs $250 or $350; what they care about is the $40,000 to $50,000 downtime loss that they face when a key piece of welding equipment isn't working. By responding quickly to the demands of such customers and by being the only major supplier of many types of vacuum tubes, Richardson has placed itself in a position that many companies in growing industries would envy—a monopoly position. In 1997, however, a new company, Westrex, was formed to take advantage of the growing popularity of vacuum tubes in high-end stereo systems, and by 1999 it was competing head-to-head with Richardson in some market segments.[30] Clearly, competition can be found even in a declining industry.

Harvest Strategy As we note in Chapter 6, a harvest strategy is the best choice when a company wishes to get out of a declining industry and perhaps optimize cash flow in the process. This strategy makes the most sense when the company foresees a steep decline and intense future competition or when it lacks strengths relative to remaining pockets of demand in the industry. A harvest strategy requires the company to cut all new investments in capital equipment, advertising, R&D, and the like. As illustrated in Figure 7.8, the inevitable result is that the company will lose market share, but because it is no longer investing in this business, initially its positive cash flow will increase. Essentially, the company is taking cash flow in exchange for market share. Ultimately, however, cash flows will start to decline, and at this stage it makes sense for the company to liquidate the business. Although this strategy is very appealing in theory, it can be somewhat difficult to put into practice. Employee morale in a business that is being run down may suffer. Furthermore, if customers catch on to what the company is doing, they may defect rapidly. Then market share may decline much faster than the company expected.

Divestment Strategy A divestment strategy rests on the idea that a company can maximize its net investment recovery from a business by selling it early, before the industry has entered into a steep decline. This strategy is appropriate when the

FIGURE 7.8

A Harvest Strategy

company has few strengths relative to whatever pockets of demand are likely to remain in the industry and when the competition in the declining industry is likely to be intense. The best option may be to sell out to a company that is pursuing a leadership strategy in the industry. The drawback of the divestment strategy is that it depends for its success on the ability of the company to spot accurately its industry's decline before it becomes serious and to sell out while the company's assets are still valued by others.

SUMMARY OF CHAPTER

The purpose of this chapter is to discuss the competitive strategies that companies can use in different industry environments to protect and enhance their generic business-level strategies. Developing a generic competitive strategy and an investment strategy is only the first part, albeit a crucial one, of business-level strategy. Choosing industry-appropriate competitive tactics, gambits, and maneuvers is the second part of successful strategy formulation at the business level. Companies must always be on the alert for changes in conditions within their industry and in the competitive behavior of their rivals if they are to respond to these changes in a timely manner. The chapter makes the following main points:

✓ In fragmented industries composed of a large number of small and medium-sized companies,

the principal forms of competitive strategy are chaining, franchising, horizontal merger, and using the Internet.

✓ In embryonic and growth industries, developing a strategy to profit from technical innovations is a crucial aspect of competitive strategy. The three strategies a company can choose from are (1) to develop and market the technology itself, (2) to do so jointly with another company, or (3) to license the technology to existing companies.

✓ Mature industries are composed of a few large companies whose actions are so highly interdependent that the success of one company's strategy depends on the responses of its rivals.

✓ The principal competitive tactics and moves used by companies in mature industries to deter entry are product proliferation, price cutting, and maintaining excess capacity.

✓ The principal competitive tactics and maneuvers used by companies in mature industries to manage rivalry are price signaling, price leadership, nonprice competition, and capacity control.

✓ Companies in mature industries also need to develop a supply-and-distribution strategy to protect the source of their competitive advantage.

✓ In declining industries, in which market demand has leveled off or is falling, companies must tailor their price and nonprice strategies to the new competitive environment. They also need to manage industry capacity to prevent the emergence of capacity expansion problems.

✓ There are four main strategies a company can pursue when demand is falling: leadership, niche, harvest, and divestment strategies. The choice of strategy is determined by the severity of industry decline and the company's strengths relative to the remaining pockets of demand.

DISCUSSION QUESTIONS

1. Why are industries fragmented? What are the main ways in which companies can turn a fragmented industry into a consolidated one?

2. What are the key problems involved in maintaining a competitive advantage in a growth industry environment? What are the dangers associated with being the leader?

3. Discuss how companies can use (a) product differentiation and (b) capacity control to manage rivalry and increase an industry's profitability.

Practicing Strategic Management

 SMALL-GROUP EXERCISE
How to Keep the Hot Sauce Hot

Break up into groups of three to five people, and discuss the following scenario:

You are the managers of a company that has pioneered a new kind of hot sauce for chicken that has taken the market by storm. The hot sauce's differentiated appeal is based on a unique combination of spices and packaging that allows you to charge a premium price. Within the last three years, your hot sauce has achieved a national reputation, and now major food companies such as Kraft and Nabisco, seeing the potential of this market segment, are beginning to introduce hot sauces of their own, imitating your product.

1. Describe the generic business-level strategy you are pursuing.

2. Describe the industry's environment in which you are competing.

3. What kinds of competitive tactics and maneuvers could you adopt to protect your generic strategy in this kind of environment?

4. What do you think is the best strategy for you to pursue in this situation?

 STRATEGIC MANAGEMENT PROJECT
Module 7

This part of the project continues the analysis of your company's business-level strategy and considers how conditions in the industry's environment affect the company's competitive strategy.

1. In what kind of industry environment (for example, embryonic, mature) does your company operate? (Use the information from Strategic Management Project: Module 3 to answer this question.)

2. Discuss how your company has attempted to develop a competitive strategy to protect its business-level strategy. For example, if your company is operating in an embryonic industry, discuss the ways it has attempted to increase its competitive advantage over time. If it is operating in a mature industry, discuss how it has tried to manage the five forces of industry competition.

3. What new strategies would you advise your company to pursue to increase its competitive advantage? For example, what kinds of strategy toward buyers or suppliers should it adopt? How should it attempt to differentiate its products in the future?

4. Based on this analysis, do you think your company will be able to maintain its competitive advantage in the future? Why or why not?

 ARTICLE FILE 7

Find examples of the ways in which a company or group of companies has adopted a competitive strategy to protect or enhance its business-level strategy.

 EXPLORING THE WEB
Visiting Wal-Mart

Enter the Web site of retailer Wal-Mart (www.wal.mart.com/). Click on "Corporate Information," and then click on "Corporate Timeline." Study the events in Wal-Mart's timeline, and from them outline the way Wal-Mart's competitive strategy in the retailing industry has developed over time.

Search the Web for a company that has recently changed its competitive strategy in some way. What precipitated the shift in its strategy? What strategy changes did the company make?

The Burger Wars

DURING THE 1990S, in the mature and saturated fast-food industry, competition for customers between the different hamburger chains has been intense. McDonald's, the industry leader, has been under pressure to maintain its profit margins, because, as the price of fast food has fallen, price wars have periodically broken out. Taco Bell started a major price war when it introduced its $.99 taco, for instance, which pushed McDonald's and other burger chains such as Burger King and Wendy's to find ways to lower their costs and prices. As a result of price competition, all the burger chains were forced to learn how to make a cheaper hamburger, and they have been able to lower their prices.

With most fast-food restaurants now offering comparable prices, the focus of competition between the burger chains has shifted to other aspects of their products. First, the major chains are all introducing bigger burger patties. The battle was started by Burger King, which is still waging an aggressive campaign to increase its market share at the expense of McDonald's. In 1994, Burger King added a full ounce of beef to its 1.8 ounce regular patty and followed this with an intense advertising campaign based on the slogan, "Get Your Burger's Worth," directed at McDonald's burger, which was more than 40 percent lighter. The campaign worked for Burger King, and the chain's market share rose by 18 percent in 1995. As a result, in May 1996, McDonald's announced that it would enlarge its regular patty by 25 percent to beat back the challenge from Burger King and from Wendy's, which has always offered a larger burger (and whose "Where's the Beef?" slogan helped it gain market share in the 1980s).[32]

Developing bigger burgers is only one part of competitive strategy in the fast-food industry, however. The main burger chains are constantly experimenting with new and improved kinds of burgers to appeal to customers—burgers that add cheese, bacon, different kinds of vegetables, and exotic sauces. They are also trying whole-meal offerings, such as McDonald's "value meals," to provide a competitive package to attract customers.[33]

Furthermore, recognizing the competition from other kinds of fast-food chains, such as those specializing in chicken or Mexican food, the burger chains have moved to broaden their menus. McDonald's, for example, offers chicken dishes, pizza, and salads; it also allows restaurants to customize their menus to suit the tastes of customers in the region in which they are located. Thus, McDonald's restaurants in New England have lobster on the menu, and those in Japan serve sushi. Product development is a major part of competitive strategy in the industry.

Another major competitive strategy that Burger King and McDonald's have adopted is market penetration: opening up new restaurants to attract customers. Because all the big chains have thousands of restaurants each, many analysts thought that the market was saturated, meaning that it would not be profitable to open more restaurants. However, McDonald's in particular has opened hundreds of restaurants in new locations such as gas stations and large retail stores (for example, Wal-Mart), all of which are profitable and have helped it protect its market share and maintain its margins.

Finally, a major aspect of the burger chains' competitive strategy has been to take their core competencies and apply them on an international level by building global restaurant empires. Indeed, so important have global operations become that both McDonald's and Burger King earn a significant part of their profits from their foreign operations. In the mature fast-food industry, developing new competitive strategies to fend off attacks by other companies within the industry and to protect and enhance competitive advantage is a never-ending task for strategic managers. Even McDonald's is currently experiencing many problems because of the intense competition in the industry.[34]

Case Discussion Questions

1. Describe the nature of competition and the industry environment of the fast-food industry.

2. What strategies are fast-food restaurants pursuing today to protect their competitive position?

End Notes

1. *www.ebay.com* (1999).
2. Press releases, *www.amazon.com* (1999).
3. M. Porter, *Competitive Strategy: Techniques for Analyzing Industries and Competitors* (New York: Free Press, 1980), pp. 191-200.
4. S. A. Shane, "Hybrid Organizational Arrangements and Their Implications for Firm Growth and Survival: A Study of New Franchisors," *Academy of Management Journal,* 1 (1996), 216-234.
5. Much of this section is based on C. W. L. Hill, M. Heeley, and J. Sakson, "Strategies for Profiting from Innovation," *Advances in Global High Technology Management* (Greenwich, Conn.: JAI Press, 1993), III, 79-95.
6. The importance of complementary assets was first noted by D. J. Teece. See D. J. Teece, "Profiting from Technological Innovation," in *The Competitive Challenge,* ed. D. J. Teece (New York: Harper & Row, 1986), pp. 26-54.
7. M. J. Chen and D. C. Hambrick, "Speed, Stealth, and Selective Attack: How Small Firms Differ from Large Firms in Competitive Behavior," *Academy of Management Journal,* 38 (1995), 453-482.
8. E. Mansfield, M. Schwartz, and S. Wagner, "Imitation Costs and Patents: An Empirical Study," *Economic Journal,* 91 (1981), 907-918.
9. E. Mansfield, "How Rapidly Does New Industrial Technology Leak Out?" *Journal of Industrial Economics,* 34 (1985), 217-223.
10. "Reshaping the Body Shop," *Global Cosmetic Industry,* (July 1999), 10.
11. This argument has been made in the game theory literature. See R. Caves, H. Cookell, and P. J. Killing, "The Imperfect Market for Technology Licenses," *Oxford Bulletin of Economics and Statistics,* 45 (1983), 249-267; N. T. Gallini, "Deterrence by Market Sharing: A Strategic Incentive for Licensing," *American Economic Review,* 74 (1984), 931-941; and C. Shapiro, "Patent Licensing and R&D Rivalry," *American Economic Review,* 75 (1985), 25-30.
12. J. Brander and J. Eaton, "Product Line Rivalry," *American Economic Review,* 74 (1985), 323-334.
13. P. Milgrom and J. Roberts, "Predation, Reputation, and Entry Deterrence," *Journal of Economic Theory,* 27 (1982), 280-312.
14. S. M. Oster, *Modern Competitive Analysis* (New York: Oxford University Press, 1990), pp. 262-264.
15. D. A. Hay and D. J. Morris, *Industrial Economics: Theory and Evidence* (New York: Oxford University Press, 1979), pp. 192-193.
16. Porter, *Competitive Strategy,* pp. 76-86.
17. O. Heil, and T. S. Robertson, "Towards a Theory of Competitive Market Signaling: A Research Agenda," *Strategic Management Journal,* 12 (1991), 403-418.
18. Scherer, *Industrial Market Structure and Economic Performance,* Chapter 8.
19. The model differs from Ansoff's model for this reason. See H. I. Ansoff, *Corporate Strategy* (London: Penguin Books, 1984).
20. Ibid, pp. 97-100.
21. R. D. Buzzell, B. T. Gale, and R. G. M. Sultan, "Market Share—A Key to Profitability," *Harvard Business Review* (January–February 1975), 97-103; R. Jacobson and D. A. Aaker, "Is Market Share All That It's Cracked Up to Be?" *Journal of Marketing,* 49 (1985), 11-22.
22. M. Maremont and G. Bowens, "Brawls in Toyland," *Business Week,* December 21, 1992, pp. 36-37.
23. S. Eads, "The Toys 'R' Us Empire Strikes Back, *Business Week,* June 7, 1999, pp. 55-59.
24. Ansoff, *Corporate Strategy,* pp. 98-99.
25. S. L. Brown and K. M. Eisenhardt, "Product Development: Past Research, Present Findings, and Future Directions," *Academy of Management Review,* 20 (1995), 343-378.
26. The next section draws heavily on M. B. Lieberman, "Strategies for Capacity Expansion," *Sloan Management Review,* 8 (1987), 19-27; and Porter, *Competitive Strategy,* pp. 324-338.
27. K. Pope, "Out for Blood, For Compaq and Dell Accent Is on Personal in the Computer Wars," *Wall Street Journal,* February 13, 1993, pp. A1, A6.
28. M. Stepanek, "What Does No. 1 Do for an Encore," *Business Week,* November 2, 1998, pp. 44-47.
29. A. Taylor III, "Compaq Looks Inside for Salvation," *Fortune,* August 16, 1999, pp. 124-129.
30. P. Haynes, "Western Electric Redux," *Forbes,* January 26, 1998, pp. 46-47.
31. J. Willoughby, "The Last Iceman," *Forbes,* July 13, 1987, pp. 183-202.
32. R. Gibson, "Bigger Burger By McDonald's: A Two-Ouncer," *Wall Street Journal,* April 18, 1996, p. B1.
33. D. Leonhardt, "McDonald's: Can It Regain Its Golden Touch?" *Business Week,* February 28, 1998, pp. 22-27.
34. D. Leonhardt and A. T. Palmer, "Getting Off Their McButts," *Business Week,* February 22, 1999, pp. 65-66.